D0290392

UNFINISHED JOURNEY

A WORLD WAR II REMEMBRANCE

Kerry P. Redmann

The Lyons Press
Guilford, Connecticut
An imprint of The Globe Pequot Press

To Morris Jr.
and
Mom and Dad

Consummatum est.

The Lyons Press is an imprint of The Globe Pequot Press

10 9 8 7 6 5 4 3 2 1

Printed in the United States of America

Designed by Stephanie Doyle

Library of Congress Cataloging-in-Publication Data

Redmann, Kerry P.
Unfinished journey : a World War II remembrance / by Kerry P. Redmann.
p. cm.
Includes correspondence by Morris Benjamin Redmann, Jr.
ISBN 1-59228-761-1 (trade cloth)
Redmann, Morris Benjamin, 1925–1945. 2. Redmann, Morris Benjamin, 1925 1945—Correspondence. 3. United States. Army. Infantry Division, 94th—Biography. 4. World War, 1939–1945—Personal narratives, American. 5. World War, 1939–1945—Campaigns—Western Front. 6. Ardennes, Battle of the, 1944–1945. 7. United States. Army—Biography. 8. Soldiers—United States—Biography. I. Title.

D769.3194th.R43 2005
940.54'21'092—dc22
[B]

2005044466

Special thanks to the memory of
Stephen E. Ambrose
whose encouragement and direction
kept me ever dedicated to the task.

There is no chosen age for war
No perfect time of life
To leave the easy shelter
For the bullet, gun, and knife
How can the choice be wholly right
As long as it must lie
Between the men too old to fight
And those too young to die.

—"A Soldier's Diary"
Anonymous

CONTENTS

FOREWORD

by Ronald J. Drez

Twenty-four overseas cemeteries are the final resting place for 124,000 United States War Dead from World Wars I and II. Each cemetery is immaculately landscaped and gleams with white Christian Crosses and Stars of David, and visitors walking among those perfect rows are transformed by emotions of sadness, joy, wonder, and curiosity.

The laws of combat and war deign that these final resting places belong mostly to young men, whose futures were hidden from their eyes, whose children were never born, and who remain forever young while their friends, family, and comrades travel the longer road.

As an author of a number of books about the events and men of World War II, I have had the honor to walk in many of these special sacred places, and on one particular day in Normandy, while researching with my dear departed friend, Dr. Stephen E. Ambrose, I asked, "What if the ground could speak? What if each stone could tell us about the man beneath: his joys, family, dreams, and the people he left behind?"

My question was nothing new. It's an easy question to ask when surrounded by the fallen youth of war; the mind staggered by the seemingly endless field of stars and crosses. Songwriter Eric Bogel asked the question most eloquently in his heart-stirring song, "The Green Fields of France." He tells of a traveler, resting from a long walk, sitting in the summer sun in a WWI cemetery. The weary traveler noticed the name "Willie McBride" etched on the cross nearest to him, and his wondering began. He saw by the cross that the fallen soldier was only nineteen, and he wondered how Willie McBride died. Was it well and quick, or "slow and unseen"? And what of those he left behind? Was there a wife, or a sweetheart, and was he buried with dignity and honor?

In the American Military Cemetery in Luxembourg, among the more than five thousand graves of fallen soldiers, one undistinguishable cross bears the name: "Morris B. Redmann Jr.", and like Willie McBride in

1916, Morris was only nineteen when he died in 1945. His end came during the biggest battle in which the United States Army ever fought: the Battle of the Bulge in the frozen forests of the Ardennes in Belgium. And one could pause at the grave and wonder about Morris and ask the same unanswerable questions that Bogel asked of Willie McBride.

But through a remarkable effort by a surviving brother, Kerry Redmann, Morris is not consigned to the obscurity of the grave. His story is not sealed forever in its silence. Young Morris Redmann was a prolific letter writer, and he wrote to his parents and nine siblings and aunts and uncles and friends, and told of his dreams, and his experiences, and his training, and his observations of war, and his enemy, and the countries he was helping to liberate. At times he waxed poetic; other times he wrote in French, and was unabashed in proclaiming his faith and spiritual devotion, and the consignment of his life to the will of the Almighty. Anyone would have been happy to know Morris Redmann. He was certainly a jolly, good fellow.

He was exceptionally smart, having finished high school when most young men were just beginning, and received his college degree and enrolled in law school at eighteen. That career, cut short by the Army's draft, sent this remarkable young man with poor eyesight, on his mission to help bring an end to Nazi tyranny in a strange land.

After his death in 1945, his accumulated letters languished in an attic for more than fifty years, neatly bundled by his heartbroken mother. They were finally rediscovered, organized and published by a devoted brother who was only fourteen when Morris left for war. Kerry Redmann's *Unfinished Journey*, encouraged by the late historian Dr. Stephen Ambrose, brings to life Private Morris B. Redmann Jr. who died liberating Europe in 1945. His letters speak to us from the past, from a time of innocence and great peril, and of one young man's call to duty. I'm glad he was on our side.

—Ronald J. Drez

Author: *Voices of D-Day*
Twenty-Five Yards of War
Remember D-Day
Voices of Valor
Voices of Courage

ACKNOWLEDGMENTS

Stephen E. Ambrose,
renowned World War II historian and author

Sergeant Robert J. Anders,
Co. L, 376th Inf., 94th Div., Crown Point, IN

Alex Arendt,
94th Infantry Division Association, European contact,
Remich, Luxembourg

United States Senator John Breaux

Staff Sergeant Angelo B. Brocato,
Co. B, 302nd Inf., 94th Div., Mobile, AL

Captain Robert N. Cassel, IHQ,
301st Inf., 94th Div., Sewell, NJ

Sergeant Vincent J. (The Count) Cinque,
Co. L, 376th Inf., 94th Div., Pompano Beach, FL

PFC William S. Connolly,
Co. H, 376th Inf., 94th Div., Clearwater, FL

Captain Ronald J. Drez,
Co. H, 2nd Bn. 5th Marines, New Orleans, LA

Eisenhower Center for American Studies—
and the United States Army Signal Corps

Lt. Robert E. Foster,
Co. L, 376th Inf., 94th Div., Atlanta, GA

Corporal Harry N. Helms,
Co. G, 376th Inf., 94th Div., Downington, PA

Lt. Herndon Inge, Jr.,
Co. D, 301st Inf., 94th Div., Mobile, AL

Lt. Robert H. (Snapper) Johnson,
Co. L, 376th Inf., 94th Div., Tyrone, PA

Tech Sergeant William W. Lehfeldt,
Co. L, 376th Inf., 94th Div., Potomac, MD

Tech Sergeant John R. Milroy,
Co. L, 376th Inf., 94th Div., Alpena, MI

Tech Sergeant Albert A. Moraldi,
Co. L, 376th Inf., 94th Div., Palm Springs, CA

PFC Donald E. Mulry,
Co. F, 301st Inf., 94th Div., Tenafly, NJ

Corporal Mervin Ruff,
Co. M, 301st Inf., 94th Div., Altamont, IL

PFC Shelby C. Trice,
94th Signal Company, 94th Div., Mobile, AL

Staff Sergeant Oliver Weisdorffer,
319th Medical Bn. 94th Div., New Orleans, LA

PFC A. E. (Gene) Wise,
Co. L, 376th Inf., 94th Div., Stone Mountain, GA

History of the 94th Infantry Division in World War II, edited by Lt. Byrnes

History of the 376th Infantry Regiment, compiled, edited and printed by the Regimental Historical Committee Information and Educational Office

PREFACE

Morris B. Redmann Jr.'s journey through life was interrupted by World War II—yet he freely accepted his obligation to serve his country in time of great need. The word "interrupted" implies that his life would have resumed at some point in the future. However, his death, and the finality therein, left his journey unfinished. Nevertheless, his letters did survive, and through them we come to know and identify with his strength of character and remember him expressly from his own words.

This book's original purpose was for the enlightenment of Morris's younger brothers, two of whom were only three and four years old at the time he was drafted; these two were not aware of what was going on in the world at the time, nor did they understand the military significance of his absence from home, as did his other brothers and sister. I was fourteen years old when my older brother Morris left for the military at age eighteen.

But as I absorbed myself in Morris's letters, which were carefully and meticulously preserved by our mother and father in the attic of their home for so many years, I felt it increasingly important that the story which emerged be told to the world. Mom and Dad kept every letter Morris wrote, and he was a prolific letter writer with very legible penmanship. Dad died in September 1955 at age fifty-nine, and Mother followed eight months later in May of 1956. The death of Morris Jr. was our father's great sorrow, particularly since Morris had already graduated from college and had begun law school. Our father had hoped to see his own footsteps retraced in the budding career of his firstborn.

So these letters of Morris Jr. continued to be stored in the attic of the family home for many years after our parents' deaths, and even while one of our brothers lived in the family home with his children. It was when the family home was sold years later during a general going-through of personal belongings that the letters again surfaced. It was at that time I decided to become "keeper of the letters." I brought them to my home and stored them in my own attic for safekeeping. The boxes not only included Morris's letters, but letters from our parents, which he always kept with him until he went overseas, at which time he sent them home, along with letters from his brothers, sister (some in French), aunts, uncles, friends and college classmates. These boxes also contained his two Purple Hearts and other medals described later in this book, and, of course, his "personal effects" package forwarded from the Quartermaster Division after his death. This package included items removed from his person such as his Rosary, Sacred Heart Badge, his Lady of Prompt Succor scapular, his prayerbook, a sterling silver chain and cross from his good friend Kent Zimmermann, his Boy Scout knife, his wallet with German and French paper money, and his small coin purse with some French and German coins—items that he had carried with him.

During the ensuing years I made a few attempts to organize the material in some fashion, but it required a substantial amount of time that I didn't have when I was still employed full-time.

The matter of doing something with this material became more pressing when I received a phone call out of the blue from a Shelby C. Trice in October of 1999, saying that he had known Morris, was inducted into the Army with him, and had spent a lovely weekend at our parents' home with Morris prior to going overseas.

We then made arrangements to meet in Mobile, Alabama, where Shelby and his wife, Georgine, live, and we spent several hours together. We made additional trips to talk more about Morris, their military service, and Morris's death. Shelby told me that he was in line directly behind Morris for the eye exam at Fort Benning, Georgia, and how the eye doctor, after examining Morris's eyes, said, "Here, son, sign this form and get out of here. Your eyesight is 20/400 in each eye. Without your glasses, you are blind." Shelby Trice said Morris asked the eye doctor to pass him, as he wanted to serve his country.

These meetings and discussions about Morris and the 94th Infantry Division, from the time the two of them had been inducted to the landing at Utah Beach in Normandy on D-Day Plus 94 (September 8, 1944), made up my mind to present this material in book form. I began working on it as soon as I retired in the end of January 2000 at age 70.

Morris had such a love and devotion to our mother that on receiving a letter from her on his nineteenth birthday, June 27, 1944—in which she spoke of how much she missed him, how much she loved him, and recalled memories of him from the day he was born—so moved him (as written us by PFC Vincent A. DeMase) that he immediately sat down and composed a poem as a tribute to her, which is offered elsewhere in this book. When

Vincent DeMase read the poem, he was so touched that he asked Morris if he could copy it and send it to his mother. Morris nodded his approval. Upon Morris's death, this same PFC Vincent A. DeMase of Albany, New York, wrote to our parents about the details of Morris's death, the incident of the poem, and how he was with Morris when he "got it."

The letters contained herein, written when he was eighteen and nineteen years old, are the sum total of letters written to his parents, friends, and relatives. They speak for themselves, attesting to his strength of character, his religious upbringing and convictions, his education and dedication, his exemplary life—yet covers a mere year and four months of his military service from October 1943 to January 1945. He was killed in action on January 14, 1945, a Sunday, in the dead of a frozen winter during the Battle of the Bulge—the largest land battle fought by American troops in the history of the United States.

Morris was baptized Catholic, as were all members of his family, and he remained devoted to his faith throughout his lifetime. He began kindergarten at the age of three at St. Rita's Parochial School, in New Orleans, where he assumed his first altar-boy responsibilities. He graduated at age ten and went to Jesuit High School in New Orleans under the tutelage of the priests of the Society of Jesus. Morris continued as an altar boy during his four years at Jesuit, and it was here that he received and knew the value of his Catholic education at the hands of the Jesuit Fathers and Scholastics. The Jesuit Latin motto—*Ad Majorem Dei Gloriam*—would remain indelibly imprinted upon his character.

His four years at Jesuit High brought him the realization that man does not live by bread alone, and with the excellent role models of his parents, he grew in strength both intellectually and spiritually. Upon graduation at age fourteen, he entered Loyola University, the College of Arts and Sciences, where he hoped to prepare ultimately for law school. He participated in many campus activities throughout his years at Loyola—chairman of the Activity Heads Committee, president of Le Cercle Français (the French club), president of Thespians (day school dramatic club), and an artist on the *Wolf* (Loyola's yearbook). He was a member of Beggars Social and Academic Fraternity, the Pegasus Poetry Society, the Edward Douglas White Debating Society, and the Academy of Fine Arts, and was a regular participant in the weekly student broadcasts over WWL Radio. In the summer of 1940, at age fourteen, Morris had two art exhibits, with some of his paintings at the Delgado Museum of Art, Young Artists Program.

In 1941–1942, he received the Student Council Citation for Extracurricular Activities and the first-place trophy in an Oratorical Contest sponsored by the College Sodality Union. In 1943 he received the A. J. Bonomo

Award for the best individual acting for his portrayal of Lear in Shakespeare's *King Lear*.

Although Morris was very active in school organizations, he also found time for healthy sports participation—not on the organized school teams, as he was very young and not physically maturing as fast as the older boys in school. However, he did manage to stay active with the St. Rita's CYO Program (Catholic Youth Organization) in basketball and softball. In 1940 in a softball game against the St. Joseph's CYO team at St. Joseph's Field on Tulane Avenue in New Orleans, Morris hit a home run that went out of the field of play, bouncing off the brick sidewall of the church. This was related by team member Donald Palmer of New Orleans.

Morris received his A. B. degree from Loyola University in May 1943 at age eighteen and immediately entered Loyola Law School. He had completed almost a semester of law school when he was drafted into the Army and ordered to report to Local Board No. 14, Orleans Parish, on September 27, 1943, at 7:30 A.M. at the induction station at 1851 Melpomene Street in New Orleans, Induction Order No. 13574.

On the early morning of October 18, 1943, Morris, with other inductees including Shelby C. Trice, whom he had met at the induction station, boarded a train at the L & A Passenger Terminal on South Rampart and Julia streets for their trip to Alexandria, Louisiana, home of Camp Beauregard. With a tearful embrace and good-bye from his mother and father, Morris began his journey into the military.

His letters—commencing with his first letter dated October 20, 1943, from Camp Beauregard, Louisiana, and ending with his last letter dated January 11, 1945, from "Festung Europa," three days before he was killed—reflect the values he held throughout his short but happy life.

> The highest obligation and privilege of citizenship
> is that of bearing arms for one's country.
>
> —*General George S. Patton Jr.*

INTRODUCTION

Morris B. Redmann Jr., was born on June 27, 1925, in New Orleans, Louisiana, the eldest of ten children from the marriage of Morris Benjamin Redmann and Esther Alice Joyce. He had eight brothers—William, Kerry, Richard, Ralph, Ronald, Jerome, David, and Robert—and one sister, Esther. His sister was second to oldest and was affectionately called "Missy" by their father. Esther is an Ursuline nun and the prioress of the Ursuline community in New Orleans.

Morris's father was an attorney of eminent ability with an integrity that multiplied his worth. In addition to his law practice, he taught a course in Corporation Law at Tulane University. His mother was a schoolteacher and accomplished pianist, who taught piano in addition to her school responsibilities prior to her marriage in 1924.

Morris's parents had planned on having a large family, and following their wedding on September 3, 1924, they set out for an extended honeymoon in Europe, feeling it would be their first and last vacation together for some time. Thus Morris's life began in Paris, in utero, during this honeymoon. At this same time, during a private audience at the Vatican in Rome, Morris was blessed by Pope Pius XI. His French lace christening dress was purchased in Paris, and his sister and eight brothers, later on, wore this same French lace dress for their christenings. Morris's life began in Paris, and, ironically, a scant nineteen years later ended a short 330 kilometers from Paris. Little did his parents realize, at that joyous time, that their firstborn would meet his fate in this same area. Morris remains buried with his comrades-in-arms in the American Military Cemetery in Luxembourg (Hamm).

All of Morris's eight brothers and one sister are still living, and this is why the story must be told before time becomes increasingly our enemy.

The crux of the book is a compilation of Morris's letters to his mother, father, sister, brothers, aunts, and uncles. The original handwritten letters are still available in their preserved entirety. Also included are a few handwritten letters from close soldier friends who were with him when he was killed, and selected letters of condolence to his parents from family, friends, and dignitaries, as well as selected letters from friends and classmates.

Morris's military record shows that he was inducted on September 27, 1943, and ordered to report to Camp Beauregard, Louisiana, on October 18, 1943. He left Camp Beauregard on October 29, 1943, by train, by way of Monroe, Louisiana; Meridian, Mississippi; and Birmingham, Alabama, arriving at Fort Benning, Georgia (Columbus) on October 31, 1943. Morris became a member of the Army Specialized Training Program (ASTP) at Fort Benning, Eighth Company, Fifth Training Regiment. This would be his home for the next thirteen weeks of basic military training.

The ASTP was a program consisting of over 100,000 inductees of high school graduates and some college students who scored high grades in the Army General Classification Test (AGCT). These inductees participated in programs conducted at 200 colleges and universities in the United States upon completion of basic training, usually thirteen weeks. After completing their courses at the colleges and universities, they were to be commissioned as Second Lieutenants in the U.S. Army.

Fort Benning, Georgia (Columbus), was the most complete Army post and training camp in the United States. It comprised 220,000 acres of ground, including many types of terrain. It made good use of its woods and clearings, its creeks and rivers, its hills and flats. Because of all these natural assets, a wide variety of battle conditions could be simulated. The Infantry School at Fort Benning had become the greatest institution in the world for military education and the development of military leaders.

Morris's basic training ended on February 5, 1944, with a battalion parade in dress uniform with rifle, belt, and bayonet. Those thirteen tortuous weeks of his young life were finished. Rumors were rampant of who would go where and if they would get a much-deserved furlough before reporting to the school they had been assigned, which at that point had yet to be decided. One rumor was Georgia Tech; another UCLA; another University of Oklahoma.

On February 18, 1944, Morris was told that he was being sent to engineering school at University of Oklahoma, Norman, Oklahoma, and upon graduation would be commissioned a Second Lieutenant. However, Morris was cautiously aware that legislation before Congress was considering doing away with the ASTP because of the need for larger numbers of infantrymen in Europe.

On February 27, 1944, all hopes of going to engineering college were dashed, with the Captain advising the hopefuls that infantrymen were direly needed in Europe, and they would soon begin advanced infantry training. Many of the men were very bitter, and some dreams were shattered. Congress formally enacted legislation abolishing the ASTP, and on April 1, 1944, 110,000 students were sent directly overseas. (Ironically, the Navy had a similar program called the V-12, which followed through on its commitment to the young hopefuls.)

Morris's group left Fort Benning, Georgia, on March 8, 1944, by troop train for Camp McCain, Mississippi, arriving March 9, 1944, at 10 A.M. His new assignment was the 94th Infantry Division, a good line outfit. Camp McCain is approximately 100 miles south of Memphis, Tennessee, and the nearest town is Grenada, Mississippi. On March 11, 1944, Morris was assigned to the 376th Infantry Regiment, 3rd Battalion, Company "L," 1st Platoon, 2nd Squad.

It was at Camp McCain that he would complete his advanced infantry training as a rifleman and BAR (Browning Automatic Rifle) man. Morris qualified as Expert in the M-1 rifle, BAR, and carbine, and also as Expert in the 30-caliber machine gun, scoring 226 out of a possible 256. (Expert is from 218 to 256.) The 376th Infantry Regiment became "The First Expert Infantry Regiment in the United States Army," and the 94th Infantry Division became the first "Expert Infantry" Division in the U.S. Army.

On July 23, 1944, the entire 94th Infantry Division began leaving Camp McCain by train for Camp Shanks, New York, the designated port of embarkation. On July 26, 1944, the men of the 376th Regiment boarded Pullman cars and departed—through Georgia, the Carolinas, and Virginia, through the nation's capital into Maryland, Delaware, Pennsylvania, New Jersey, around New York City, finally arriving at Camp Shanks, New York. Camp Shanks was a pretty camp nestled in the pine hills of the lower Catskill Mountains, near West Nyack, New York. Their stay at Camp Shanks would be for only two weeks. The movement of the 94th Division was completed by July 31.

After the necessary drills, abandon-ship drills, and censorship rules were rehearsed and emphasized, the men were issued twelve-hour passes to New York City, to see as much as possible of America's largest city.

On Saturday, August 5, the entire 94th Division then moved by rail to New York City where they were loaded aboard the converted British luxury liner, the *Queen Elizabeth*. On the morning of August 6, the *Queen Elizabeth* weighed anchor, sailed down the Hudson River, and out into the Atlantic. The *Queen Elizabeth* received no military convoy other than an aerial escort the first day out. Beginning on August 7, the *Queen* was on her own, her only protection being her speed and her deck guns, which were added when the British luxury liner was converted to a troopship.

Her excellent speed was her protection, although she also changed course every two to four minutes in hopes of avoiding the hunting ground of German submarines.

On the morning of August 11, 1944, the *Queen Elizabeth* sailed into the Firth of Clyde to Greenock, Scotland, near Glasgow, in stately grandeur. The *Queen* had to anchor in midstream as there were no wharfing facilities capable of handling a ship of her tonnage. The morning of August 12, the troops of the entire 94th Division began debarking. This was accomplished by means of "lighters" (smaller vessels) which steamed alongside the *Queen* to receive the troops from unloading ports located at approximately the deck level of the lighters. Looking up from the decks of the smaller vessels, the enormous size of the *Queen Elizabeth* was a striking sight to behold. And what an amazing trip—New York to Scotland in less than six days, continuously zigzagging across the Atlantic.

From the lighters, the troops boarded trains to Hullavington, England, where they located at Pinkney Park, about one mile from the village of Sherston, Wiltshire, England. The train trip to Hullavington was filled with the lovely scenery of southern England, and it was the first time the men heard the historic plea, "Any gum, chum?" Whereas the troops were billeted in tents, the 94th Headquarters was established in Greenway Manor House at Chippenham.

Immediate training began on hedgerow tactics, conditioning marches, and weapons' firing. Helping them were officers who had returned from Normandy with experience in hedgerow fighting.

All wars experience disturbing and disheartening situations. In August 1944, the failure of the British Second Army to close the Falaise-Argentan gap in France was one of these regrettable events, which allowed large German forces and equipment to escape eastward through the gap, while Generals Patton, Haislip, and LeClerc watched in disbelief. Patton's Army was in full gallop, moving northward of Argentan, when it was ordered to pull up and halt its XV Corps from advancing to meet the Canadians under General LeClerc. The order came from General Bradley, but had the approval of General Eisenhower. The decision was to let the British Second Army under General Montgomery advance and enter Falaise, thus sealing off any chance for the retreating German Army to escape the trap that had been set.

The British Army's inability to close the gap enraged General Patton, as he was convinced had he been allowed to continue his movement northward of Argentan, his XV Corps could have easily entered Falaise, closing the gap and annihilating the German Army, and capturing its tough commander, Sepp Dietrich. Patton remained convinced of this to his dying day. This opinion was unanimously shared by the German commanders involved, and subsequent research supported it. Had the gap been closed, one could conclude such action would have facilitated the end of the war in 1944.[1]

On September 6, 1944, the 376th Regiment filed up the gangplanks onto the HMS *Cheshire* at Southampton Docks. That evening, under cover of darkness, they left England behind with their destination somewhere in France. Throughout his training and during the European missions, Morris's close Army buddies were Tom (Buddy) Moore, Vincent DeMase, Ed Gallagher, Elmer Smith, Hamby (I don't recall his first name ever being mentioned), and Shelby Trice. In France they would enjoy weekend passes in places such as Nantes.

On the afternoon of September 8, 1944, the HMS *Cheshire* dropped anchor off St. Mère Église on the Normandy coast, and the 376th Regiment boarded LCIs and landed on Utah Beach, D-Day Plus 94.

Visible from offshore were the wrecks of more landing craft and liberty ships than anyone could imagine, with masts, funnels, sterns, and bows thrust up from the waves in all manner of angles. On Utah Beach, the sea had coughed up all types of military equipment that was dug into the sand. In the dunes behind the beach, heavily camouflaged, were the *widerstandsnests* (pillboxes), gun emplacements, communication trenches, dugouts, and shelters that had formed the German beach defenses. The long tapered-barrel 88s still protruded from their firing slots. The rusted tangles of barbed wire, old shell casings, and artillery craters stood in mute testimony to the assault that took place ninety-four days earlier on this same beach—and its deadly consequences.

Since there was no transportation available, the men marched twelve miles through the flat, uninhabited moorland that stretched endlessly in the darkness from the beach, eventually coming to the marshaling area between Carentan and Ste.-Marie-du-Mont. The bivouac area was an assortment of orchards and pastureland, and they settled in fields surrounded by hedgerows. They had walked through areas where they saw crashed gliders and planes that the 82nd Airborne Paratroopers came in on, behind the German lines. The 94th Infantry Division opened its first combat command post on the continent of Europe, in the outskirts of the village of Ste.-Marie-du-Mont in Normandy, a few miles inland from Utah Beach.

They began training again in hedgerow tactics, and on September 12, 1944, moved out by truck to another bivouac area near Nozay. To overcome the obstacle of the hedgerows, American Sherman tanks were fitted

[1]British Major General H. Essame's book, *Patton: A Study in Command*

with large steel spikes or blades, which were welded to the front of the tanks for cutting through the thick hedgerows. They were popularly referred to as "Rhinos."

It was at this marshaling area that the 376th Regiment learned for the first time that its mission in France was to contain and screen the enemy in and about St. Nazaire on the Atlantic coast of France. It was then the regimental convoy moved out by truck for the coast of Brittany. This area, which included the Breton ports of Lorient and St. Nazaire, was called "the forgotten front." At Lorient and St. Nazaire, the enemy strength consisted of approximately 60,000 men. The ports of Lorient and St. Nazaire were Germany's chief Atlantic submarine bases. The port of St. Nazaire is on the Bay of Biscay at the mouth of the Loire River. German U-boats continued to enter and leave the huge submarine pens in Lorient and St. Nazaire, and neither American field artillery nor American and British heavy bombers were able to penetrate the reinforced concrete roofs and walls to damage any of the submarines.

The 376th Regiment was assigned a defense line that ran nearly 22 miles north and south from the Loire, below Le Temple de Bretagne, up through Fay and Blain, to an area of a road junction five miles north of Blain where ten roads came together like the spokes of a wheel. The men of Company L, 3rd Battalion called this road junction the "spider." The area of Blain was the responsibility of the 3rd Battalion, and a great deal of patrol activity took place. Its proper name was Forêt du Gâvre, a much tangled and gloomy forest. It was here that Morris was wounded in action on September 18, 1944, by a German artillery shell. He received shrapnel in his knee and thigh. He was operated on in a rear hospital, but only the shrapnel in his knee could be removed—the shrapnel in his thigh was probed for, but was too deep to be removed, and trying to do so would cause more harm than good. He returned to his outfit ten days later on September 28, 1944. For a few weeks he was returned to the rear hospital weekly by jeep to receive clean bandages. On approximately October 3, 1944, Morris and several other wounded men were decorated by the Commanding General and given the Purple Heart.

The Germans in Bouvron had an excellent observation post in the church steeple, and were always on watch for any signs of change in the landscape and artillery; patrol activity was engaged by both sides on a regular basis. The Germans would shell into both Blain and Forêt du Gâvre. During the period at St. Nazaire, from September 17, 1944, through December 31, 1944, besides the normal patrol activities, there was an offensive action by the 3rd Battalion to straighten the lines north of Bouvron. The center of action during this advance was the area along the Brest-Nantes Canal in the vicinity of La Pessouis. The area of most combat patrols was the "spider," the Brest-Nantes Canal west of Blain, and the country around Bouvron.

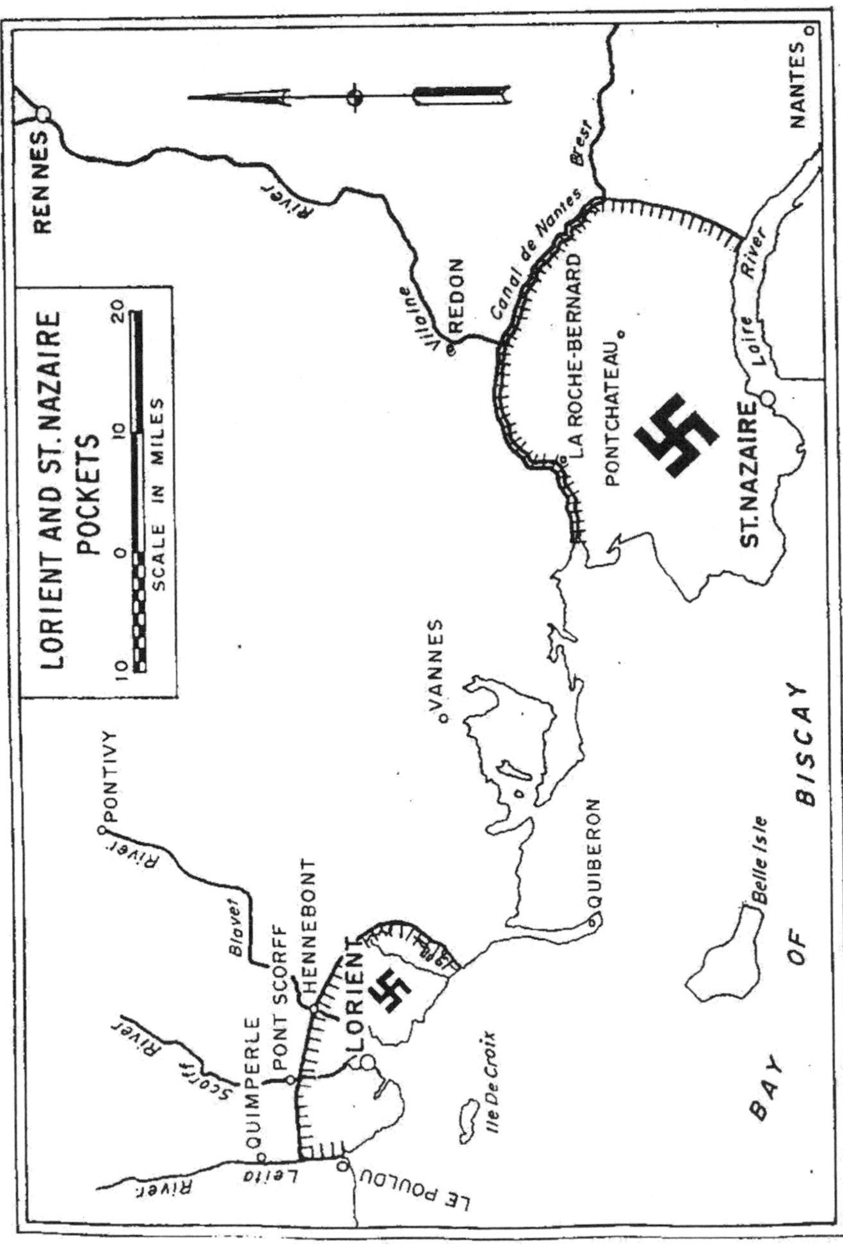

The three battalions of the 376th had been taking turns in Division Reserve at La Gacilly. Twelve-hour passes to Nantes were granted, where members of the 376th had their first experience with cognac, French beer, and the famed "Calvados." Actually, during their reserve periods they would be engaged in intensive training programs, the purpose of which was clear—it was training of the sort to prepare them for the type of obstacles they would encounter when and if they hit the Siegfried Switch Line. All of this aggressive training at La Gacilly made everyone in the battalion realize they would not stay on the forgotten front of the St. Nazaire-Lorient pockets, as the entire 94th Infantry Division was now too well trained not to shove off for some important mission.

With the German Ardennes offensive from Belgium commencing on December 16, 1944, the rumors and stories were numerous on where the regiment was heading; they knew for certain they would no longer remain in the comparative quiet of St. Nazaire.

The Battle of the Bulge, militarily known as the German Ardennes Forest offensive, began at 0530 hours on December 16, 1944, when a lightning counterattack by three German armies—comprising twenty-nine infantry divisions and twelve armored divisions, under the command of Field Marshall Gerd Von Rundstedt—swept across the northern half of the Grand Duchy of Luxembourg into Belgium, with Antwerp as their objective. The assault was timed to coincide with inclement weather to effectively limit the use of Allied air power. Under cover of fog and rain, the counterattack was initially very successful, breaking through the American lines on a 45-mile front, and penetrating 60 miles at its furthest point. This attack destroyed one American infantry division as a unit, badly crippled two other infantry divisions, and cut one armored combat command to pieces.

To stem this onslaught, the United States Third Army, under the command of Lieutenant General George S. Patton Jr., was diverted from the Saar region of France. Swinging northward, General Patton's troops re-liberated northern Luxembourg, and ten days later on December 26, 1944, relieved the beleaguered forces at Bastogne, Belgium, hereafter referred to as the "Bloody Bastards of Bastogne." The United States First Army, fighting to the north, met with Patton's Third Army on January 16, 1945, at Houffalize, Belgium. By January 25, 1945, the enemy salient no longer existed.

In his letters Morris referred to this Ardennes Forest Offensive as the "final roar of a dying lion."

On December 29, 1944, Colonel Harold H. McClune assumed command of the St. Nazaire sector, and for the first time since its entry into combat, the regiment became the 376th Infantry Combat Team. On the next day each battalion and each company, except Headquarters and Service, were formally awarded the Combat Infantry Streamer.

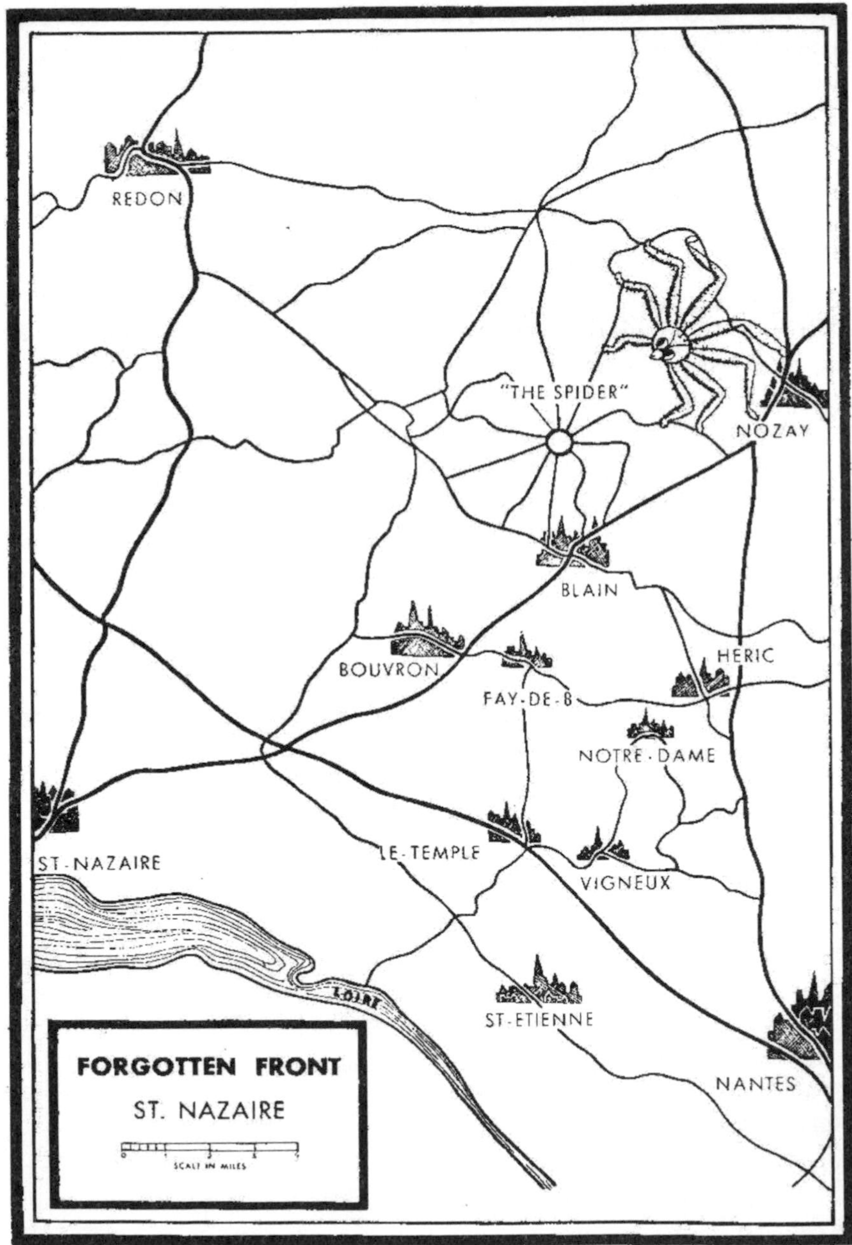

By the end of December, the true story became apparent. The 66th Division was appearing on the lines, and trucks and equipment of the incoming 263rd Infantry were assembling in rear areas. The first days of the "Battle of the Bulge" were so alarming that all major offensive plans had to be temporarily abandoned. Liquidation of the "Bulge," which by Christmas Day, 1944 had reached near-catastrophic proportions, had first priority. A reason that the 94th Division had not been transferred to a more active front during the most crucial days of the Bulge was that reinforcements could be sent more quickly direct from the ports of debarkation on the English Channel. It is entirely possible that if the 66th Division had not lost one of its two transport ships, His Majesty's transport, the *Leopoldville*, off Cherbourg on Christmas Eve, it would have gone directly to the "Front" that first week in January 1945, while the 94th Division continued its holding assignment in Lorient and St. Nazaire on the Atlantic coast of France. The *Leopoldville* was torpedoed crossing the English Channel by the German U-boat 486, with the loss of 784 enlisted men, 14 officers, and equipment, vitally sapping its fighting strength. The U-boat 486 was a new, snorkel-equipped submarine whose Captain was Oberleutnant Gerhard Meyer.

In early December 1944, the strategy was to have the 11th Armored Division relieve the 94th in Brittany, as General Malony had been promised a front-line assignment at the next available opportunity. The first elements of the 11th Armored Division landed at Cherbourg on December 16, the very day the Germans launched their Ardennes Forest Offensive. Thus, the 11th Armored Division moved at full-speed into the Bulge, canceling the replacement of the 94th. However, in late December, the 66th Infantry Division did relieve the 94th and the 94th became part of the XX Corps commanded by General Walton H. Walker—a unit of General George S. Patton's Third Army.

On January 1, 1945, the 376th Infantry Regiment, after 106 days on the line at St. Nazaire, was officially relieved. That evening, after a turkey dinner with all the trimmings, they began the seven-mile march to Vigneux. Here they bivouacked for the night and the next morning, January 2, 1945, they boarded trucks for the assembly area at Châteaubriant. Châteaubriant was the last stop before setting out for the new and unknown destination. At Châteaubriant they waited three days for the trains that would take them across France. Passes were issued and eagerly welcomed, if not for a final celebration before moving on, then for a pleasant means of finding shelter from the freezing and snowy beginning of winter that had set in on a harsh note.

The only trains available were the "Quarante Hommes ou Huit Chevaux" (forty men or eight horses) boxcars of World War I fame, as passenger coaches had become scarce during four years of war in France and the Occupation. These French boxcars were shorter than their American counterparts, and many wondered how they ever got forty men or eight horses into one of them. Although the 376th Infantry Regiment loaded 100 pounds of straw for bedding and twenty-seven men in each boxcar, it was still a cold and uncomfortable ride for the occupants. The boxcars pulled out on January 5.

For three days the trains moved eastward, skirting Paris to the south, passing through Rennes, Lorraine, LeMans, Chartres, Reims, Metz, and finally, on the evening of January 8, 1945, they pulled into Thionville near the junction of the French, German, and Luxembourg boundaries. It was here that the men of the 376th first heard the guns of the western front. At Thionville there was a brief stop for coffee before the trains moved on to their final destination, a small town south of Thionville named Uckange. Here the men of the regiment got off the trains and immediately were loaded into trucks and taken to nearby towns, where billets had been arranged for the night.

Not all of the 376th Regiment traveled by "40 or 8"; this was mainly the foot soldiers. The vehicles had to be driven across France in time to reach their destination when the bulk of the troops arrived in the boxcars. So, the motor convoy left a day earlier from Châteaubriant on January 4, 1945. Thus, the motor columns of Combat Team 376 arrived at Reims, France, on January 6 and left the following morning, while the foot troops of the regiment remained on the 40 or 8s when they arrived in Reims and continued on by rail.

The motor convoy got off to an early start the morning of the seventh, and by late evening the same day had arrived at their assembly area near Sierck, France. At 2300 hours on the eighth, the foot troops arrived in Sierck, and early on the morning of January 9, the 376th relieved the Third Cavalry reconnaissance squadron and was then assigned to the XX Corps of General George S. Patton's renowned Third Army, under the command of Major General Walton H. Walker. The XX Corps had played a dramatic and brilliant role in the Third Army's blitz through France. Now, the 376th, with the rest of the 94th Infantry Division, would join it and take up defensive positions facing the Siegfried Switch Line.

As part of General Patton's Third Army, the 94th Division entered the front lines of Germany facing the Siegfried Line on January 7, 1945, with orders to occupy the area at the base of the Saar-Moselle triangle. The three regiments of the division, the 301st, 302nd, and 376th, had spent several days traveling across France in the bitterest winter in fifty years. Before arriving in the Saar-Moselle triangle, the 94th Division had fought to contain Germans corralled in the Breton ports of Lorient and St. Nazaire, the home of many German submarine pens.

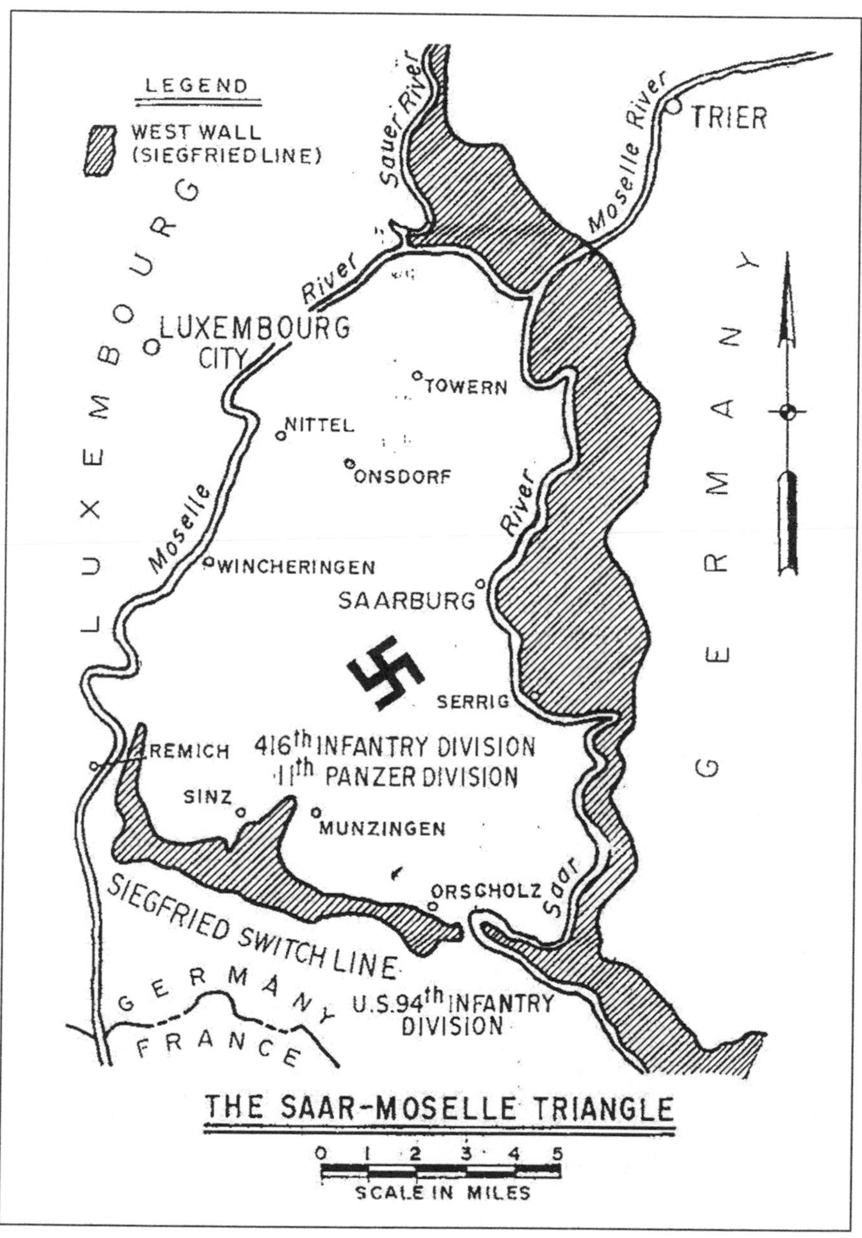

The 94th Division entered Germany at Perl and proceeded to a wooded area near Wochern, in close proximity to Tettingen, Butzdorf, and Nennig. The 376th Regimental Command Post would remain at Sierck; the 1st Battalion CP at Perl, the 2nd Battalion CP at EFT, and the 3rd Battalion CP at Kirsch. Here began its first mission in Germany.

Earlier, on January 3, 1945, the American First Army attacked from the northwest with Houffalize, the center of the German penetration, as its objective. This great counteroffensive began to seal off the German

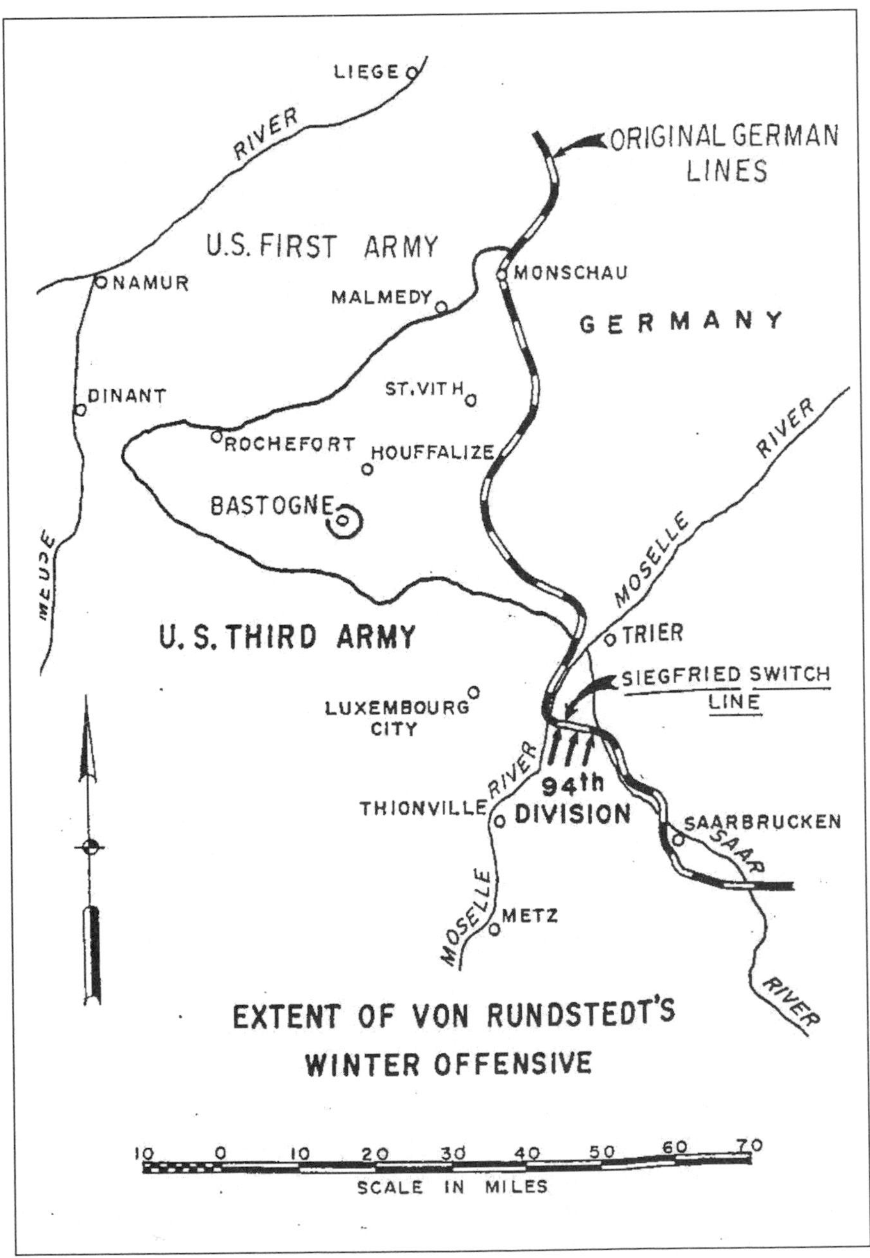

bulge in the American lines. This second half of the Battle of the Bulge began during the bitterly cold winter. To the south, General Patton's Third Army exerted strong pressure in the drive toward Houffalize. This was designed as a huge pincer, cutting into the flanks of the "Bulge" to cut off as many of Field Marshal Rundstedt's troops as possible, isolating them from the main German forces, annihilating them and forcing them to surrender.

These young minds could not fathom what was in store for them—the blood and gore, the human carnage and suffering—images they never could have been prepared for—inhumanities forever burned in their memories. But they knew what they were trained to do and went out and did it, because so much was riding on their actions—the freedom of the world—and they would endure and prevail.

Thus the first mission in Germany for the 94th Division was to make thrusts into the left portion of what the Americans called the Siegfried Switch (the Germans called it the Orscholz Switch). The Germans continued to occupy the area known as the Saar-Moselle triangle, formed by the confluence of the Saar and Moselle rivers, southwest of Trier, Germany. The base of the triangle extended about twelve miles, from Nennig in the west, to Orscholz. The 94th Division faced the entire twelve-mile stretch of the Siegfried Switch from the Moselle to the Saar.

The Siegfried Switch Line was not thought of as part of the west wall, though it was almost as formidable. It was a narrower belt of fortification, running at right angles to the main line, from the Saar River above Merzig to the Moselle River, in the vicinity of Remich on the

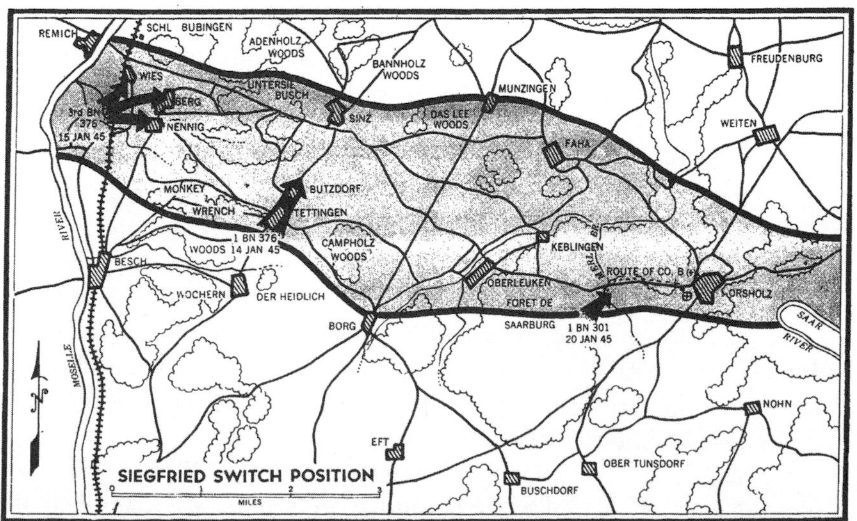

Luxembourg side. For twelve miles the switch wound its way over steep hillsides terraced with vineyards and dotted with thick clumps of spruce forest, passing near the towns of Oberleuken, Borg, Tettingen, Butzdorf, and Nennig. The purpose of the Switch was to guard the approaches to Saarburg, and especially Trier—a very vital communications center for the Germans.

The 376th Infantry Regiment in their new positions were within sight of the Dragon's Teeth and snow-filled anti-tank ditches, communication trenches, and barbed wire. The approaches to towns like Besch, Wochern, Borg, Hellendorf, and Oberleuken were guarded with mines and pillboxes which had perfect observation from neighboring steep hills. From January 9 to January 13, the 376th remained in their position—poised, waiting, and watching—as did the enemy. The frozen ground made the widening of foxholes and the deepening of emplacements almost an insurmountable task. These were the last five days of any kind of quiet for a long time to come.

On January 13 the warning order came: 94th Division will conduct offensive operations within the Switch; 376th Infantry will attack at daylight 14 January '45—mission: to seize and hold Tettingen and Butzdorf. Be prepared to repel counterattacks from the west, north, or east.

In the darkness before dawn on January 14, the 376th attackers were given a hot breakfast and enough C rations to last the rest of the day. Everyone draped himself with as many bandoleers of ammunition as he could carry, and hung grenades from every buttonhole. In spite of the intense cold, no man carried more than one blanket. The idea was to attack aggressively with speed and maneuverability. The 1st Battalion of the 376th Regiment launched its attack on Tettingen at dawn on January 14, the first village behind the Dragon's Teeth on the western slope of a high ridgeland overlooking the Borg-Munzingen highway, leading northeast to Saarburg. Colonel Russell M. Miner, 1st Battalion Commander, requested and obtained from the Regimental Commander two additional companies—namely "I" and "L," from Colonel Benjamin E. Thurston's 3rd Battalion—for the attack. The operation was so successful that the regimental commander, Colonel Harold H. McClune, ordered Colonel Miner to take the adjacent village of Butzdorf. By midafternoon of the same day, Butzdorf was in American hands after two hours of desperate fighting. Scores of German riflemen lay dead in the snow as evidence of the fierce fighting that had taken place.

Colonel Thurston reclaimed his two companies "I" and "L" from Colonel Miner's 1st Battalion for his attack on Nennig, Wies, and Berg the next day, January 15. These three towns anchored the German line on the banks of the Moselle River. Nennig was a town of about fifty stone houses situated on the extensive mudflats bordering the Moselle River. Wies was a smaller town about fifteen hundred yards to the northwest. Berg, the last of the three villages included in the 3rd Battalion's mission, was located about six hundred yards north of Nennig and comprised about twenty stone houses and a strongly fortified castle. The castle was shown on the map as Schloss Berg and was strongly fortified, with a commanding view of all the area in the vicinity of Nennig and Wies. These three towns formed the base of the Saar-Moselle triangle switch position and were heavily defended by Germans. Company L, 3rd Battalion, 376th Regiment, was involved in heavy fighting in the area of Tettingen, Butzdorf, Nennig, Schloss Berg, Wies, and Sinz—the Saar-Moselle triangle of the Siegfried Line.

It was during this action in Tettingen and Butzdorf, in the vicinity of a wooded area known by the 376th as Monkey Wrench Woods, that Morris B. Redmann Jr. made the supreme sacrifice on Sunday, January 14, 1945. He was nineteen years old.

During a lull in a German artillery barrage, only minutes prior to being killed, Morris helped take casualties from the woods to the road for evacuation. To quote his commanding officer, Lieutenant Charles P. Macke, in a letter to Morris's mother: "After helping the wounded out, Morris returned and again the Germans started shelling and it was at this time that he was killed and as Fate would have it, in the same hole that he had just helped one of his wounded buddies out of. There are no words of praise that I might use that I should consider praiseworthy of his act, so I shall not try." Lt. Macke was killed in an automobile accident in 1951, when he went with a neighbor to pick up the neighbor's son from college to bring him home for the holidays.

Morris was killed by a German 88-mm artillery shell. A piece of shrapnel entered his back and hit his heart, and another piece of shrapnel entered the spinal column of his neck. His close friends, PFC Tom (Edward Thomas Jr.) Moore of Columbus, Georgia, and PFC Vincent A. DeMase of Albany, New York, got to Morris in a matter of seconds after he didn't answer their call when the barrage ended. Tom Moore crawled to Morris's hole and lifted him up, but he was already gone—he died instantly. He was hit by the last shell of the second barrage. Tom Moore became despondent after Morris's death, as they were such close friends; he stepped on a German *schützen* (*schü*) mine on January 26, 1945, just twelve days after Morris's death, which blew off his right foot.

About three weeks after Morris was killed, Staff Sergeant Oliver Weisdorffer of the 319th Medical Battalion wrote from Germany to his father in New Orleans, his letter dated February 3, 1945:

> *"If you are ever asked about Morris Redmann, two weeks after he got it, I got the chance to reach his outfit. I found out about him from his buddies. They were Sergeants Milroy and Rasmusen, and I also spoke to his platoon commander. The platoon was digging in after moving up and fighting off counterattacks. The Jerries started tossing in 88's. A sergeant near Morris, his squad leader, was hit during the barrage.*
>
> *A while later another barrage came in and another shell landed in the same spot. Checking later they found him, and he had a piece of shrapnel which had entered his back to his heart, and another piece in the spinal column of his neck. He had a quick, easy death. No pain, plus the fact that his person was not all chewed up.*
>
> *He was very popular and had lots of steady buddies. He was a crackerjack doughboy and one of the reasons the Jerries are strewn all over the sector like fertilizer.*

The 319th Medical Battalion of the 94th Infantry Division was commanded by Lieutenant Colonel Richard P. Johnson. The battalion was split in half to serve both pockets of Lorient and St. Nazaire when in Brittany. They set up two clearing stations—one near Nozay, and the second in the vicinity of Plouay.

Elsewhere in this book are very moving letters from PFC Tom Moore, PFC Vincent DeMase, and Lt. Charles P. Macke to Morris's parents after his death.

PFC Tom Moore returned to the States in May 1945 to Lawson General Hospital in Atlanta, Georgia, for his revision operation on his right leg. All soldiers who have had an amputation have to have this operation to prepare the stump for the artificial limb (prosthesis). He was fitted with the prosthesis in August 1945 and wrote his first letter to Morris's parents on August 13, 1945, giving details of Morris's death. On September 14, 1945, Tom Moore wrote again, advising that he was leaving Atlanta for California on September 18 for a visit with his sister, Margaret Moore Colbert, in Oakland. He had planned his train trip through New Orleans to meet them and would arrive on Wednesday, September 19; he would have a few hours' layover to be with Morris's family. Dad picked him up at the train station and brought him to our home, where we just relaxed. Mother had sent the smaller children out

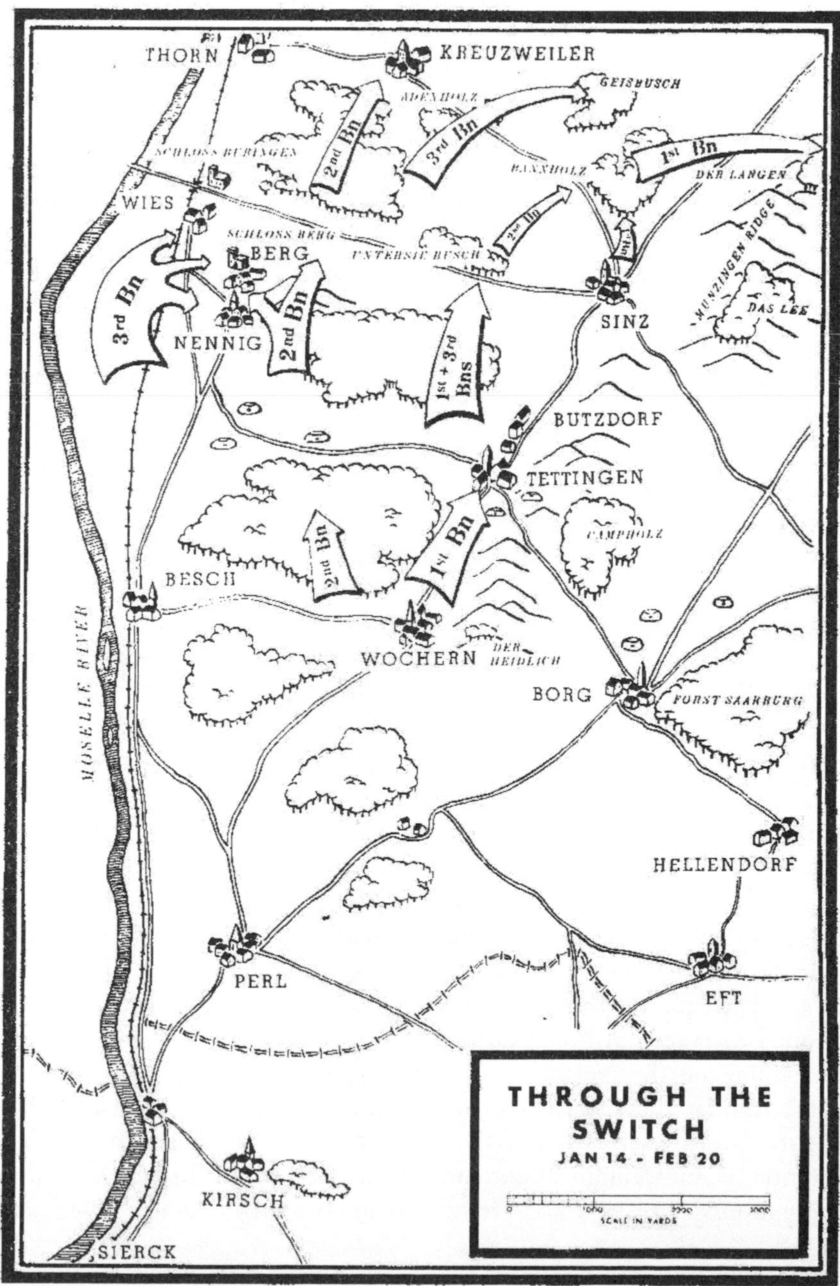

into the yard to play, for obvious reasons. Tom Moore proceeded to tell Mother and Dad the particular details—where they were, what action they were engaged in, and that it was on a Sunday that Morris was killed. He answered any questions they had. Though I was just sixteen when Tom Moore visited us, I remember the occasion quite well. Afterward, Mother and Dad took Tom, my sister, Esther, and my older brother, William, for a nice dinner at Antoine's Restaurant in downtown New Orleans in the Vieux Carré (Tom Moore especially liked Antoine's famous "Absinthe Frappe" aperitif), after which Dad drove him to the train station to continue his trip to California. They all said their good-byes with hopes of meeting again, but for some reason that never happened, other than a nice letter dated October 14, 1945, thanking Mom and Dad for a lovely visit.

PFC Morris B. Redmann Jr. is buried in Luxembourg American Military Cemetery at Hamm—and has been since his interment within days of his death during the Battle of the Bulge. It was the expressed wish of his parents that he remain where "fallen," with his comrades-in-arms, and through the years, we, his eight brothers and sister, have respected this wish.

In quiet reflection, a somber thought emerges—that in his supreme sacrifice, in the flower of his youth, Morris gave up all his tomorrows, as did so many young men, that we could continue in freedom and live a full life. It is incumbent on us and future generations to remain forever a grateful nation. Morris's unfulfilled legacy on earth will never be known—perhaps he would have been a United States senator; perhaps an international lawyer striving to alleviate the injustices of the world. But the additional sadness is that his parents would never realize the brightness of his mature years, nor ever hold his children in their arms.

During the sojourn of the 94th Division in the ETO, Company "L" of the 376th Regiment was commanded by Captain William A. Brightman of Massachusetts, who was later killed in action on February 22, 1945, when the 376th crossed the Saar River between Ockfen and Ayl about two miles north of Saarburg. He was killed by German artillery fire falling on the crossing site. I mention this because after Morris's death, the family letters to him were returned, marked DECEASED 1-14-45, the face of each envelope signed by William A. Brightman, Captain Infantry. Upon Captain Brightman's death, Lieutenant Robert E. Foster, the executive officer, took over the company. Lieutenant William M.

Goldenzweig was Platoon Commander of the First Platoon (Morris's platoon), and the letter censor for the platoon.

After Morris's death, the assault on the Siegfried Switch continued in earnest, and General Patton's Third Army finally breached this major obstacle and went on eventually to capture Trier. Hitler had proclaimed that the Siegfried Line could not be broken, nor the city of Trier captured.

Trier was Germany's oldest city and birthplace of Karl Marx. It was once the capital of the Roman Empire and contains the Basilica of St. Matthew, the only grave of an apostle north of the Alps. Constantine the Great beautified the city. His mother, Empress Saint Helena, presented it with the "holy coat," or seamless tunic (shroud) of Christ, which remained the chief treasure of Trier's fourth-century cathedral.

Lieutenant General George S. Patton Jr. wanted desperately to capture Trier and breach the Siegfried Line, and for his Third Army to be the first Americans to reach the Rhine River and, even more satisfyingly, to beat the British crossing the Rhine. General Patton did both, and celebrated the occasion by relieving himself in the Rhine River. On March 22, 1945, General Patton's Third Army crossed the Rhine River at Oppenheim, a prelude to the final offensive of the European war.

By war's end on May 8, 1945, the Third Army had liberated towns and cities in France, Luxembourg, Belgium, Germany, Czechoslovakia, and Austria. In all, it had killed approximately 145,000 of the enemy, wounded approximately 386,200, and captured 1,280,688 prisoners.

One of the statistics recently revealed by *VFW* magazine and John Kline, editor of the 106th Infantry Division Association *CUB* magazine, is that of the deadliest U.S. Campaigns of World War II, the Ardennes Campaign (the Battle of the Bulge) had the most deaths sustained daily. At first glance, the Rhineland Campaign shows the most deaths at 50,410—but by breaking the various campaigns into days, there is a startling difference. The Battle of the Bulge has a far higher daily kill ratio than any other campaign in the European Theater of Operations.

When the war in Europe ended in May 1945, the 94th Division was located on the Rhine River near Solingen. Later in June, the division moved to a north/south line through Pilsen, Czechoslovakia, facing the Russians across the Elbe River. Later in the summer, the division troops were redeployed, with the next step being deactivation of the 94th Division on February 7, 1946, at Camp Kilmer, New Jersey. Thus ended the saga of one of the finest fighting units of the Third Army.

Germany: The Saar-Moselle Triangle
94th Infantry Division
A Tribute

The highest honor that could possibly be paid the Artilleryman is respect and gratitude from his Infantry buddies with whom he serves. In February 1945, when troops of the 376th Infantry Regiment were coming out of the Line, they marched in single file past the Battery position of Battery "A," 356th Field Artillery Battalion of the 94th Infantry Division. They glanced over and saw the Artillery Guns in position and the Cannoneers standing by. One by one, each Infantryman in the column took off his helmet and brought it to his chest. One Infantryman broke a smile across a mud- and ice-caked, bearded face and said simply, "Thank you."

Letters of Morris B. Redmann Jr. to His Family October 20, 1943, through January 11, 1945

P A R T   O N E

CAMP BEAUREGARD, LOUISIANA

October 20, 1943–October 30, 1943

Camp Beauregard, Louisiana
October 20, 1943

Dear Mom,

The Army is all right. The food is wonderful. Here is our menu for today:

Breakfast
2 hard-boiled eggs
1 serving of preserved apricots
1 small box of cornflakes
1 cup of coffee
bread and butter

Dinner
serving of meat loaf
mashed potatoes and gravy
1 cup of lemonade
white beans seasoned with diced ham
stewed apples
bread and butter

Supper
short ribs of beef (Wow!)
string beans
potatoes
lettuce and tomato salad
rice and gravy
pineapple juice

These are some portions too. Everything is fine but the water—it tastes like diluted Clorox.

Today I was interviewed. I'm ASTP but at present am an Air Corps cadet—wait until they make me take the eye test: I'm classified as an artist (ho-ho). Out of a possible 140 in the Army General Classification Test, I scored 129—tied for highest with an Elroy James, a very well-educated Negro graduate from Dillard. On the mechanics test I made 135 out of 150 (average was 73). On the telegraph operator reception test I made only 84.

I have just come home from the "day room"—all the latest magazines, pool, cards (gambling is a court-martial offense), ping-pong, etc.

Well, all's well that ends well and this has been a perfect day. Kiss all the kids and tell all the folks hello.

Lovingly,
Morris

* * * * *

Camp Beauregard, Louisiana
October 20, 1943

Dear Mom,

This is just a short note to tell you that my clothes are on the way home. I am fine. The meals are very good, extraordinarily so. The weather is warm and carrying around some $300 worth of equipment on your back is no picnic. Already I have met Harry Cain, Frank Hennessey from WWL, and Irwin Poche. Poche says he might, if I so wish it, fix it so I can be permanently stationed here—teaching illiterates. If so I should be home almost every week-end. We have all the latest magazines. Can get all the candy we want, ditto for soft drinks or what have you.

I will go see *This Is the Army* for 50¢ for Army Emergency Relief.

I do not send my address, because you move around a lot here. You don't know where you will be next. Usually I wind up on the end of a line of 4,000 waiting on chow.

There are eight fellows to our tent—all swell guys. There is never a fight—always a lot of joking and language.

When new recruits come in, it is the funniest thing in the world. All the other veterans—of two days, or only a few hours—start yelling "Fresh meat" or "You poor fellow; you had a good home and you left it."

When they line up for typhoid shots and physical inspection the "veterans" scare the devil out of those guys—some of the new recruits pass out—by telling them of the different places in which they get the shots. Oh, well . . . oh, for the life of a sailor.

Lovingly,
Morris

* * * * *

Camp Beauregard, Louisiana
October 23, 1943

Dear Mom,

Here is my insurance policy and some other papers that I wish you would keep as souvenirs for me.

I shall know Monday what they're going to do to me. I still have to take the Air Corps test.

I have the rest of the day off—but don't know what to do. At present I have a big hut all to myself—all the other fellows having moved out. These same fellows are all stationed here for the duration, one teaching (Charles Schwarz—he knows Daddy and Ludwig Eisemann, says he's signed many documents with Daddy, he's a Phi Beta Kappa from Tulane and had one yr. of law), another going to school (H. Thibodeaux, big-hearted Cajun), one as a cook (Clifton Morris, formerly the manager of St. Regis), and the other fellows as clerks.

I hope everybody is well at home and is doing well in school.

Do not write yet because I am liable to move out at any time.

Kiss Robert and David for me.

Your loving son,
Morris

* * * * *

October 28, 1943

Dear Mom,

This has been the worst week I have ever spent. These have been the longest days of my life. As I told you over the phone, I had KP on Tuesday. Twenty-four hours divided into 6 hours of sleep and 18 hours of work—and I mean work.

I had various jobs all day long, the hardest of which was peeling 25 pounds of onions for the meat loaf. My crew went on at 4 o'clock and the only time I got to sit down was when I had a bowel movement.

Here are some of the jobs I performed.

1. Peeled 800 lbs. of potatoes in an electric peeler
2. Helping pick out the eyes
3. Clean up the machine
4. Store 1,000 loaves of fresh bread
5. Help cut up and store some 16 sides of beef (enough for 2 meals)
6. Supervise the storing of waste fat
7. Cleaning out the bread boxes
8. Peel onions
9. Help clean the 100-gal. capacity electrically operated cooking pots
10. Prepare 750 gals. of lemonade
11. Help break 13 cases of eggs for Wednesday's breakfast
12. Load garbage
13. Store butter
14. Help cut butter into small pats (48 lbs. for breakfast alone)
15. Serve at breakfast some 3,500 dishes of cereal
16. " " supper some " " of fruit
17. Help mop and scrub with soap and lye the floors and walls of the kitchen

These are only a few of the many hundreds of jobs that must be done each day.

However, at the end of the day I chalked it up as "experience" and considered the day one well spent.

Wednesday at 2 P.M. until Thursday at 2 P.M. I had 24 hours' guard duty—two hours on and four off. On the ten o'clock watch five Negroes made a run thru my post. I got one with my nightstick but the other four got away. So I yelled at the top of my lungs for the Corporal of the guard. Such a call goes all around the camp, being repeated by the guard marching each post.

On the two o'clock watch about thirty Negroes came running thru the post (the post I marched was right along the woods). I was about 100 yds. away when I first sighted them. They ran like the wind. I just stood there and watched. First I yelled "Ha! Grand Central Station," then I burst out with "Corporal of the Guard Post No. 12." Most of them were rounded up before they reached their tents.

Today I got off at two o'clock and watched the German prisoners of war dig ditches. These men receive their pay according to their rank in the German Army, plus 80¢ a day for working. They don't have to work if they don't want to. One of these POW's asked me for a cigarette. I told him I didn't smoke. He turned away. A Negro soldier standing next to me asked me what he wanted. I told him. The Negro said, "You reckon he'll take one of mine?" I called the soldier back. The Negro held out a fresh pack. The German took one and bowed graciously and smiled his thanks. Guards stand ever ready with machine guns.

Tonight I had guard duty over at the Negro PX (Post Exchange) from 7 'til 9.

Tell the Kellys, Stuarts, and Sellers hello. Tell them too that I'll write as soon as I'm permanently stationed.

What happened to Mrs. Fonseca? Ask Will to get the dope for me on Numa's draft status.

C'est tout.

Lovingly,
Morris

* * * * *

POSTCARDS

Camp Beauregard, Louisiana
October 29, 1943

Dear Mom,

I write this seated on my barracks bags. I am leaving in a few minutes. Will write when I reach destination. Give love to all.

Morris

Dear Jerome,

I hope you are studying hard and making good marks. Please be a good boy so that I can send you something for Christmas.

Morris

Dear Robert,

I am writing this on a big choo-choo train. Tomorrow I shall be a long ways from home. Help Mother all you can.

Morris

Dear Kerry,

Glad to hear you made the team. I owe you a quarter. Try also to make the grade in school.

Morris

Dear Dad,

Well, I'm on my way. I know where I'm going but cannot say. Am riding on Mo. Pacific train as I write.

Morris

Dear Kerry,

This is one of the many big buildings in this big city. However, all of the tall buildings are hotels. There are here also the Holton and the Bankhead, named for the senator from Alabama.

Morris

Dear Will,

I am glad to hear you are doing fine on the *Maroon*. Tell my friends at school hello.

Morris

* * * * *

Birmingham, Alabama
October 30, 1943
Arrived at 10:00 A.M.

Dear Mom,

I have been on and off trains for the past twenty hours. Our first stopover was at Monroe where we had dinner at a very nice restaurant which was owned by the father of one of the five other fellows traveling with me.

I am going to Fort Benning in Ga. for ASTP which suits me fine. I'll probably get there late tonight (Sat.) or early tomorrow morning. I intend to look up Lucas right away.

This morning we passed the huge Bessemer iron and steel works. The little settlements around these works are very dirty and squalid, and Birmingham resembles them quite a bit.

We have a six-hour stopover here because the coupling on our coach broke last night and it was four hours before we started out again. No air-conditioned cars were the ones we rode in. They were the oldest cars I have ever seen. No cushion seats but wooden slats provided us with little comfort.

In the toilet there was a campaign poster suggesting Jeff Davis for the presidency. I thought at the time that even the infamous Jesse James might have held up the passengers of this coach of 150 yrs. ago.

I have had very little sleep and am getting ready now to eat breakfast, since our cattle cars had no diner. After eating I'm going to look over the city. Already we have passed through several large cities.

Do not write me until I write from the Fort. Love to all.

Morris

P A R T T W O

FORT BENNING, GEORGIA

OCTOBER 31, 1943–MARCH 4, 1944

Fort Benning, Georgia
October 31, 1943

Dear Folks,

Happy Hallow'een (?)! By the time you get this you should have received about 20 postcards and letters written en route (catch dat French). I left Camp Beauregard—that wonderful place (really)—on Friday, Oct. 29, and arrived here at Fort Benning, today, at one o'clock in the morning.

The first big stop was at the nice city of Monroe. Here I was really surprised to see the large buildings and the very nice restaurants. One of my barracks-mates, Nick Kokinos, a good-looking Greek, took us to his father's restaurant to have a free meal. We insisted on the acceptance of our meal tickets, which were limited to 75¢ in restaurants and $1.00 on trains. Although Nick swears he didn't have anything to do with it, we got:

vegetable soup
lettuce and tomato salad
very large steak, 12" x 1/2" x 5" (approx.)
french-fried potatoes
lemon pie and ice cream
coffee

From Monroe we went through almost all of the big towns in Miss. We transferred at Meridian to the Birmingham train. In the middle of nowhere the Smithsonian relic we were riding in broke down and we were delayed 7 hours—with no breakfast car.

We arrived in Buminham—as I've heard it called by all the natives—at 10 in the A.M.

Adjoining their very grand station and a large part of the station itself is the USO—a very fine organization. Here we took showers, shaved, and checked our baggage. I wrote you a letter and some postcards there. The stationery is provided free, along with cake, candy, and fresh fruits, late magazine, etc. From the USO we sallied out, having 7 hours between trains. We had breakfast at the Beverly. Then I went into the big hotels, the Bankhead, the Tutwiler, the Holton, looked around, had a beer. Then I went to the department stores. There are more 5 and 10's in Birmingham on one street than there are in all of La.

But I got what I wanted. There are three ties there, one each for Daddy, Kerry, and Will. For Richard there is a big jigsaw puzzle. Ditto for Ralph. Ronald gets the Lone Ranger set. Jerome, the paints and book that colors by just passing a wet brush over the pictures. Divide the little plastic ships between David and Robert. The other little things (I forget what they are), you might give to Ronald or to somebody I might have kinda skimped.

For Mom & Es, there is a separate package—one box apiece.

I guess that covers everybody.

I'll miss this Christmas and I'll celebrate New Year's in the field. We start the rugged physical on Nov. 8. Then at the end of the month we get the "mental conditioning" only one day—of machine-gun fire, bursting shells, dynamite charges at three feet, etc. Oh well, such is life.

Sincerely,
Morris

* * * * *

Le Fort Benning
le 2 novembre 1943

Ma chère Esther,

Comment allez-vous? Et votre mère et votre père, et mes frères? J'espère que tout vont bien. Ici la nourriture est mal, c'est affreuse ça, épouvantable. Surtout, c'est triste. Hélas, sapristi!

A l'USO à Birmingham les gens sont bons aux soldats. Donc, j'ai donné un dollar aux charités unies de la guerre. C'était un dollar bien donné.

Je suis heureux que mes cadeaux sont arrivés. J'espère que vous les aimiez.

Je regrette que M. Douglas est mort.

Je me souvenirai M. Fonseca dans mes prières.

Je n'ai pas trouvé mon ami Lucas. Je suis mis en quarantaine pendant deux semaines. Donnez mon adresse à sa mère et lui demandez de le lui envoyer par lettre. Je ne peux pas sortir de cette partie du fort pour lui rendre visite, mais il peut venir me voir. Cependant, je vais lui écrire une lettre et découvrir où et quand je peux le voir.

J'espère à recevoir vos nouvelles bientôt, et je reste le frère d'une soeur charmante.

Morris

* * * * *

Fort Benning, Georgia
November 4, 1943

Dear Aunt Winnie,

I certainly was glad to hear from you and appreciate very much the money you sent me. It will come in handy. You can never realize all the things that you have to buy yourself in the Army. Then too we have all the latest shows here, many of which have not shown yet in New Orleans and won't for a long time. There is almost a new show every night. Tonight there is a double feature. Admission is fifteen cents. Ordinarily, I wouldn't go out to the show that much, but if you sit around the hutment, you get to think of home too much. It grows on you. You feel like a lost soul—you'd give anything to see home again. The shows are the only thing to keep your mind off home. I feel that if ever I can lose this homesickness, I'd be a darn good soldier.

My basic training lasts until Feb. 1, 1944. I go out on bivouac on New Year's Eve for two weeks in the field. I won't be home again for years, I guess, unless by some small chance I would be sent to LSU for advanced engineering. There is absolutely no commission attached. The highest rating I can hope to attain in this program is that of a Buck Sergeant. OCS is closed, so if I want to become an officer I'll have to wait till the next war.

As regards your letter, the Army does give me gloves. They're all wool and very warm. I suppose if ever you have some little cakes lying around, you might wrap up a few and send them out.

I'm sorry that Claude got a bad mark in Greek. I know Claude is a very bright boy and am inclined to believe that this mark is not due to any shortcoming of his own.

As regards having my picture taken, I'm afraid that's out. Columbus is a rotten town—I don't want to go into it.

I haven't lost any weight yet but expect to before I finish here.

Give my regards to Uncle Claude and to the two little Kellys.

I hope to hear from you again soon and I remain,

Sincerely yours,
Morris

November 5, 1943

Dear Mom and Dad,

I waited until today to write because the Army was undecided as to what to do with me. I am considered as overeducated—as far as the Army is concerned. I was told also that I would be ineligible for ASTP. However, at noon yesterday, the classification of candidates began. Every soldier was interviewed. My interviewer, thank goodness, was a WAC. After a few minutes' conversation I had her in the palm of my hand. But she, as had the other interviewers before whom I had gone, said that she was afraid that there was no place in the ASTP for me because I was a college grad. I asked her to consider the fact that most of the fellows of my age had just finished high school and were going to be sent to engineering. Why couldn't I? I was only eighteen. She admitted that I had finished school very young and was surprised at my "wealth of education." After a few pensive moments she went into consultation with an elderly Captain and a Lieutenant. Some minutes later she came back and put me in Basic Engineering. I got in because I was so young. We talked for a few minutes more about school, etc. Finally, as the interview closed, she wished me good luck. I rose to attention and saluted. She returned the salute and smiled. I left the building a member of ASTP. Today we took physics and mathematics tests at high school level. I think I did all right. When I go to college it'll be just my luck to be sent out West or up to Yankeeland. Oh well—ours not to reason why, ours but to do and die.

I am glad that the two packages got there. Glad am I, too, that everybody was pleased. I tried to get what I could with the money I had. I assure you it was as much a pleasure for me to go shopping (the stores there were already decorated for Xmas) as it was for the children to receive them.

I heard from Aunt Winnie and Aunt Ogie. Each sent me a buck, so my finances are stable.

Max Derbes and several other fellows are out of ASTP but will go through basic training here.

If you can get a sweatshirt my size, I could use it. It gets awfully cold here at night but gets awful hot in the day.

Well, give my love to all and congratulate Kerry and Rich.

Lovingly,
Morris

Daily Communiqué
Area: Battle of Fort Benn
Troops: ASTP

Dear Mom and Dad,

Today the officers and non-coms forged ahead on all fronts in their greatest attempt so far to make us soldiers. With preparation that started yesterday with the chopping down of trees and with a withering fire of calisthenics, lectures, and drills that started at eight in the A.M. but spent itself near noon today, it was foreseeable that the battle would be just beginning. However, at about 1:30 we were besieged by Sergeants, Corporals, and Cadres and forced downhill to the supply room where our forces held the enemy from two till six, cleaning and unpacking rifles of the 1917 vintage. At 7 P.M. we began general retreat and had to sweep and mop the barracks. However, at nine tonight, all's quiet on the Fort Benning Front.

For dessert tonight I ate a pt. of ice cream bought at the PX. Sun. night I saw *Lassie Come Home* at our theatre. There are more good pictures coming at the end of the week.

I shall remember Mr. Douglas in my prayers. I shall pray also for the safety of Mr. Fonseca.

There is a boy in my barracks named McIntyre who is the very image of John H. Redmann, even to the glasses.

Most of the people here are Republicans—except the fellows from Louisiana.

I'm convinced that Georgia was a desert and that the Army engineers just put the trees here for ornaments. No kidding. I never saw so much sand in all my life—nor did I ever sink so deep in sand as I do here with every step.

But I'm worn out and need sleep. A fellow just told me that we don't get paid till the 30th, so I guess I'm sick now too.

Please give Mrs. Bruno my address. Tell her to give it to Luke and ask her to ask him if he could get to see me soon or let me know what time he'll come around. I'm quarantined and can't leave here to go see him, but he can come see me. I'm not quarantined because of sickness or anything. The Army does this because any kind of disease will show up in two weeks if we have any.

Oh well, I remain your tired but loving son,

Morris

Le Fort Benning
le 6 novembre 1943

Ma chère Esther,

Aujourd'hui j'ai parlé avec des prisonniers de guerre. Ils sont italiens. Ils sont très heureux à leur nouvelle maison. Ils reçoivent de l'argent pour leur travail dans les forêts et les bois. Après la guerre ils aimeraient rester ici et devenir citoyens des États-Unis.

Les collégiennes, comment vont-elles? Peggy, Susie? J'espère qu'elles vont bien. Combien y-a-t-il dans votre classe au collège? Mon français est mieux, n'est-ce pas?

Quelques jours passés nous avons marché pour deux heures au soleil chaud.

Lundi je commencerai à étudier d'être un bon soldat dans la plus grande armée du monde. J'espère que je puis être un bon étudiant.

Je m'en vais au collège bientôt. Peut-être au milieu de février. J'ai fait beaucoup d'amis ici.

Mon sargent s'appelle Garner. Il a vu le combat en Afrique et en Italie. C'est un bon homme et un bon sargent. Mon lieutenant, appelé Barnette, était autrefois avocat.

Il fait mal ici. Il pleut toute la journée, aussi pendant la nuit. Il fait froid pendant la nuit et très chaud pendant le jour, quand nous marchons.

Ah, moi, ma foi, c'est triste, cette vue, comme-ci, comme-ça.

Affectueusement,
Morris

* * * * *

Postcards

Fort Benning, Georgia
November 7, 1943

Dear Missy [Esther],

I certainly am glad to hear that you are as studious as ever. Dites allô aux jolies filles que tu saches pour moi.

Morris

Birmingham, Alabama

Dear Es,

I passed this statue this morning when we came into the city. I saw it from my train window. It stands atop the mountains in which rich iron ore deposits are found.

Morris

Dear Mom,

Well, I'll be eating Ga. peaches soon. Don't worry. I'm fine, in good health. Don't expect to be home until about 17 wks from now.

Morris

Dear Ralph,

I'm glad to hear that you can read my letters. I will send you some more postcards soon.

Morris

Dear Davie,

I hope you are behaving yourself and not giving momma any trouble.

Morris

Ft. Benning, Georgia
Sat. 1:15 p.m.

Dear Mom,

Have just returned from shopping. Am sending home presents for everybody. They should arrive in day or two.

Morris

Dear Ronnie,

Do you still listen to the Lone Ranger? I hope you are studying hard and that you don't give Mother any trouble.

Morris

Dear Fatso [Richard],

Well, they found a uniform for you, did they? I hope when I come home again you are taller and not so round. I hope you beat Easton.

Morris

Fort Benning, Georgia
Monday, November 7, 1943

Dear Aunt Winnie,

I received the package from you on Friday night. Thank you very much. That was one of the things I forgot to get in New Orleans.

Mother has one picture of me which was taken by Mr. & Mrs. Reinecke at Camp Beauregard. Today we were shown the results of our posing on Saturday morning. The picture came out pretty good. It is the 8th Co. 5th Regt. ASTP. I'm on the top row, seventh from the last man on the left. I'm sending home 5 copies so you can get them from Mama when she receives them. Anyone in the family who wants one is welcome to them.

Although we have had two days of rain—which has turned the fort from a sea of sand and dust to a sea of slush and clay—the morale here is high. We stood for about 30 min. in the pouring rain this morning to get breakfast. The whole company was singing in the rain. Singing songs of all types, songs of your day, of mine, of the First World War, even to "The Battle Hymn of the Republic."

After breakfast we spent four hours disassembling the gas-operated, semi-automatic Garand rifle, a wonderful masterpiece from a genius's mind.

After lunch we were taken to the Co. theater where we saw *Prelude to War,* a film dealing with the reasons for the clash between the democratic ideology and the fascist ideology, and also with the world events that led us into war.

After the show we had a couple of hours on poisonous gases. We wore masks, were given sniffs of the gases so that we could recognize them in combat.

After a 10-min. break we spent an hour learning how to roll a full pack. Now that we have learned how, we shall march tomorrow with the full pack, rifle, canteen, bayonet, and cartridge belt, with first-aid kit attached.

If ever I can get to be anybody in the Army, I would consider making a career of it.

The temperature now (9:25 P.M.) is about 35°. It'll be even colder tomorrow morning.

Thanks again for the present. Give my regards to Uncle Kelly and the little Kellys.

Your loving nephew,
Morris

Le Fort Benning
le 8 novembre 1943

Ma chère Esther,

Aujourd'hui j'ai reçu votre lettre. C'est bon. C'est une bonne idée que nous écrivons en français. Ma mère pense bien.

Tu es fâchée que je n'aime pas la nourriture ici! Ha! Comment penses-tu que je me sens? Il faut que je la mange.

J'aimerais lire les éditions de votre journal du collège et aussi le journal de mon collège. Les envoyez-moi, s'il vous plaît.

Mon éducation, maintenant, consiste de tout ce qu'un soldat doit savoir pour survivre en bataille. J'étudierai tous les fusils. Je saurai vivre dans toutes les conditions de bataille. C'est une bonne éducation.

Demain nous marcherons à travers les forêts pendant vingt kilomètres à pacquet plein.

Bientôt j'enverrai cinq photos de ma compagnie, le 8-5 Regt., de quoi je suis un membre. En donnez un à qui le veut.

Comme aller à LSU!—La Dame Fortune n'était jamais avec moi. Hélas! Probablement je serai envoyer au nord au collège. C'est ma fortune! Fortune, à moi, est "la femme fatale."

Dites aux vendeurs de la glace et du lait "hello" de ma part.

Affectueusement,
Morris

* * * * *

Fort Benning, Georgia
November 8, 1943

Dear Dad,

Thank you very, very, much for the five. I found out today that we have to pay laundry fees, so much a month, whether you send or not.

The Army, Navy, or Marines is a good life for anybody as long as there are no mental setbacks or psycho-neuroses caused by the effects of actual combat.

Today we learned to disassemble the gas-operated, semi-automatic Garand rifle. Really a honey. Then we learned to roll a full pack, then something about chemical warfare and the use of the gas mask. Tomorrow we're going on a hike with full pack.

The weather has been terrible here but we're well dressed with fine warm clothes, raincoats, and plastic helmet liners. It's pretty cold tonight and will be colder tomorrow. The rain has stopped and left a sea of slush and clay—all in red, yellow, and orange colors.

Will you please ask Mama if she can get a pasteboard box that she could put about 12 hangers in. I need them bad. I could use also a pair of woolen underwear—2-pc., and a pair of leather gloves. Of course, if Mama has any extra space in the box she might put in as a filler some fudge or something.

Oh, yes, I could use a knee-high pair of wool socks—if Mother can get them.

Give my love to all. It's now 9:40 and I need sleep.

Morris

* * * * *

Fort Benning, Georgia
November 8, 1943

Dear Kerry,

I am glad you liked the tie I sent you. I bought them in a hurry and did not know which one you would get.

I am glad that Jesuit has won all of its games so far, and I hope they will go through the season undefeated.

Congratulations again on making the team. I hope you move up to 1st string soon. You can do it. Work hard but don't neglect your studies. Write me a simple letter in Spanish. I will try to understand it and I will write you back my translation.

Morris

* * * * *

Fort Benning, Georgia
November 9, 1943

"Aux Petits"—

I am glad that you like the presents I sent you. By the time I come home, I am sure—or at least, I hope—that David will be able to write without Mama holding his hand. As for Robert—I cannot get you a real gun because it costs $87.50, which is more than I can afford. However, if ever I can go into Atlanta where they have big department stores, I will send you a good play rifle.

I hope too that my two pals, Robert and David, are behaving themselves and helping Mother.

Ronald—don't send me any more paintings; I have no place to hang them. Do a lot of painting and keep the pictures in a folder so I can see them when I come home. The one you sent me was very good.

Ralph—you are very welcome for the presents I sent you. When you have completed your puzzle, work on the other one.

My thanks to all of you for your prayers. I pray for you little fellows, too.

Morris

* * * * *

Fort Benning, Georgia
November 10, 1943

Dear Mom and Dad,

Have your letter of the ninth. Would like to get a letter a day but realize how rushed you both are.

The fellows that are ruled out of ASTP go through their basic training here, but transfer to some other outfit when we start college.

I certainly will be glad to get the sweatshirt. I'll sleep in it.

I didn't ring Sunday because I didn't think it was necessary. Although I would have liked to have heard your voices, I decided not to call because first, I choke up when I go to speak, and secondly, there flashes through my mind all the swell things about a good home. I miss you a lot. On Sundays too I get homesick when I hear Mass. I miss Fr. Castel's sermons. I get the desire to want to serve at Mass. Last Sunday I asked about it, but there are many, many Catholic soldiers on a list awaiting their turn to serve at Mass. By the way, are there any altar boys left in our family?

I heard today too from Aunts Hy and Ogie.

I can't do anything about David's birthday except send my best wishes. I'll try to keep Aunt Winnie's in mind though.

I got the $2 and the one today. Thanks a lot. If you want to send me a Christmas box of food, I would appreciate that more than anything else. If you send, send plenty. There are fellows in the hut that have gotten packages from home and have been very generous with us.

Don't send me a bracelet yet.

I am glad that all are well and I hope to hear from you very soon.

Loving Son,
Morris

Fort Benning, Georgia
November 10, 1943

Miss Ogie Joyce
1905 Calhoun St.
New Orleans, Louisiana

Dear Ogie,

I was happy to receive your letter because it came at a most opportune time. I had just come back from a six-mile hike over the very hilly country of Georgia.

Our schooling began on Monday morning and we haven't had a moment of peace since. Monday A.M. we spent four and a half hours on the M-1 rifle—the Garand. Then from one till two, we had an hour on chemical warfare, then an hour of picture shows on why we had to go to war, then the rest of the day, the rolling of light packs and full packs and marching and drilling.

Tuesday we had—starting at eight o'clock in the A.M. in a temperature close to freezing, with only our fatigue clothes on—one hour of vigorous calisthenics, then till one o'clock, military sanitation and personal hygiene. In the afternoon—two hours of the "Interior Guard"—then two more hours on Extender Order, Hand and Arm Signals. (I have pages of notes.)

To-day we got up at 6:30, got dressed, and made our bunks. Fell out for reveille at 7:00. Went to chow, finished at about 7:40, got back to the hut, swept and mopped it, emptied all trash cans, and took down wash hanging from rafters (if you hang it outside, it freezes). Fell out for the day at 8:15. Had an hour of calisthenics. Put our clothes and field pack, cartridge belt, and rifle back on and marched over to theatre No. 12 for lecture on "personal hygiene." Then drilled for two hours. This afternoon had lecture on gas mask, and then gas drill. Finally a short lecture on what to wear to go on a hike. Then hiked till six.

This is an average day. The morale is high here even though we get up in a hut with no fire or anything; even with taking baths and shaving and washing in ice cold water. Everybody has a good time laughing and yelling at each other in the showers. I guess if you could stand still in the cold showers you wouldn't be natural.

The food is fine here. I'm losing my homesickness and I'm beginning to even like the place. There is no aim in griping. A smile goes a long way and I have to live here for a great portion of the next thirteen weeks. Already I've lost about fifteen pounds, even though today as every day I had seconds on breakfast and dinner and only one supper, making five meals to-day.

As regards Armistice Day: The intervening twenty-five years was a period of truce. This is really not World War II, it is only a continuation of the First World War. The terrible misjudgment of the Versailles Treaty was the mother of the conflagration of today. Christian principles were ignored, if not aggressively violated. Man's greatest attempt at peacemaking failed the hope of mankind—a lasting peace.

Tomorrow I shall spend in prayer. Praying that the vengeance of the battlefield shall not again dictate the terms of the covenant. Praying that my sons, if I ever have any, will not have to fight for their freedom as we fight today for the freedom of the world.

I may sound like I'm preaching, but in the Army I have learned to appreciate my religion and its unchanging principles. I have met many soldiers who have no god, no church, no principles, no reason, if you want, for living or for observing any set standards of morals. These I can only pity. Then too I have been given strength to answer the many jabs of the d——d Yankee, high Anglicans, from Deacon or Beacon Hill in Boston who went to Tufts College and who think they know everything. There is plenty of power in a prayer well said.

Give my regards to all. I'm glad that everyone is well.

Sincerely,
Morris

* * * * *

Fort Benning, Georgia
November 11, 1943

Mrs. Joseph R. Sellers
3020 Paris Ave.
New Orleans, Louisiana

Dear Aunt Hy,

Thank you very much for the "buck." Also for the very nice letter. I was certainly pleased to hear from you.

I am glad that you have finally settled down and feel comfortable. I guess a telephone does help, too. I'm sorry, though, to hear that Jodie Boy is not well. I shall pray for his recovery and continued good health. I have loved my little brothers at home, but it has been some time since I have seen a new pink and white package. I don't believe Jodie Boy and I ever had the pleasure of meeting each other.

I'm writing this at 9 P.M. over in the huge recreation hall—a rather large building, filled with tables and chairs and standing lamps, huge wall maps, and hundreds of games. There is a radio-phonograph set here complete with all the latest swing records, also many card tables and Ping-Pong tables. Here, too, are Coca-Cola machines, always full.

Yes, I had a good home but I left. Ha! Ice-cold huts, showers, winds, and rain. However, most of the fellows here are grand guys. Standing in the rain the other morning waiting for breakfast, I saw a fine example of morale. It was very cold, the rain came in sheets, but the fellows stood there in the cold, shaking their mess kits and singing "Jingle Bells," and singing other songs, too—songs of the last war, songs of the days of yesterday, good old songs that I thought were lost forever under the pile of swing and jazz of the present generation. I couldn't help joining in. It was natural. The spirit of these buddies permeated every fiber of my body. It raised me from the depth of melancholy—for I had never stood in the rain waiting for a meal I wasn't sure I'd like. I actually enjoyed the period of waiting. By the time I arrived at the mess hall door, everyone was in high spirits. Yes, the Army is a grand organization, if you make it such—and it was such to me on that morning and the rest of the day.

Letters from home also give a fellow a lift, as did yours this evening. I got it just after coming from a six-mile hike.

Give my regards to Uncle Joe and the little ones.

Sincerely,
Morris

* * * * *

Fort Benning, Georgia
Sunday, November 12, 1943

Dear Mom & Dad,

I tried to get to Confession this morning, but even though I was twenty minutes ahead of time, the line was so long that the chaplain wasn't able to hear all the confessions. Next Sunday, however, I think I will be early enough to be heard.

When you lay around this place at night all the happy scenes of your life flash before you in one continuous reel. This is what makes you feel bad. But at other times when you're being instructed or when you're marching, or in a bull session over at the PX, you're feeling good then. As long as you're doing something, even if it's KP, the longing for home leaves.

My Lieutenant's name is Barnette, and there is a fellow in my hut named Schwarz. Barnette was a lawyer in civilian life.

Except for a few melancholy moments, I am enjoying myself. Every time I have been interviewed I've heard the surprised exclamations of the interviewers regarding my age and my education. Yesterday was the final day for interviews. The WAC officers arrived together with several Lieutenants & Captains who composed the ASTP acceptance board. When my turn came I walked up to the WAC interviewer, saluted, and sat down. She told me that she was afraid that my eyes were too bad, and that it was up to the board to decide whether I would remain in the Army or not. So I waited to go before the board. Since here I have taken about five exams of every type. To the board I carried all my records of everything I have done since I got into the Army.

I sat down at the table before the board, composed of two Lieutenants, two Captains, and one civilian, who had a false right arm. He seemed to be the one running the show. Then the questions began.

The Capt. told me I really had no background as a college student for ASTP. He then asked me to explain briefly what the radio course consisted of that I had taken in college. I told him. He then told me that I was the youngest college grad he had ever heard of. The Lieutenant on the left asked if I didn't feel a little strange going through school at such a young age. I replied that I had been rather backward as a social being in high school, but had snapped out of it after my first year of college. Then I gave a brief history of my life. They listened very attentively. Finally, when I had ended, the Capt. asked what I would like to study at school. The choice was given to me, he said, because I had "done brilliantly" in the tests. On the classification tests, I made 129 out of 140. On the mechanical aptitude test, I made 180 out of 200. On the General Cooperative test in physics, I made 130 out of 135. On another test dealing with definitions and applications of scientific terms, I made 178 out of 200. All of these were the highest marks in the company. On the math test I made only 84 out of 120—the only test I didn't do well in. So, I told the Captain I thought I could do best in engineering. The Capt. asked if I knew anything about engineering. I told him I didn't. Before he could reply, the Lieutenant on the left said that he thought I could start off from scratch and learn anything. The Capt. agreed. So they put me in Basic Engineering, term 1. And so for the next two years, I go to college. I was then told by the board that I would never be in combat service because of my eyes. However, each member said that my case was unusual, that they expected me to keep my nose in the books all the time, to make the highest marks, and if the war lasted long enough, to be commissioned a Lieutenant and teach other trainees.

Well, that board certainly made me feel good. I walked out whistling.

There are no newspapers here and no radios. I don't even know who is winning the war. What I miss most is news about New Orleans. I'd like to know, too, how Jesuit is doing in the prep league. Ask William to see about my getting the *Maroon*. It is sent free, I believe, to all alumni in the service. Let him give my address to Marion Schlosser, the editor. Tell him to say hello to Frs. Chapman, Crandall, Mullins, Gaul, Soniat, Quirk, Dr. Bonomo, and others with whom I was affiliated through classes or organizations.

I pray that I can get through these next thirteen weeks. These will be the hardest of all. We will learn how to break down, repair, and fire the Garand rifle (the M-1), the Enfield rifle, the grenade rifle that fires grenades, the 30 mm. machine gun, the old trench mortar, the 57 mm. cannon, the French 75, and the 105 mm. field gun. Then, too, we shall use anti-tank guns, including the famed bazooka. It'll be quite an education.

Yesterday we spent two hours among some Italian prisoners of war. We gave them cigarettes and chocolate. I have never seen a happier group of men in all my life, even though some had been in the Italian Army for as much as 12 years. Their ages ranged from 19 to 31. I honestly believe they are better off than we are. There are no guards, and the American officers in charge all speak Italian. I spoke with one in French, asking how old he was, how long he had been in the Army, and where he was from. He told me he was from Naples and that he had been captured in Sicily.

We are having very nasty weather here today.

Send me some clippings of the political situation, too.

Your loving son,
Morris

* * * * *

Fort Benning, Georgia
November 14, 1943

Dear Mom & Dad,

Sunday, today, I went to Confession and Communion and prayed for everybody. At this time too I remembered that this being the second Sunday of the month, the Holy Name Society was receiving Holy Communion and holding a breakfast and meeting afterwards. I offered my Mass also for this intention.

Last night, right after I had finished speaking to you, I was called to the orderly room and told that there was a man from the 4th Rgt. coming to see me. I waited until after 10 o'clock, but he never showed up. I suppose it was Luke. However, our regiment is hard to find at night and I guess he missed it in the dark. Today being Sunday, though, I expect to hear from him sometime today. I won't be able to go see him as I had planned because I am restricted until I get some more clothes.*

At ten I went back to the hut where there was a feast in progress. Two, or rather three, Italian boys had received food boxes from home. Their names are Santelli, Scioli, and Ruffrano. Other fellows had cake and candy. I had a box of pralines that somebody sent, I guess you, for which I am very grateful, and a box of cookies that Aunt Winnie sent me. So we pooled our interests and sat down to a big meal. I went down to the PX and got the soft drinks. There were loaves of Italian bread, cakes, Italian salami, cheese, little candies, one large cake, and chocolate bars. We sat around until eleven when the lights went out, then went to bed. These certain moments make you realize what kind of fellows you're with, and the boys in my tent are the most generous you could find anywhere, and they certainly possess a fine spirit of fellowship.

This past week certainly went by fast. It seems as if it were just yesterday that we sat down to Sunday dinner. Every day is packed with work, marching, and lectures. The time passes quickly, and most of us look forward to mail call. Mail call here is an institution. I always run and wait for it, sometimes in the rain; the other fellows drop everything they're doing. I've seen guys taking cold showers run out in the cold weather with only a towel wrapped around them to be present at mail call. They get their mail and then run back to the showers. That's what mail means to us.

Yesterday, on Saturday, we took another hike with full equipment. This time it was a little longer than the last one. This time, too, we pitched our tents in the forest under the trees, and then camouflaged them. After a few minutes' rest, we marched back home.

I haven't written in some days because I haven't had time. I've had night detail or work twice. On Thursday night we hiked over to the Greek theatre over at the Officer Candidate School. Here we heard some talks by some lecturers of the National Conference of Christians and Jews (to whom Loyola was host at their convention in New Orleans about a year ago). The first speaker was a Fr. Redden from Montana, followed by Dr. Spears, a Protestant minister, and then by Rabbi Rosenblum.

The Rabbi told a joke about the young man who took his grandmother to church services with him. As they were standing in church watching the procession, the young man pointed out one of the members of the procession.

*Editor's note: Morris had just returned from an Army exercise in the woods and his fatigues were torn and muddy.

"That's the new deacon," he said to the old lady. "What?" she asked, for she was a little hard of hearing. "That's the new deacon. NEW DEACON," he said very loudly. "Oh" she replied. "A new dealer." Exasperated, the young man exclaimed, "He's the son of a bishop." "Oh" said the old lady. "I thought they all were."

And that's all the news for now.

Lovingly,
Morris

P.S. I enclose $1 for David. Don't worry, we'll be paid in December. I signed the payroll the other night.

* * * * *

Fort Benning, Georgia
November 14, 1943

Dear Aunt Winnie,

Thank you very much for the cookies and the "Soldier's Housewife." Both came in very handy. Saturday from two 'til three we had inspection. I don't know what I would've done had it not been for the needle and thread. We had to wear woolen ODs (olive drab). The woolen shirt I had on was missing a button, and the only other OD shirt I had was dirty. But I got the needle and sewed the button on in time and passed the inspection.

I would have written sooner but honestly, you don't have a minute to call your own here. Every day is jammed full of action. Every minute is accounted for by lectures, picture shows, tactics, etc. Every hour sees the increase of our knowledge.

It really is, beyond a doubt, good to lead the Army life. Even with the cold showers and the cold weather, I haven't been sick once. I eat like a horse and in spite of this, I've lost about 15 pounds. Before I come home I'll have to go to a tailor's shop and get all my clothes cut down in the waist. I feel fine and haven't been homesick in about a week, and don't think I ever shall again. Our officers and non-coms are all fine men. The reason that we are worked so hard, they say, is to keep our mind off home and things it shouldn't be on. These officers believe that the idle mind is the devil's workshop, and therefore, our minds are never idle. We are taught to be attentive and alert at all times.

This morning I went to Mass and Communion and prayed for all the family. The chaplain gave a short sermon about rendering to Caesar the things that are Caesar's and to God the things that are God's. He's a very good priest and a fine man.

This Christmas and New Year's will be spent on the rifle range.

The other day a collection was taken up in the mess hall for something extra for Thanksgiving. Cigars, cigarettes, candies and cakes, ice cream, too, all you want, will be placed on the tables. They collected about $65 from the 250 men in my company.

And that's all the news for now.

Lovingly,
Morris

* * * * *

Le Fort Benning, Georgia
le 15 novembre 1943

Ma chère Esther,

Aujourd'hui j'étais le chargé d'affaires de ma "platoon." Il faut que je fasse échec des lits pour confirmer que tout le monde est là. Si quelqu'un n'est pas là, il faut que je l'accuse.

Ici, la nourriture est très bonne. Aujourd'hui, c'était un beau jour. Je me suis bien amusé. Nous sommes allé au cinéma pour voir le film *Pourquoi Nous Sommes aux Armes*. C'était bon. Il raconte l'histoire de l'avancement d'Adolf Hitler.

Les nuits ici sont belles. La lune éclaire toute la nuite.

Maintenant il faut que j'aille.

Sincèrement,
Morris

* * * * *

Fort Benning, Georgia
November 16, 1943

Dear Mom & Dad,

Today we learned a lot. We advanced through the woods under strafing from the air (simulated attack by planes) and actual gas attack. This evening we went through chloropicrin, lewisite, mustard, tear gas, and phosgene. We wore special clothing and carried rifles and ammunition belts besides our gas masks. The charge was up the hills and through the woods until we finally stood on the crest of the drill field. This is the kind of work I like. Maybe I'm still childish, but I get as much fun out of this as Ralph or Ronnie get out of playing Lone Ranger.

Tomorrow we're going on a long hike. We'll eat out of cans in the field and pitch tents again. I don't know how my feet will hold up, but so far they've been grand.

The food is swell now and gets better day by day.

I got some candies from Aunt El and Lala. Please express my thanks, for I don't have time to write and may not get another chance to write until Sunday. However, I'm thinking always of everybody and remember all in my prayers.

Well, it's almost midnight now, and I've got to get to bed. I'll write again as soon as possible.

Your loving son,
Morris

* * * * *

Fort Benning, Georgia
November 17, 1943

Dear Folks,

I received the kids' letters today and was certainly happy to read them. I thank you very much. I would like to thank Esther for the fudge. The other fellows enjoyed it as much as I did.

The weather is really cold here and I wear the longies Mother sent me all day.

Today we went on a march out into the hills. In the morning we had demonstrations of several of the shells and guns used by the infantry, of which one was the famous bazooka. This is one of the most deadly, the most powerful weapon against mechanized warfare. It is only five pounds and fifty-four inches long. At 300 yds. it will smash four inches of armor plate or twelve feet of solid concrete. We had lunch in the field from field kitchens set up on trucks. Then after a brief rest we set out on some practical work. We went over the infiltration course—100 yds. over a cactus-covered, brush- and log-studded Georgia hill. Your helmet is to the front, the nose of your face is scraping the ground, your back flat, and your heels down, feet out. (Some guy just spilled a bottle of ink on my writing table.) That's OK, bud! A little ink never—no, really, get off your knees. I'll forgive you. Yes, I know you're sorry. That's OK.

Later on we dug slit trenches and foxholes. I was issued a shovel last night and I really used it today. A while later we had lessons in concealment—how to hide yourself among the places afforded by the terrain, such as fallen logs, brush, tall grass, etc. This is the kind of work I like—the practical end. I don't care at all for the calisthenics or group games. I believe that practice as a soldier makes perfect as a soldier. It was some grind today. At times during the infiltration course I felt I couldn't pull my body another inch, but as it was, I was fifth out of 250 to finish. You don't go around cactus, you go through them. After it was all over I felt good, and as I write I am confident I shall sleep well tonight. I don't know what tomorrow brings, but whatever it is, I know I'll make it after today.

That's all the news for now. I remember you in my prayers, especially for the success of Daddy in his case, and I remain

Your loving son and brother,
Morris

* * * * *

EIGHTH COMPANY
Fifth Training Regiment, ASTP
Fort Benning, Georgia

le 18 novembre 1943

Ma chère Esther,

J'ai reçu la dragée. Je vous remercie beaucoup. Je l'aime beaucoup. Je suis heureux que vous faites bien en français. C'est bon.

Est-ce-que *L'autobiographie de M. Chesterton* est en français?

Il y a vingt garçons, ou mieux, soldats, dans ma hutte.

Ils ne sont pas tous italiens, mais ils sont des bons hommes. Les photos de ma compagnie seront envoyés bientôt, j'espère.

J'espère que vous avez gagné une victoire contre les jeunes filles du Collège Dominicain. Bonsoir. Il est minuit maintenant, et il faut que je dorme.

Sincerement, votre frère,
Morris

Fort Benning, Georgia
November 18, 1943

Dear Mom & Dad,

To-day was the first monthly anniversary of my entrance into the Army. I am feeling fine and am enjoying good health.

By way of celebration I went through the tear gas chamber. First time through you go in with your mask on. When a whistle blows, you take it off. When the next whistle blows, you leave the chamber. Well, now I realize what a powerful weapon gas can be. I was only exposed to the gas for about fifteen seconds. But in those fifteen seconds I got enough to last a lifetime. The second time, we go into the chamber with our mask all packed up. Well, having learned a lesson only some minutes before, I was pretty darn quick to get that mask on. I think I got it on in about five seconds. After a few minutes in the chamber we were permitted to leave. This was a grand experience, though, even with its tears.

Tomorrow, Friday, we will march ten miles out to the bivouac area and back. I guess I'll be pretty worn out and I don't think I'll be able to write.

I don't care for the sweets much. Your suggestion of olives, spreads, cheeses, crackers, etc. sounds swell. There are twenty in the hut, but all are never there at one time.

I am glad David liked his present and had a truly Happy Birthday.

I'm sorry that I left out Jerome. So this part is for him. Well, Jerome, old man, I hear you have made all A's on your report. But what happened to you in Deportment and Application? I hope you shall do better next time. Work hard and you shall lead your class. I hope that you obey your mother and father and your teachers. There is one thing that I have learned in the Army that I hadn't really learned until now—and that thing is obedience. Without obedience you cannot have discipline; without discipline you cannot run an Army. And without a well-behaved Army, you cannot win wars. Your ability to obey and do is the first step. After you have learned this, Jerome, then you can command. A man is not measured by his looks or height or weight in the Army. The true man, here, is judged by his ability to follow orders. Therefore, obey, Jerome, that some day you may command!

Well, that's all the news for now.

Your loving son and brother,
Morris

P.S. I got Will's letter & the *Maroon*s [Loyola University campus newspaper].
Thanks. Morris

I haven't rec'd the paper yet.

EIGHTH COMPANY
Fifth Training Regiment, ASTP
Fort Benning, Georgia

November 18, 1943

Mrs. C. J. Kelly
4139 Gen. Taylor
New Orleans, Louisiana

Dear Aunt Winnie,

There is no doubt about it: Fr. Chapman is one of the more brilliant men of our time. He is truly a genius. Sociologist, Historian, Lecturer, Economist, and Author, he was a very fine teacher from whom I learned very much. It was on his final exam in his course "The Philosophy of the American Way of Life" that I made 100%—the highest mark he ever gave in thirty years of teaching.

The Belgian priest you heard was probably Fr. Victor J. Dossogne, S.J. Des Lettres et Des Philosophies de Louvain at Belgium. He was a professor of law at Loyola until the demand for his talks was so great that he became a lecturer. Fr. Dossogne is probably more concerned with the causes that led up to the war—the corruption in French politics, and the corruption of the French as a nation. He is exceptionally well informed along these lines, and is a member of the national board for Belgian War Relief.

Fr. Chapman's principles are deeply rooted, and his far-seeing wisdom has searched out the only plan for true world peace. His books on world economy and business and banking can be found in London, Calcutta, Washington, Chunking—in any place where democracy still flourishes. He has met and dined with the Rockefellers, the Fords, Wm. Nelson, and almost all the cabinet members and bureau heads appointed by the present administration. He is truly a wonderful man and a grand professor. If ever you have occasion to meet him again, mention me and see what happens. He and I were very good friends.

I hope all are well. Give my regards to Uncle Claude and the two little Kellys.

And that's all the news for now.

Your loving nephew,
Morris

Fort Benning, Georgia
November 21, 1943

Dear Mom & Dad,

After a pretty rough week I spent a pretty swell week-end. Saturday we had a general inspection by the Major. Inspection of shoes, of foot lockers, of rifle, of equipment, of hut, and of mess cans. Our hut passed the hut inspection, but there were only six of the twenty fellows in the whole hut that had everything perfect. I was one—even though I was scared to death when the Major picked up my rifle and started looking over the parts. After three hours the inspection was over. Those who passed were given their passes and permitted to leave for the week-end. Well, I was going to go to Columbus but I decided not to; Lt. Tyler talked me out of it. He told me that if I just wanted to see the city and go to the USO club, I could do better by waiting until this morning. I took his advice.

Last night I went with some of the fellows up to the Service Club over by Luke's regiment. We had a swell meal there and it was ridiculously cheap. It's a cafeteria arrangement. As I came down the line some beautiful pieces of freshly broiled meat were brought in. It looked like veal cutlets with the bread. So I asked the waitress for it. Instead of giving me one, she gave me three. I would say that I had a pound of meat there! Then I got a tremendous serving of some of the most beautiful cauliflower I have ever seen. Next I got carrots, creamed potatoes, and string beans. Also I had pocket rolls (hot) and butter. I had a gelatin salad and a huge piece of angel food cake with icing and a cup of coffee. This wonderful meal was had for only fifty-five cents! It was really good.

I talked with Luke a while after and he suggested going to town and to Mass there. Then I started the long walk home with the rest of the fellows. Some caught the last show at the theatre on the way home. I got in before ten but wrote Charlie Brennan, Warren Mouledoux (who in six weeks will be a Lieutenant), Bobby Broussard, and Aunt Ogie. I thought I'd wait until tonight to write to you.

This morning I got up at eight, went to breakfast, and fooled around until about 9:30 when I went to meet Luke. We came back to my place where I waited for mail call, and received the Thursday paper and the swell package of food. I rounded up two of the other fellows, Scioli and Rich, and the four of us walked about two miles to the cab station. It's twelve miles into town and the cab driver charges only 60¢ per passenger, which is very, very cheap. We got off on Broad Street and Luke and I went over to the Catholic Church, a building of the stone Gothic type. It was a very lovely little church with a huge mural of the crucifixion on the wall behind the altar. There were officers of every rank there with their wives and families. It being dinnertime when Mass was over, we went to a nice little restaurant called the Victory Café. Here we had another good meal, but it cost more and we got less. I had a western broiled steak which was on a big platter surrounded by tomatoes and lettuce, french fried potatoes, rice and gravy, and early June peas. For dessert I had lemon meringue pie and coffee.

After dinner I had my shoes shined and took a walk around town. There are one or two high buildings here, but they are hotels. The town itself is fair, and cleaner than Birmingham in appearance. Finally, we decided to go to the show, and at the Bradley we saw Olson and Johnson in *Crazy House*. It was all right, but not as funny as Abbott and Costello. The theatre itself was very beautiful on the inside—more beautiful than any of the New Orleans theatres.

When the show was over we went over to the USO. I gave the lady at the big reception desk my name, phone number, and all that. She told me to go ahead and wander about the building wherever I wanted and that I'd be paged when the call came through. I had no sooner gotten into the next room when the loudspeaker boomed my name. I rushed up to the desk and was told to use booth two. So I talked with you.

Luke, having completed his call, showed me around the place, and I played the piano for awhile in one of the upstairs rooms. After this we caught the 7:00 bus for the Harmony Church area and came home. Tonight I rounded up Derbes and some of my other friends, and their food too, and went over to my hut and had a pretty good time eating. I still have the oranges and apples and chocolate syrup malt and milk, but everything else except the peanut butter is gone. Everything was swell. Thank you very, very much. I walked halfway home with Luke and then came back to write.

Well, tomorrow is an easy day for a change. I will try to write again then.

That's all the news for now, and I remain

Yours, gratefully and lovingly,
Morris

Fort Benning, Georgia
November 22, 1943

Dear Mom & Dad,

It is now 1540 Fort Benning time. I have been latrine orderly since 0800 this morning. As I write this I am sitting in the shower room on some of the benches we scrubbed this morning. This afternoon is loafing time. What am I saying? We loafed all morning. The thing I can't see is why they put four fellows on an easy detail like this. All we had to do was clean 16 toilets, 19 urinals, 21 basins and their brass-work, mop the floors, and clean the shower room. We finished this after about three hours and then read funny books. Around eleven-thirty the Major came around for inspection and told us we had done good work. At twelve-thirty the Captain came over and told us to go back to our barracks and prepare for chow. He said that the Major said we had the best latrine in the whole battalion. Oh, well, the man with a B.A. degree can do well in any field.

Tonight Hedy Lamarr is coming to our theatre with a USO Club show. If I don't get any mail I shall go over and see the show.

I can't think of anything to write about now but will write again tomorrow.

That's all the news for now. I hope all are well and I remain

Your loving son,
Morris

* * * * *

Fort Benning, Georgia
November 22, 1943

Dear Aunt Winnie,

Just a few lines to wish you a very Happy Birthday and many more.

Of course the card looks nice and all that, but I don't know how you'll like its scent. I'll confess that I didn't pick it out myself. I got it last week through my Corporal because I didn't know when I would be able to get to town. Although the taste is his, the sentiments are mine.

So once again I wish you many happy returns of the day, and I hope that all the Kellys are well. Give my regards to all.

Your loving nephew,
Morris

Postcards

Fort Benning, Georgia
November 23, 1943

Dear Ralph,

I am glad to hear that you are studying hard and I hope that you will make all A's. I thank you for your prayers, but I hope that you are still an altar boy. You must realize that being an altar boy is the greatest act that you, at your age, can do with regard to the worship of God.

Happy Thanksgiving to you.
Morris

Dear Robert & David,

Well, how are my two little pals? I hope you are well. The next chance I get, I will try to send you some picture postcards.

Morris

Dear Jerome,

When I can get it, I will send you the insignia that I will wear on my sleeve. I can't buy it yet because they aren't on sale.

Morris

Dear Ronald,

I am sorry to hear that you weren't feeling well on Sunday morning. That's too bad. When you have finished the book, write me and tell me what it was about.

Morris

Letters

Fort Benning, Georgia
November 23, 1943

Dear Mom & Dad,

Well, the hard stuff has really started. Today we had one hour of physical drill, one hour for obstacle course, one hour of judo, and one hour of the motion pictures—No. 3 of *Why We Fight.* Then an hour off for lunch.

In the afternoon we had two hours of map reading, and two hours and a half of bayonet drill. This is really tiring. I had wanted to go to the show tonight, but having received a few letters from you and some of the Tri-Sigs, I decided to spend the evening writing. I have received all the papers up to and including Monday's. It's certainly good to hear from the old town.

I'm going to write George to-night. I didn't know his mother was dead. When did she die? Recently or what?

I heard from Charlie Brennan and Warren Mouledoux the other day. They seem to be doing fine. Charlie is over in Mississippi and Warren is in Texas.

Well, that's all the news for now and I remain

Your loving son,
Morris

* * * * *

Fort Benning, Georgia
November 25, 1943

Dear Mom & Dad,

Today is Thanksgiving. However, it isn't any different than any other day. We marched all yesterday, went on night tactical operations that lasted almost all night, and this morning were permitted to stay in bed until 8:30, if you wanted to miss breakfast, which I did. We worked until lunch when we had bread, water, red beans, and fried sausage.

I have just returned from a long march that started immediately after lunch and lasted until six o'clock. I have already bathed and am now waiting mess call at 7:30. We're supposed to get all the turkey we want. We shall serve ourselves, and I know that after missing breakfast, having so little for lunch, and after marching for so long, little Morris is going to look after little Morris wherever the food is concerned.

As for the day itself, I said little prayers for the most part. While on tactical work last night, while in the early hours of the morning in the depths of darkness, while resting during our "breaks" during the march, I thought of the numerous graces and blessings that have been bestowed on us during the past year. These graces are rather negative.

We can be thankful that this nation as a whole has not felt the deep pains of hunger and starvation that now grip almost half the world. Thankful that our skies are still blue and our fields green. Thankful that our people hover not in fear, trembling at the sound of the exploding aerial bombs. Thankful that our little children's faces are not stained with live horror and mortal fear. Thankful that our churches stand, not as hollow shells, devoid of roof or floor, but as the sacred castle of "our Lord and *Souverain,*" whom we all adore. Thankful that our cities have been spared, because of geographical position, the tragedy of Warsaw, the horror of Hamburg, the rocking devastation of Rotterdam and London, the criminal and barbaric destruction of Naples. Above all that the air we breathe is free, that free men fight to keep it free. Thankful that perhaps this time we might win, not only the war, but also the peace. Thankful that we have, in the teachings of the Catholic Church, the only solution to the problems that are creasing the brow of mankind. Thankful that these teachings, if adopted in a world covenant, would bring new life, peace, and joy, once more to mankind. Yes, we have a lot to be thankful for.

I have now returned from supper. It was really a very splendid meal, enjoyed by all.

The tables were beautifully set with their white tablecloths and glistening silverware, the salads—already set out—the huge cake already cut on each table, two different pies one at each end of the groaning boards, the golden biscuits and butter, the handsome red tomatoes alongside the celery and olives, the mounds of green peas and mashed potatoes, the smaller dishes of corn, the little dishes of cranberry sauce and other jellies, the steaming pots of coffee and finally, "in media res," the king of the delicacies, the Thanksgiving turkey and dressing, all gleaming white meat, wonderfully sliced and plentiful—the grace by the rugged, slightly hunched-back, stern Captain, and his command "seats,"—the introduction of the company's guests of honor, the wives of our commissioned and non-commissioned officers—the resounding applause to the few words uttered by the Mess Sergeants at the end of the feast—this was the Thanksgiving celebration the Army gave us. And it was swell. Everybody was really happy.

Last night I ran into Luke Bruno; he had been looking for me all evening, but I hadn't been there. He had come to say good-bye and to borrow $10 until he got home—the lucky sonofagun. He'll drop by to see you sometime during the coming week. The ten dollars I lent him I had just received from Dad. But don't worry; I'll have it back within a week, in plenty of time. He certainly looked happy and I guess he was.

They've really been working me hard lately. I only go on from mail call to mail call and from Sunday to Sunday. Tomorrow night I have guard duty. And then the regular work for Saturday inspection.

I would like to thank Dad for the money, but I am afraid that in Luke's case, I could *not* "neither a borrower nor a lender be." "For it were poor fraternity indeed that would forsake a brother in a hole." (With apologies to M. B. Redmann, Esq.)

I am sure that the income Uncle Sam gives me will be plenty after I get settled. I don't spend much on the "luxuries of life." I haven't had time to go to a show here.

As soon as you can I would like a small volume of Shakespeare's plays, a small English dictionary, and if Esther wants to write in French in the future, a small French dictionary. You could send these as a Christmas gift because there is nothing I need or want. I refuse to ask for any food now, because after the meal we finished a while ago, the very name itself is repulsive.

Well, that's all the news for now. Tell everybody "Hello" and that I will write on Sunday. I got a swell card from Ogie. I wish you a Happy Thanksgiving and I remain, ever

Your loving son,
Morris

* * * * *

Fort Benning, Georgia
November 28, 1943

Mr. & Mrs. Joseph Sellers
3020 Paris Ave.
New Orleans, Louisiana

Dear Folks,

Although it's rather late, I would like to get this letter done before I go to bed. I have been meaning to write for the last few days but hadn't had the time. I heard that everybody had a very nice time on Thanksgiving Day down at the Kellys. I wish I could have seen all of you. Although I really missed home, there was some consolation, and compensation too, in the Thanksgiving supper served us here at Camp. It was really swell.

I know how "little" Joe is. I hear about him in all the letters I get from home. Mother says he is adorable, and Aunt Winnie says he's one of the grandest babies she's ever seen. But I never hear about Margaret anymore. Joe seems to have taken over the spotlight from her. How is the young Miss? I hope everyone is well.

This past week was a rather hectic one. However, the more work done means the less there is to come. The obstacle course here is not very hard. The only thing I can't do is go over the eight-foot wall. Already we've had a good bit of tactics and night work. I have liked it all so far. Of course at night I'm worn out, but every morning when I get up I feel fine. I've lost plenty of weight and waistline inches, which necessitates the alteration of all my clothes.

I offered my Mass & Communion this morning for you all and for any special intentions you might have.

Well, that's all for now.

Your loving nephew,
Morris

* * * * *

Fort Benning, Georgia
November 28, 1943

Dear Ogie,

I would like to thank you very much for your sweet remembrance on Thanksgiving Day. I am sorry, however, that I did not get a chance to write you sooner, but last night (Saturday) was the first night this past week that I was off and I decided to sleep. On Friday night I got only three hours of sleep, and last night, I slept like a log.

We are now beginning our fourth week of Basic. This week, running, we will be out every night on tactical operations, so I don't think I'll be able to write until next Sunday perhaps. Lately we've had a lot of map reading and work with the compass. So this week we will have to go through the swamps and woods by compass and arrive at a certain point before or at a certain time. I went through the other day at the head of a squad of six men, and we missed the stake only by five paces, which for our first attempt was pretty good. Of course, when we finished we had a little mud on us, and we were a little damp, but we had fun. One fellow who I picked to read the compass was named Raczykowski. He was supposed to get the compass reading and pick out a prominent object in the terrain in line with the reading and then lead us there. Well, he picked out a tree. So I told him to keep his eye on the tree and lead us to it. Well, he started out staring straight at the tree, fearing lest he lose it. At that time we were walking on comparatively hard ground. He was about fifteen paces ahead of me and the other fellow when all of a sudden, I saw him fall. I rushed up and saw him pulling himself out of the mud and water. He had fallen into one of the many concealed streams that flow through the woods. But he was still looking at the tree he had sighted.

This Tuesday we have to go over the same course, approximately, but at night. There is no moon out now, and since the operation is tactical we are not allowed the use of matches or flashlights. But I know we'll make it all right.

This morning I offered my Mass and Communion for the continued health of all the family and for any particular or general intentions you all might have.

At this moment there is a soldier in here playing the piano. He is playing all the songs that Mother used to play. It recalls to my mind all the happy moments we used to have, whenever all the uncles & aunts & cousins got together at the house for somebody's birthday or for 4th of July or other holidays. I know Thanksgiving must have been a wonderful celebration with you all. I missed it. I really did. All day we worked and sweated. Finally at 8 P.M., all dressed in our GI best, we entered the mess hall led by the Captain, our Lieutenants and their wives, and the non-commissioned officers and their wives. There were tablecloths and plates and silverware, flowers—almost like home. It was really swell. All you could eat.

I hear that we'll get Christmas off. That means another swell day I'll miss at home, but I know it'll be pretty good here.

With love to all,
Morris

* * * * *

Fort Benning, Georgia
November 28, 1943

Dear Aunt Winnie & Uncle Claude,

The past week has been terrific. We've been hit with everything under the sun. However I consider everything in a passive light and thus, time passes very fast. The work is very interesting and had I been in better physical condition when I entered the Army, I would enjoy every hour of it. I now believe it should be a matter of personal pride as to one's physical fitness and stamina. I'll never ride Kerry for taking Charles Atlas courses, for doing exercises. Had I done this I wouldn't have the tired feeling I do when I go to bed each night.

This past week we've marched a lot, gone on tactical operations and night movement that sometimes extended our day from 12 hours to twenty hours. Friday night, for instance, I got only three hours' sleep but made up for the loss last night. In the past few days, too, we've had a lot of map reading, contour lines, and profile work. Also we've had a lot of experience with the compass. On Friday, at the head of a detail of six men, I had to take an azimuth of 310° on the compass, basing the direction in a line from myself to a prominent object in the terrain in line with the azimuth. When I reached the first object I took an azimuth of 310° again on another object, walked to it, and so on, until I reached our destination. We arrived only five paces off, which was fairly good for our first attempt. Our course led us through dense jungles & swamps and hidden streams that make up this part of Georgia. It was quite an experience. On Tuesday night we will go out and proceed from one point to another by compass. This compass, by the way, is a very fine one, with luminous dial and sighting instruments. Since this operation on Tuesday is tactical, we will not be allowed the use of matches or lights. But we'll make it, and probably do better at night than during the day.

Yesterday evening I spent some of my free time out at the obstacle course trying to get over the 8-foot wall. I met with little success. I can get over everything else but the wall, and frankly, I like this obstacle course.

Life is not dull here by any means. Every morning we have an hour of calisthenics, one hour of dismounted drill, two hours of bayonet drill, an hour of class. From one until two we have lunch. In the afternoon we have about three hours of class and one hour of competitive sports or group games. We play football or have Indian hand wrestling or Indian leg wrestling or running games or horseback fighting. It's a pretty good setup. We never walk anyplace anymore—we run from one field to another, or from one class to another.

Yesterday afternoon after the regular Saturday inspection, we had the battalion parade. Of the sixteen platoons participating in the competitive drill, mine was second by only 1/3 of a point. But next week we'll win it. The platoon in our company that wins the most places in the competition will, at the end of 13 weeks, be feted at a dinner paid for by the other platoons, and will receive a huge silver cup.

This morning I offered my Mass & Communion for the whole family and for any special or general intentions you all might have.

With love to all,
Morris

Fort Benning, Georgia
November 28, 1943

Dear Richard,

Well, how are you getting along in school? Jesuit certainly must have a good team. I was glad to read that they beat Holy Cross. I hope they go on and beat Easton by a good score. However, win or lose, I know the Jesuit team will be in there fighting hard.

Are you getting any thinner? I am. I've lost so much weight that I will have to get all my clothes taken in before I can go into town again. My pants which once would hardly button are now about five inches too large.

The Pepsi-Cola people will send home a record of any boy's voice. All that is required is that you make the record. There is no charge or anything.

I hope you make good marks and I remain

Your loving brother,
Morris

* * * * *

Dear Ralph,

I am glad to hear that you are doing well in school, but you really ought to try to watch your spelling. A good speller is a good reader and a good reader is a good speller. I have noticed at times that I myself make mistakes in the spelling of little simple words that I once knew. That's because I don't get a chance to read as much as I used to.

When I come home I'll show you some real tricks that I have learned in the past few weeks.

The next time you see Richard Treuting, please ask him for Frank's & Billy's address. Then send me their addresses in your next letter.

Your loving brother,
Morris

* * * * *

Fort Benning, Georgia
November 28, 1943

Dear Mom & Dad,

Today I attended Mass and received Holy Communion and got off on the right side of the new Church year that starts on this, the first Sunday of Advent. I received your letter in this morning's mail. I was certainly glad to get it. Also, I got a very nice letter from Uncle Billy Hume. It was a very good letter and a pleasure to read.

I missed Mass this Thanksgiving because there wasn't any said in our regiment or near here. But I prayed throughout the day. This Friday coming is the first Friday of the month, and Mass will be at 6:15 P.M. I don't know how fasting requirements will be met, but whatever they are, I am going to try to get to Communion, too. This morning after Mass the chaplain gave out prayer beads, religious pamphlets, and missals. I took the missal even though I have my own, because I prefer to read the Latin of the Mass.

I am glad that everybody had such a good time on Thanksgiving Day. I enjoyed myself at dinner here that night, but not to the degree of former, more happier days. I wish I had been there to see all the family and Joe Jr. That is one young man in the family that I never met.

(I have just finished talking with you on the phone.)

The other day we had to go through the compass course. I was at the head of my group and we came out pretty close to the finish stake—only five paces off. This was very good considering that this was the first time I had ever used one of their compasses. Some of the other groups missed their stakes by as much as twenty-five paces. Last week we had all kinds of work—marches, tactical work, night problems, and what not. This past week was really terrific. This coming we will have much to do. On Tuesday coming we have to go through the Georgia jungles & swamps by compass at night. This is going to be a panic. We fell all over when we went through it in the daytime.

I'm getting along all right now. I've got the Capt. and Looies and the Sergeants working for me. I felt that I had to remain here at the post to see that they attended to their duties. No, really, I don't care to go into town. I have no reason to go. We get all the latest shows here, sometimes weeks before you do. Last night I went to the show to see *Thousands Cheer.* It was the first show I have had the chance to see in quite some time. Many of our classes consist of training films made by the Army Signal Corps. These are much better than the usual dry lectures we get on grenades, malaria control, or what-not.

I get paid on Tuesday. I don't know how much, but at least it'll be plenty for me, I know. I shall write William on Monday, because I won't have time on Tuesday. The 3rd is Friday, n'est-ce pas?

Enclosed you will find a picture of Fr. Jimmie Hyland. I cut it out of the Catholic newspaper, *The Register.* He still looks as young as ever.

This morning I offered my Mass & Communion for everyone and for any particular or general intentions they might have. I also remembered Fr. Pat Walshe in my prayers.

Are you affected by the milk shortage down there? I had read in the paper that there was a shortage of dairy products due to seasonal let-up and increased demands from the increasing population.

I am sorry to hear that you lost Kerry's ration book. I hope that the OPA will soon act right and kick up with another.

That's about all I have to say now. I try to write as often as possible but there is so little spare time that I am often found wanting in that regard.

Your ever loving son,
Morris

P.S. Tell Lizzie, the iceman, milkman, and postman hello for me.

* * * * *

Fort Benning, Georgia
November 29, 1943

Dear Dad,

To-day began our fourth week of Basic. We were awakened at 5:30 A.M. EWT [Eastern War Time], which is really 3:30 Sun Time. So around nine o'clock here, the sun begins to come out and shed its feeble rays over the ice-covered roofs and cold pines that make up this section of the camp.

This morning was rather easy, as we didn't have too much calisthenics. This was because of the rain—not a heavy one, but a nasty little drizzle mixed with a cold wind. We then had two hours of bayonet drill in which we used training sticks. They're about 1" by 1" by 8'. On one end is a heavy wire loop, on the other a pad about the size of a large orange. One fellow takes the stick and holds it near the middle, parallel to the ground, with either end to the right and left. When the loop end is held high, the movement indicated is a long thrust; when held low, a short thrust. When the stick is brought parallel to the ground but perpendicular to the body, with the padded end forward about chest high, the butt stroke, smash, or slash is indicated. These sticks are better than the other work we did with the bayonet. At least we now have something tangible and solid to hit at. The last hour before lunch we had grenade practice with dummy grenades.

This afternoon we went on a hike. That's the reason I'm writing this letter in bed. It was really a march. We covered 10.25 miles in two hours and forty-five minutes, which was practically running. It was raining too. I got a funny feeling marching along with the rain coming down. There was a bleak sky overhead, and when my platoon reached the top of one of the hills, they beheld a sight not often seen—a line of troops stretching over the winding road as far as the eye could see. There they were, silhouetted against the dark gray sky, flanked on either side by deep red ditches and bare trees. Under their tramping feet was the blood-red slush of their Georgia roads. Marching, marching, marching. You can't look up because it rains in your face. So you look down at the tramping feet. Feet & slush, hour after hour. This is the only unpleasant part of a march. There is usually singing, talking, or joke telling, that keeps everyone in high spirits. But while it was raining I recognized in the somber scene a certain touch of realism. I realized that in many parts of the world men were marching just as we were. It was perhaps the same scene in many places of the world, only the conditions were different. The guns we heard as we passed the field artillery were friends', not foes'. The concrete pillboxes sunk in the fields with their twelve-foot walls were there for training purposes, not otherwise.

This is our training. As Uncle Billy says, it's a certain type of education, and you can never get enough education, no matter what kind or type it is.

I must say that Uncle Billy writes a very fine letter and has some very fine thought content in it. He also told me that he had lunch with you several times a week.

Well, there goes Taps.

Lovingly,
Morris

* * * * *

Fort Benning, Georgia
November 30, 1943

Dear William,

I never did get a chance to answer your letter, or perhaps I kept putting it off. However, any communications from you in the future will be promptly answered.

However, the purpose of this letter is to wish you a very Happy Birthday. Enclosed you will find $2, because we got paid today. I know you will save this, for you are such a thrifty person.

Well, tell all your lady friends hello for me, and study hard.

With best wishes I remain

Dein Bruder,
Morris

Fort Benning, Georgia
December 1, 1943

Dear Mom & Dad,

Well, the Army is rolling on. This week is really passing fast. That's probably because of the high volume of work we've been doing. Last night I didn't get a chance to write, for we had to run the compass course. This was as I predicted—a panic. Those woods are really dark at night, and those marshes are pretty marshy at this time of year. Of course, the temperature is pretty low too. When I returned home I was covered with mud, sweat, and tears. (With apologies to Winnie.) However, and this is the happy part, my squad finished first of the whole battalion, was first back at camp, and first for the doughnuts and hot coffee.

Another bright spot in these fast-moving days was yesterday noon. At that we were paid. I received exactly, to the penny, $52.47, which was far above my expectations. This sum included laundry deductions, three months' insurance, and bond allotment.

Tomorrow we go on another long hike, I believe. If it's much longer than the last one they'll have to carry me home. No, I'll make it. The only thing in this Army I can't make is the eight-foot wall of the obstacle course. And if I lose any more weight I'll be able to wave my arms and fly over it.

I skipped breakfast "ce matin" because I didn't have to stand reveille or any formations until 10:30. We were given the extra time to rest, so, why spoil it by going to breakfast. We had a swell noon meal complete with ice cream and chocolate-iced cake.

I skipped supper in order to take a bath. I hadn't had one in about three days. Afterwards I got dressed, walked down to the PX, and had combination sandwiches and 3.2 beer. It was the first beer I had tasted since I left home, and it didn't taste too bad. The sandwiches were pretty good, too.

Well, I hope William enjoyed his birthday, and also, that all are well. That's all the news for now and I remain

Your loving son,
Morris

P.S. Enclosed find the stamps off the fudge. Please give to William.

Fort Benning, Georgia
December 5, 1943

Dear Richard,

I am very pleased to hear that you are doing well in school. Keep up the good work. Don't worry about the Yankees. I'm getting used to them now. I'm afraid I've even picked up some sort of accent.

I am in hopes that you will beat 1-A for the championship and win the intramural title. Unless Easton has something hidden in its sleeve, I think you should beat them for the city title. You have some good men in the Jesuit line and in the backfield, and a few of these should make all-prep—perhaps all-state. But remember, Easton has some good men. I know it will really be a fight. Whichever team wins it will be a good game, and I am only sorry that I am not there to see it.

Well, good luck,
Morris

* * * * *

Fort Benning, Georgia
December 5, 1943

Dear Jerome,

It was a decided pleasure to hear from you. I certainly enjoy reading your letters. Except for a few mistakes in spelling you write a very good letter for such a young man. But keep it up and soon you won't make any mistakes. Remember, practice makes perfect.

I was disturbed to hear that you weren't feeling too well. Try and bear up. Never complain; a good soldier never complains. Always remember that your pain is small compared to the suffering of the countless millions of enslaved people in the occupied territories.

I do not have any pictures of commando tricks to send you, but in about ten weeks I might be home to show you some, if I'm lucky.

Well, study hard in school. You can never learn enough. Every day I live, I learn new things and so will you.

Your loving brother,
Morris

Fort Benning, Georgia
December 5, 1943

Dear Mom and Dad,

Well, I have just completed the first four weeks of Basic—supposedly the hardest. However, this remains to be seen. It is now three o'clock on this sunny Sunday afternoon. A more beautiful day couldn't come, even in the month of June. The sun is just warm enough, there is a slight breeze, and in the towering pines a few birds sing. It is a very peaceful day—a far cry from the days of the past week. I cannot clearly remember what happened at the beginning of the week, but Thursday and Friday were awful hard. From 8:15 A.M. 'til 12:15 P.M., we had two hours of bayonet fighting and two hours of grenade practice. From after the lunch hour until eleven-thirty at night, I had KP. Then the rest of the day the program called for "the training of the individual soldier."

With full field pack we hiked out in the vicinity of Hell's Half-Acre. There were nine problems to be worked out. The toughest was one in which we were to attack a village on the other side of a stream. We were given our instructions, and under the guidance of our squad leader we set out.

We crept through the woods and underbrush until the scouts, who had crossed the river and were lying in firing position on the other bank, signaled for us to advance. Our squad leader signaled by hand "up, over, and at 'em." I have never hesitated on an order yet and I'm rather proud. Where I get the nerve to act on the instant, whether the order is to jump out of a second-story window or as it was in this case, to jump into a freezing, roaring stream from a comparatively high bank, I don't know. But, in this squad I was the ammunition bearer for the Browning Automatic Rifle team. When I got the signal I rushed "up and at 'em" all right, but I didn't get quite over. No, I landed in a rather shallow hole about five feet deep. I wasn't as lucky as one of the other fellows who went through the shallows. But—and here is the mark of a good soldier—I kept my rifle high and dry above my head, and as a result of this, when I pulled myself freezing out of the water, I was ready for action. I won't say what kind of action. But I was ready for action. Yesirree!

On Saturday morning we had one hour of physical drill and the number-four film of *Why We Fight*. It depicted the Battle of Britain. These films are rather amazing in that they are made up from captured German film of the bombing of London, and of the conferences of Hitler and his staff planning the annihilation of the British race. It is shocking in that it shows the partial destruction of "the fortress built by Nature for herself." It is terrible in that it depicts the wealth of human sorrow and heartbreak pressing the people of "this England." It is truly a tribute to a stubborn, unpredictable, courageous people, who, in a great hour of peril, in the midst of their devastated cities, their broken homes, their peoples' blackened bodies strewn in the pockmarked streets, fought back, man, woman and child, and finally after two years, won the Battle of Britain.

In the afternoon we had a battalion parade. Everybody was dressed in their GI best. There was a military band and flags and all the hullabaloo that goes with parades. After the parade we were off for the weekend. I went to the show and saw *Riding High* with Dorothy Lamour, Wm. Powell, and Victor Moore. It was pretty good and very funny.

This morning I started right after Mass, writing out Christmas cards and answering mail. I am so far behind I went right on through the lunch hour. Thus far I have written thirty-four cards. I would like you to send me the addresses of several people. I would like William to ask Arthur Appfel for Howard Taylor's, Tom Gaudry's, and some of the other Tri-Sigs' addresses. You can help me out there. I would like to know the address of the Redmanns on Magazine Street and Uncle Hickey's and Aunt Jeanne's. You might also send me the Convent's address so I might send a card to Sr. Kevin and the other nuns. I could use, too, a Loyola Directory.

All this week coming we will have night problems, infiltration, etc. Looks like work.

Eh bien, c'est tout pour maintenant. Je reste

Votre fils amant,
Morris

P.S. I don't know when I'll get another chance to write, but don't worry.

* * * * *

Fort Benning, Georgia
December 5, 1943

Mein Bruder, Wilhelm der Groz,

Today being Sunday, I find the opportunity of writing you. I read with interest your letter of December 2nd. I am glad to see that you go in for all that hullabaloo. That's a good sign. Stick with it. It'll carry you a long way. However, you neglected to tell me what happened, what the outcome of your attempt was, or who won. Since I don't get the *Maroon,* I am totally ignorant of happenings at school. The few issues I received from you were welcome and I was under the apprehension that they would be continued. However, such has not been the case. Now you get on the ball and make those women editors get on the ball so I can be on the ball as to what G's at skule.

How's the political situation at school? Have you been elected to any offices since I left? Let me know what offices you hold, what organizations you belong to, and other personal data so I can know how my "big" brother is doing. Are the frat dances coming up soon? If so, when? By the way, give my regards to your friend "Legs." What other rackets are you running around school? Don't let the big-time operators get ahead of you. By the way, Will, what happened to Jimmie McGovern, Tommy Blouin, and some of the other fellows I knew? If they're not in the Army or Navy, or even if they are, send me their addresses as soon as possible. I'd like to write them. Look up or ring up Artie and get Howard's address, Tom Gaudry's, and some of the other Tri-Sigs.

I hear from Bernie Ward that exams are over now. How did you do? I imagine you had no trouble. However, I hope you did sufficiently well to keep up Fr. Crandall's interest in you. Did all of your students pass?

Thanking you in advance for the information requested, I remain,

Dein Bruder,
Mouritz

P.S. I'm sitting next to Tommy Dix, the kid that played the lead in *Best Foot Forward.*

* * * * *

Fort Benning, Georgia
December 7, 1943

Dear Mom & Dad,

This is a short one. My nerves and morale are shot to pieces. I have just gotten off detail, which was the third one to-day.

Last night we had an infiltration problem. It was very realistic. In fact, too much so. The "enemy" had machine guns, rifles, aerial flares, and dago bombs. In crossing the stream, I fell in when a burst of machine-gun fire came from the right. The night was a rainy one already, but up to that time I had remained rather dry. There was a beautiful moon in the sky, sometimes hidden by thick clouds. A low mist hung over the marshes, fields, and forests. The setting was perfect. The scene could have taken place in the Argonne 25 yrs. ago or on Guadalcanal within the past few months. The enemy was out there in undetermined numbers. Our job was reconnaissance. In this job you must avoid contact with the enemy. You must avoid capture or fail in your mission. Our course led some 2,000 yards. It sounds short. But when you're creeping and crawling, backtracking and running—past and from—enemy patrols, it takes a long time, and it seems even longer. Well, I must admit, even though freezing and wet at the end of the course, it was a proud and happy soldier who received the praise of the Major for having done so well. My squad was the first to finish intact after being almost the last to start. The first in the whole battalion to report in. The new record holder for the course with a time of one hour and twenty minutes. One of only five that accomplished its mission.

I would certainly appreciate a box for Christmas. Make it of cakes & candy, crackers and spreads. No syrup or malted milk, for I still have it from last time.

That's all for now. Give my love to all. Remember I haven't forgotten my lines from Polonius: "To thine own self be true, and it must follow as the night the day thou canst not then be false to any man."

Pray as if all depended on prayer.

Lovingly,
Morris

P.S. Put Jr. after name. Who won the Jesuit-Easton game? The papers I have don't give the score.

* * * * *

Fort Benning, Georgia
December 9, 1943

Dear Mom & Dad,

Yesterday was the feast of the Immaculate Conception. I attended Mass at 6:15 in the evening and afterwards received four letters which I don't think I will be able to answer until Saturday night or Sunday. One was from Lolita Martinez, one from Luke, one from Aunt Winnie, and the other from the kids. I certainly did appreciate them because yesterday was an exceptionally hard day. It started off with lectures, but ended with hours of physical drill and the obstacle course.

Since it was the feast of the Immaculate Conception I said a prayer every time I remembered the fact. When we reached the obstacle course I prayed as if all depended on prayer. For at that time, after two hours of physical drill, I was all but dead. It was then I made my conquest. The eight-foot wall is but a memory. Not only did I get over it once, but the second time I went over almost unfalteringly. Well, there isn't much news and there's even less time. So, good-bye.

Your loving son,
Morris

Fort Benning, Georgia
December 10, 1943, 6:30 A.M.

Dear Mom & Dad,

I am writing now because I know I won't get another chance to until Saturday evening or Sunday. Even then I might not be able to write because I think I will have KP Saturday evening and Sunday morning. Ah, what a life!? This week certainly flew by. It was one of the fastest I can remember. I must confess it was, on the whole, rather easy, but there were times I didn't think anything could be harder. Yesterday was a gold brick day. Except for an hour in the morning—we had creeping and crawling and an hour of physical drill in the afternoon—it was a loafer's paradise. We had class in the morning, and in the afternoon we had three hours of patrol scouting. I was in one of the first four scouting groups of two men each. I and my buddy finished third and laid around for an hour or so waiting for the rest of the squad to come in. I got letters from Marie Louise Salatich and George Reinecke yesterday. George says he is no longer a flying cadet but has been transferred to radio.

I am sending home two ASTP shoulder patches. One goes to Jerome, to whom I had promised one some time ago. The other I wish saved in some place where it won't get lost, perhaps in one of the secret drawers of the desk.

A recent new course of study, one might call it military strategy, has been added as a sort of sideline. In it we consider the latest battles, the loss or gain, the number of casualties, etc. Since Benning is the headquarters and news center of all the war news from all fronts where American soldiers fight, we get, of course, firsthand information. Here we are taught how to avoid the costly mistakes of the marines on Tarawa, how to avoid, by simple discipline, the unnecessary casualties of North Africa.

I have paid particular attention to each course that has dealt with the training of the individual soldier, because we were told that 40% of us would go into combat right from here. Of course I think it's a lot of bull, but you never can tell.

Well, that's all the news for now.

Your loving son,
Morris

Fort Benning, Georgia
Sunday, December 12, 1943

Miss Ogie Joyce
1905 Calhoun St.
New Orleans, Louisiana

Dear Ogie,

For some nights I have been attempting to answer your most welcome letter of last Tuesday, but incessant night details have taken much of my spare time.

The week just past was one of the fastest I have ever seen. Today the sixth week of Basic starts. This leaves only two weeks until bivouac. I am sure that time will fly and that soon I will look back on basic training with its good points and its few bad ones, all blended together, making a not unpleasant picture.

This week we will have the 60 mm. mortar. Last week we studied the 30-cal. machine gun. This is very interesting work. After studying these guns one can take them all apart and put them back together again. It is amazing how simply these guns are constructed.

I am sorry to hear about little Joe's fistula. I sincerely hope and pray that everything will be alright.

Ogie, I have heard of the book *The Robe* by Lloyd Douglas. I know that it is a very splendid book. I would enjoy reading it very much. But I wish, if you wish to give me a present, that you hold it for me until I ask for it. The reason is this: I will be on bivouac for four weeks, during which I shall have little time for anything but work and needed rest. I am writing Mother to hold everything until after Basic. Perhaps I shall be lucky to get home, or maybe I shall be so unlucky as to be sent to Brooklyn College or some other far-off place. However, I am doing what I think best. There can be no finer present than such a book, but I simply have no place to keep it just now. When and if I go to college I know I shall enjoy it all the more, so please hold it for me.

Well, that's about all for now. I remain sincerely and gratefully,

Yours,
Morris

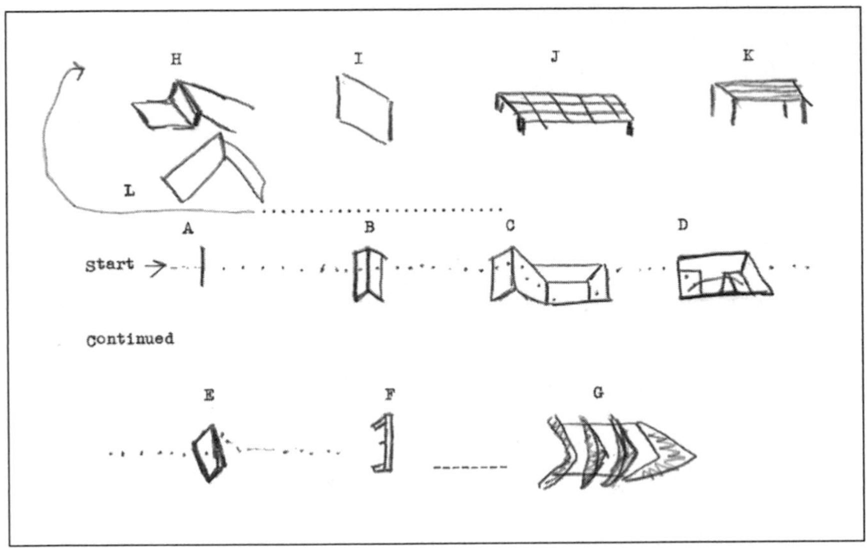

Fort Benning, Georgia
Sunday, December 12, 1943

Dear Ralph,

I am glad to hear that you made the 59-inch team at school. I am glad also to hear that you won against the Holy Name team on Friday a week ago.

The following is a diagram of our obstacle course.

- A A low fence 3 ft. high
- B You run up one side and down the other.
- C Is the same as B but there is a 10-ft. pit on the other side.
- D A pit within a pit—you jump into the first, the floor of which contains another pit; you jump across this one and then pull yourself out.
- E The eight-foot sheer wall.
- F A fence four feet high. You get over this by using one hand and a jump.
- G A pit about four feet deep in that V-shape with four logs across the top over which you must run.
- H Here you run up this hill on the right and jump over the pit.
- I A wall 20 ft. high over which you can climb just like it was a ladder.
- J This obstacle is close to the ground and will trip you if you don't step high and be careful.
- K In this you hold onto the rods across the top and swing from one side to another, hand over hand.

L Another incline board about eight feet high. You run up one side & down the other.

Then you're finished—in more ways than one.

Your loving brother,
Morris

* * * * *

Fort Benning, Georgia
December 12, 1943

Dear Mom & Dad,

Well, the time is flying fast. It's hard to believe that this is the start of the sixth week of Basic, but it is, and I'm pretty happy about it. It means that we have only two weeks before bivouac. I will be out on bivouac for two weeks and then in for a week, then out again for two weeks, and then our last week of Basic. It will really break my heart to say good-bye to this place. WHAT am I saying?

I listened to so many lectures this past week that I can't recall anything of particular interest except the night tactical problem and my conquest of the obstacle course. The week was a fast one, not too strenuous except for the calisthenics and obstacle course stuff. The time really flew by. I hope the same happens from here on out.

Today I had to walk two miles to get to Mass at 11:25. It was about 12:30 when it was over, so Scioli, Santelli, and myself decided to walk a little further and dine at the Service Club. We waited an hour in line but the meal justified it. It was really a whopper. We had a whole leg and thigh of chicken, a thick, long slice of beautiful boiled ham, creamed potatoes, green peas, butter beans, pocketbook rolls and butter, apple pie, milk (I drank a quart), potato salad, and coffee. It cost only eighty-five cents, but at present I'm in the millionaire class. The same meal in town would have cost about $1.65 at least. I'm still full, although I didn't go to breakfast and so far tonight have had no supper.

I think that I mentioned over the phone that I hadn't gotten any papers in the last three days. Well, I got all of them at mail call this evening, so I'm even.

This past week we had the study of the 30-cal. machine gun and the detection of land mines and booby traps. This coming week we have a lot on military sanitation and the 60 mm. mortar. We should have some more marches and night problems. So pray that my squad meets with the same success as it has in the past.

I think there is going to be a midnight Mass celebrated here for Christmas. I shall try to get to it instead of the later ones.

Well, that's all the news for now.

Your loving son,
Morris

* * * * *

Fort Benning, Georgia
December 13, 1943

Dear Mom & Dad,

To-day I received and enjoyed your most welcome letter of the tenth. I received one from Kerry, and also one from Kent Zimmermann.

I certainly will appreciate some of those wonderful Christmas pictures you always take. I suppose some change has taken place in the kids. I am anxious to see how handsome they are.

I guess clothes are hard to get for Richard, but I don't think I'll ever be stout again—at least not until I'm 50. God grant I live that long.

I suppose it was a shock to hear that Mr. Bergerot was dead. He always impressed me as being such a spry, active salesman. I shall remember him in my prayers.

Well, today I had an easy time of KP in the boiler room from 0600 till 1300. I have it again tomorrow from 1300 'til. If I get the same job I'll be set for a half day of rest. In the evening today, or rather afternoon, we had two hours on the aiming and firing of the machine gun, one hour of first aid, and a terrific hour of calisthenics designed to develop your stomach muscles.

The news isn't much, of course, from day to day. I heard a rumor that this Sunday is the last before bivouac and that we leave 2 A.M. on Christmas Day. However, I shall label this type of story as a latrine rumor.

Well, tell everybody hello, the iceman, etc.

Thanks for the addresses and the things to come.

By my admonition I meant that you should profit by my experience. Everything I have prayed for so far I got.

Lovingly,
Morris

P.S. Enclosed find some candy wrappers from some of Scioli's Italian candy. Picturesque, n'est-ce pas?

Fort Benning, Georgia
December 15, 1943

Dear Mom & Dad,

I am writing this during the noon dinner hour. I didn't get a chance to write last night because I was on KP. Since the weather was so bad the cook let the outside men go at ten o'clock. I wasn't strictly an outside man because I was shoveling coal in the boiler room. The easiest job I ever did. I sat around like a bump on a log for that 10-hour shift. I was pretty warm in there, but outside the temperature was about 25°, and there was a steady rain that had been continued from the day before.

The reason for this letter is the weather. The temperature is down to 20° and it has been SNOWING all morning. It's really beautiful to see the continuous rain of snowflakes upon the frozen ground.

We have been out all day, but had on overcoats and anything else we could get on.

Please if you can, send another pair of longies and a shawl. I can use anything you think I could, including long socks, etc. (The next paragraph was started after the supper hour.)

I know this is last-minute notice, but so was the weather. However, if you can't get around to it now, I can still use them for the second bivouac near the end of January. Or if you can't get them at all, don't worry. I'm sure that our Lieutenant will see that everybody will be warm enough. We'll sleep in regular six-man tents with stoves on the first bivouac. I don't know what they plan to do on the second one.

Something else I would like to mention. Please send me some food while on bivouac. Not only do they freeze you, but also they starve you, I hear.

Boy, I can't get over this weather. At the present I have on cotton underwear, woolies, woolen olive drab shirt (they cost $7.00, so they must be good), my heavy fatigue shirt, wool-lined field jacket, woolen cap that covers all the head and neck and ears, and woolen overcoat (valued at $50) and woolen gloves. Whew! And I'm still cold.

Today out in the snow, while listening to the lectures and operating the 60 mm. mortar, the instructor paused almost every 10 minutes to make us get up and run around to keep warm.

Most of the trees had put away their green leaves for a warmer day, but the towering pines merely tucked their needles under the blanket of snow and awaited the sun which never came.

Oh, well, a new day—a new experience. That's all the news for now.

Your loving son,
Morris

Fort Benning, Georgia
December 18, 1943

Miss Ogie Joyce
1905 Calhoun St.
New Orleans, Louisiana

Dear Aunt Ogie,

Before I answer your letter or give any of my news, I would like to express my thanks for your sweet remembrance of the 16th. It was really swell.

(My handwriting won't be too good because my bosom friend Michael Angelo Scioli is writing so fast, the table is all but falling to pieces!)

The past week was pretty swell. It was a week of dry-firing of the M-1 rifle, the 30-cal. machine gun, and the 60 mm. mortar. The only hard part of the week was the weather. On Monday and Tuesday it rained, the temperature at about 30°. On Wednesday it snowed all day. The temperature went down to about 20°. The rest of the week the place was coated in the winter white of ice. The place in which we washed our mess kits after chow was frozen solid. Globery-Bobs had icicles on the end of their chins. No kidding!

But really, this week was all right. I didn't get much chance to write because I had KP and then some make-up classes to attend. We didn't get much chance to run the obstacle course because everything was covered with ice.

I read in a New York newspaper where the ASTP was being discontinued in order to save 150,000 fathers from the draft by shoving us in. Of course, this story is more than just a rumor, as I have read it myself. What its immediate effect is, I don't know. But I do know that every one of us here had better do their best in all their work because most of us will be in combat sooner than we think. The only lesson learned from the Battle of Tarawa and from our losses in the young invasion of the Island of New Guinea is that the American soldier is losing the war because he didn't adhere to all the methods of warfare taught in basic and advanced training.

Well, tomorrow is the beginning of the grand finale. It starts the next week before bivouac. We will spend two days of it out on the range firing the 30-cal. carbine. That week is Christmas week, I suppose, so remember me in all your prayers. I assure you that you will be remembered in mine, and I remain,

Your loving nephew,
Morris

Fort Benning, Georgia
December 19, 1943

Dear Mom & Dad,

The freezing weather, the nipping air, the hard ground, the smoking chimneys, and the familiar, frequent strains of the Christmas carols heard over the radio in the recreation hall are the only outward signs that the great feast of Christmas is near. But throughout this tired, shattered, embattled world, the inward preparation for the coming of the Christ is almost complete. And in all Christian hearts men "make ready the way of the Lord and make straight His paths."

And with the coming of Christ comes from many lips the single prayer of salvation. Salvation from our earthly enemies, the false philosophies and ideologies that have caused the premature aging of nations by the destruction of entire generations. The prayer that the present holocaust will end and that a new joy and peace will accompany the coming of the King of peace into the hearts of men.

This past week wasn't hard. It was a week of "dry-firing" of the guns the infantry soldier will use in combat. I never realized there was so much to pulling a trigger until now. It was very interesting work and I believe I got a lot out of it. As I told you in a past letter, it snowed on Wednesday and remained around 25° the rest of the week. But we went out every day, either for work on the rifle, the machine gun, or the 60 mm. mortar. There is no such thing as "too cold" or "too rainy" or "too sloppy" in the Army. If you have a job to do, there is no excuse for not doing it.

This coming week should be pretty interesting because we are going out to the range to fire the 30-cal. carbine. It's really a peach of a gun, no bigger than some of the children's toy guns, and it doesn't weigh much more. It should be interesting to note that this week marks the half-mark of our basic training. It will be an important one for me because I will be Corporal for a week, as well as squad leader. I pray that I shall do well, as everything you do goes into your record here, and all is brought out on the "last day."

During the past week I have received many cards from many people—the Tri-Sigs, from Roy, Numa, Artie, Tom, Nat, Parker, from Lolita, Peggy, Monita, Marie Louise, from Ogie, the Kellys, Uncle Billy, from Luke, Charlie, and others. I also received a card and letter from Fr. Castel, which I hope to answer this evening.

I hope that all are well and that Christmas brings not only its customary gifts, but also health and joy and peace that only God can give.

That's all the news for now and I remain

Yours in the spirit of Christmas,
Your loving son,
Morris

* * * * *

Fort Benning, Georgia
December 20, 1943

Dear Mom and Dad,

I have not as yet received your Christmas box, but I guess that is due to the overcrowded Christmas mail.

The purpose of this letter is to deal with the situation of sending packages to me while on bivouac. It is plainly this: We have been told to write home and ask that no boxes be sent for the rest of our training because we will be here for only two more weeks; the other four will be spent on bivouac. The newspaper must be discontinued also, but not until the second bivouac. I would welcome the subscription again at my next assignment, however. This is due to the fact that the second bivouac will be tactical maneuvers, and we won't get much chance to read newspapers. However, the letters can, and for reasons of morale, must continue.

Today lasted an hour longer, as every day this will be, in order to make up for Christmas off. But the only hard thing all day was a half-hour of calisthenics.

Besides your welcomed letter, I received letters, cards, and notes from the Rev. C. Quirk, S.J., Gissie Burton, and Bernard Ward. Fr. Quirk sent me a program of the Symposium of Pegasus.

Well, that's all for today.

Your loving son,
Morris

P.S. Enclosed find a GI laundry slip. The service is 4 days and the cost comes out of your pay ($1.50 a month). R 9577—the last initial and the last 4 numbers of my ASN.

Fort Benning, Georgia
December 23, 1943

Dear Folks,

This is a just a short note—an expression of thanks, for all the swell things you have sent me during my short time in the Army. Upon opening them I was, I must say, pleasantly surprised, for if you remember I had asked that this request, namely that you send none, be granted.

I do not have the time to comment on the usefulness of each one. However, it is necessary that I say that some of them should and will be saved for "Better Places" than Fort Benning. I couldn't possibly use them here and keep them in good order.

Everything here is hustle & bustle. Tomorrow we leave for the range, and so tonight it is necessary to load ammunition belts and other things. This trip to the range will only last one day, and we will fire only the 30-cal. carbine.

We are off on Saturday, Christmas Day, but we leave for bivouac at an early hour on Sunday. I don't know when I shall write again, so if you don't hear from me for some time, do not worry. If I can I shall write.

I got a letter from Doc Bonomo the other day, which I don't think I shall find time to answer. Please have William tell Doc that I will write in about two weeks, or maybe sooner. Tell him (Wm) also to give Fr. Quirk my regards, and tell him that I shall write him when opportunity affords.

The weather has taken a turn for the better. It is much warmer than it was some days ago.

There is one thing that I wish Mother would do for me. Due to extenuating circumstances and the scarcity of time, I have not been able to send cards to everyone I wished. I request that Mother extend my Best Wishes and Kindest Regards for the Christmas Season and the New Year to all the Fonsecas at 7011 Broad Place.

Well, "ought is law when time is fleeting," and I ought to clean my rifle and I only have 45 minutes to do it in.

So, that's all the news for now. Write the news but don't expect an answer. I remain with you in the spirit of Christmas,

Your loving son,
Morris

Fort Benning, Georgia
Christmas Day, 1943

Dear Mom & Dad,

On this the commemoration of the Coming of the Christ, I again wish to take opportunity to wish you and all my brothers and sister and all the family all the blessings and happy moments that Christmastide and the New Year can bring.

I attended midnight Mass way over at OCS. I was on KP until eleven, when one of the cooks asked who wanted to go to Mass. I held up my hand and he told me to "take off." I saw him over at Mass. Even though I ran a good part of the two and some miles, I didn't get there in time for Confession, and I must say it was a great disappointment. However, it was a high Mass and was well sung.

While walking back along 8th Division Road, I noticed that the spirit of Christmas was not totally lacking. There were a few trees decorated in front of the regimental headquarters, and a few groups were singing the age-old carols. All this in the rain.

Thursday we had semi-final instruction on the mortar and the machine gun—nine hours of it. Then that night, 100 of us had to load 50,000 rounds of ammunition into the machine-gun belts. When I finished, I had blisters on my hands. The only reward for that work is that we'll fire 50,000 machine-gun rounds on the range.

Yesterday we spent a very interesting day out on the carbine range. In the morning the 8th Co. was firing and the 7th Co. was in the pits working the targets. In the evening it was the other way around. We fired at 100 & 200 yards. There was a 15-mile-per-hour wind, and the gun has set sights of 150 & 300 yds. So we had to use Kentucky windage and Tennessee elevation. Out of a possible 156, I got 130—which wasn't so bad, considerin'.

The Christmas gifts, je t'assure, are out of the generosity of my heart, given in appreciation for having such a swell family, rather than from any expert knowledge of the game of African dominoes. No gambling is allowed here. (Except among the cooks in the kitchen on Christmas Eve.)

Thank you very much for the $10. I don't think I would have needed it because I don't spend much around here. It's not such a long time between paydays, or so it seems, because there's one coming up at the 30th of the current month (I hope).

I was very sorry to hear about the bank case. It would have been a grand feather in your hat, had the decision favored your clients.

On Thursday I set a record by receiving sixteen pieces of mail in one day.

Well, this week certainly passed fast, and I hope that the remaining few do too.

Your loving son,
Morris

* * * * *

Fort Benning, Georgia
Christmas Day, 1943

Mrs. Claude J. Kelly
4139 General Taylor
New Orleans, Louisiana

Dear Folks,

I had asked Mother to tell you hello and to express my thanks for your swell presents. This note is to make sure, double sure. So I do thank you very much for the lovely presents from all the Kellys, and especially the cake and cookies which I certainly enjoyed very much. I would like to congratulate Claude Jr. upon his grand scholastic standing.

There is plenty of Christmas spirit (and some spirits) around here. Although it's pretty damp (it has reached the flood stage) around here, it isn't enough to dampen the spirits of these boys. They're a pretty swell bunch of guys. We're going to need plenty of spirit to last out bivouac in this weather, and that's one of the reasons I phoned home twice to-day.

To your question, do all boys take Basic, I say yes. That all finish, I say no. Many from our company are in the hospital, and before the next five weeks are over there'll be plenty more in the same fix. I hope it'll not be me. But whatever happens, it should be a grand experience.

Please remember me in your prayers during the following weeks. I must say that I have spent a happy Christmas. This was a day spent writing letters, phoning home, and thinking of the grand people and good times I once knew.

We're spending our Christmas this way so that we may at some future Christmas celebrate it with you in peace.

That's all the news for now. Write often if you have time. I cannot promise an immediate answer, but your letters will mean a lot to me.

Sincerely,
Morris

Fort Benning, Georgia
December 26, 1943

Dear Mom & Dad,

If it weren't for the candles you sent me, I would not be able to write you to-night. We are living in rather large tents that hold five men rather comfortably. When we got here, they (the tents) had already been set up, and the beds and mattresses placed in them.

The march here wasn't very bad. It started at nine this morning and lasted until four this afternoon. It was through some of the worst country you could find. This same march could have taken place in Italy or in Africa, or in any other land where the ravages of war have left their marks. Our course of march led through the infantry woods, over the artillery ranges, with their blackened, twisted trees; through the rows of tank traps and 16-foot concrete pillboxes, the faces of some blackened by the use of flame throwers, others dressed in camouflage. The muddy roads, chewed by the thousands of marching feet, and the heavy tread tires of the huge supply and ammunition trucks, reminded me of some of the French dirt roads of the last war that I have seen in pictures from the last war. (Not such good construction—the roads & the last sentence.)

The sky is very cloudy. There is no moon, and consequently, you can't see your hand in front of your face outside. We had to dig a deep trench all around the tent so that the rain we believe coming will not sweep us down the hill into the stream—where we must do all our washing, shaving, etc.

I mailed out four letters today that I had written on Christmas Day. There was no outgoing mail until we got here.

Give my love to all. Give my regards to the milkman, mailman, iceman, etc.

I'm going to bed now. That march pooped me out. Hope all are well.

Your loving son,
Morris

* * * * *

Fort Benning, Georgia
December 29, 1943

Dear Mom & Dad,

Well, bivouac isn't so bad—so far. We have still to go through the infiltration course. This is the worst thing that can happen in Basic.

The only hard thing about this is that we leave the bivouac area before dawn—about 2 hrs. before dawn—and we don't return until dark. Any washing you do is done in the dark in the creek behind us. Any rifle cleaning is done, rather imperfectly, tho', by candlelight.

For the past three days we have concerned ourselves with the firing of the 60 mm. mortar and the 30-cal. machine gun. Since the mortar shells cost $7.50 apiece, only one in every four men could fire. I was one of *the* ones. You can't get any medals for mortar unless you are a member of the weapons platoon, and you get to use the mortar a lot. However, I qualified as an expert with the machine gun, scoring 226 out of a possible 256. From 180 to 210 is a gunner 2nd class. From 210 to 217 is a gunner 1st class. From 218 to 256 is expert.

I get a medal for this, if I ever get a chance to buy it. They say it's really a beautiful medal.

I am also an expert "chowhound" who would, in normal times, be termed a glutton. The thing is, though, if you don't go for seconds, you don't get enough to eat. Here's how I work it.

When we come in in the evening I grab my mess kit, stand in the door of the tent, and wait for the chow whistle to blow. As soon as it blows, I run as fast as I can to the field kitchen. I get there first. One half-second later, I have 249 other guys behind me. (They're pretty fast too.) So I get served. I run, immediately, to the end of the chow line. As the line moves up, I eat. By the time I get up to be served again, I have finished round one, and so round two begins. Round three is a repetition of rd. 2. Only after the third, I usually run over to the wash lines, which is now pretty long, and while waiting my turn to wash my mess kit, I finish round three. This method saves a lot of time and I get a lot more to eat this way. Of course, you eat in line all the time instead of comfortably sitting down. But to be an expert chowhound, you have to make some sacrifices.

Today, too, we fired the grenade-launcher. This is really a tank-killer. It is an attachment that fits onto a rifle, over the muzzle, onto which you can attach a special made grenade. You fire a blank cartridge, the gas from which propels the grenade toward the target. Of course this contraption kicks like a mule, and I almost got my shoulder kicked off, but it will ruin a tank & crew anytime.

That's all for now.

Your loving son,
Morris

P.S. Got letters from Will, Ogie, and others. If you can get some more chocolate—please send. Package rule isn't enforced.

Fort Benning, Georgia
December 31, 1943

Dear Mom & Dad,

Ring out the old year. Ring in the new. And so it goes. A candle stuck on top of my steel helmet resting on the head of my cot provides the light by which I write. The hat is GI, the candle is mine, the paper and ink are borrowed.

So, on this, the last day of the year of 1943, I attempt to write the news. Today we got paid again. I received from the govt. of the U.S. $42.10. I don't know how I rate this, because $6.40 for insurance, $6.75 for bonds, and $1.50 should be deducted from my original $50. But when these three are added to the $42.10 I received, the grand total is $56.75, which is pretty good for a private.

It is now 1944. I was unable to finish last night because we had to clean our rifles. Yesterday we fired all day long out on the rifle range. First at 200 yds., then at 300, and finally at 500 yds. Strange to say, I did my best at 500 yds., getting—out of the 12 shots allowed to "zero in" your rifle—7 bulls, four fours, and one three. Since a bull is five, I made 54 out of a possible 60. Today we will fire for record. I hope I can qualify, for if I don't, I'll have to go out on Sunday, which would just about knock me out.

Give my best wishes for the new year to the Hoggs & Mr. Thomas Reagan, whose picture I saw in the paper the other day.

C'est tout.

Your loving son,
Morris

* * * * *

Camp Illback
ASTP Battle Range
January 2, 1944

Dear Mom & Dad,

It's now about four o'clock of this Sunday evening. I have just returned from Mass. The whole company was called out and the services followed almost immediately. The Catholic services were down in the woods by a small stream, the Jewish behind the last row of tents, and the Protestant at the other end of the tents.

On New Year's Day there was no services because it isn't a holiday in the Army. However, during chow time the battalion was assembled on a hill where it was addressed by the chaplain. He read to us the President's Proclamation that Jan. 1 be set aside as a day of prayer. He read the 23rd Psalm: "The Lord is my shepherd, I shall not want." Then he asked that all rise and say a prayer for our leaders and the success of our armies. It was very impressive, and I daresay that it was the first time that plenty of these fellows ever said a prayer.

Yesterday I earned another medal to wear on my chest: the expert medal in the M-1 rifle. I had prayed all the day before and all that day that I would fire expert. My prayers were answered. Marksman is from 140 to 165; sharpshooter is from 165 to 179; and expert from 180 to 210. Going into the 500-yard mark, I needed only 30 points (out of the possible 40 I could get) to be an expert. So I said a prayer and started shooting. I shot a 34 and brought my score up to 184. Thus, I was one of the few to make expert. A good many of the fellows "boloed"—that is, they didn't qualify at all. Consequently, they spent today firing. Most of them qualified, but some still have to shoot over.

We fired at 200, 300, & 500 yards. There was slow fire and rapid or sustained fire from all positions—sitting or squatting, standing, kneeling, and prone. My best position is the prone position; next comes sitting, then kneeling. My hardest position is standing. However, yesterday I did surprisingly well at standing, getting 17 points out of a possible 20 given for this position.

I got William's & Esther's letters but cannot find time to answer. I also got one from Luke, but cannot answer for a week unless I find some scarce time some place. So tell his family hello for me and that I heard from him. Tell them, too, that I'll write him as soon as I can.

The weather here continues cold and windy, but I am very warm, and at times when running I sweat a little. This coming week is going to be pretty bad. We're going out to a combat range and shall live under battle conditions. (If they're any worse than the present conditions, they'll have to be pretty bad.) I'm growing a mustache, but I have to shave off my quarter-inch beard because I can't wash my face.

Oh well, it'll all be over soon. Gen'l Ike says it should end in '44. I hope it does. Tell everybody hello for me.

Your loving son,
Morris

Camp Illback
ASTP Battle Range
January 3, 1944

Dear Folks,

I am enclosing the remnants of the *Pine Bur,* the ASTP-TIS paper. It'll give you some idea of the things we do. Read "Pilgrim's Progress." Read also the article about esprit de corps—about the kid that shot himself. He was on the range the same day I was.

There are other interesting articles, too. I shall try to get Kent something in town here for his graduation. If I'm lucky I might be in town to give it to him personally. I hope, I hope, I hope.

Morris

* * * * *

United States Army
Fort Benning, Georgia
January 4, '44

Dear Mom & Dad,

This morning the vast armies of Soviet Russia crossed the Polish border. In the past week the premier of Belgium promised his people their freedom within the next few months. Prime Minister Winston Churchill's aide has forecast the end of the conflict in this new year, and General Ike has promised that the war will definitely end in 1944. There must be some sound basis in fact for such predictions. Such an eventuality must be the grand scale invasion of Hitler's Festung Europa. From the reported disgruntled rumblings of the people, Germany must, herself, be able to read the handwriting on the wall.

To-day, while we worked in the field on our problems, we were watched by Major-General Bonesteel. "He was the very model of a modern Major-General."

January 5

I didn't get a chance to finish last night, so I shall continue to-day.

We were awakened this morning very early as usual, ate breakfast, rolled up our tent flaps, and moved out into the field. All day long we fired at silhouette targets that popped up at ranges of 200, 250, 300, 350,

400, and 500 yards. The work is very interesting and I like it a lot. Tomorrow we have anti-aircraft fire. This is firing at moving airplane silhouettes with 22-cal. guns.

The life here now is pretty slow, but within the next two days things will really be popping around here. Infiltration comes on Friday or Saturday, and this is really going to be tough.

Ask William when graduation is. Kent Z. is going to graduate in Feb. and I would like to remember him. He has always remembered me, and I wear a silver chain & cross that he gave me when I entered the Army. So let me know. I will send home some money and perhaps you could get him something rather nice.

How is all the family? I haven't heard from you in some days. I hope everybody is well and that all are doing well in school. Please write me the scores of all the bowl games and send some news of what's going on at school.

That's all for now and I remain

Your loving son,
Morris

* * * * *

United States Army
Fort Benning, Georgia
January 7, 1944

Dear Mom & Dad,

Today we went through the mental conditioning course, the purpose of which is to accustom the soldiers to actual combat conditions. It's really a cinch when you have as much cotton in your ears as I had. The battlefield over which we passed was studded with blocks of dynamite. These are exploded at intervals while we crawl by. The purpose is to simulate the explosion of shells, and to portray, as nearly as possible, to the infantry soldier, the concussion from shells. Overhead the bullets flew, spat from the mouths of the heavy machine guns fixed in their restricted positions. The only hard thing is the crawling over the ground and through the barbed wire. At one end of the field there is a trench into which we filed before starting the problem. Then across the field there are the barbed-wire aprons, the many dynamite charges. Then another trench, and finally, an assault course whereon we used our knowledge of bayonet fighting.

After running this course we're supposed to be mentally conditioned for combat. However, it's like the old story of Pvt. Smith. As it goes, Pvt. Smith was, during his training cycle, the best soldier in the whole division. Unhesitatingly, he obeyed every order. With quickness and accuracy he performed every maneuver. In tactical operations he showed up best under fire, and was always first to accomplish his mission. Then one fine day his division moved overseas. Shortly afterward, they contacted the enemy, and the opportunity to put into practice all the things taught them in training was given to all. When the order to assault was given, Pvt. Smith turned around and took off in the opposite direction. The Captain, seeing this, took out after him. After some fast running he collared the fleeing private.

"Pvt. Smith," he roared, "where are you going? You shouldn't run away like this. What's happened to you? All through training you were the finest soldier I had ever seen. You were never afraid of anything. You know how to fight and to advance. You can do well now. You did well in training."

"Oh yes, sir," he replied, "but fellows get killed out here."

So, no one is really in the correct mental condition until they go into combat.

This bivouac has, on the whole, been very interesting. We have fired all types of weapons at all types of targets. Today, our last of actual work, we had the aforementioned infiltration course and anti-aircraft firing. The latter was done with 22-cal. rifles at silhouetted targets. These rifles are specially made for the Army but would be a swell gun for any of the boys.

Today we were issued our C rations for our march home. Two cans are for Saturday night's supper. The other two are for breakfast Sunday morning. By noon Sunday we should be back in camp eating a hot meal.

Tomorrow will be, undoubtedly, the most interesting of all days here. All day long the battalion will witness demonstrations. The anti-tank grenade, a grenade fired from a rifle, the bazooka, the bangalore torpedo, anti-tank guns, and others will be fired and explained to us.

Well, it's cold and rainy out and the steady pitter-patter of the rain on our canvas ceiling is droning me off into the land of Nod. So I'll say goodbye. Give my love to all.

Your loving son,
Morris

United States Army
Fort Benning, Georgia
January 9, 1944

Dear Mom & Dad,

Thirteen very important weeks of my life are fast drawing to a close. I say important because the principles taught me here will perhaps someday save my life, if I see combat, or in the alternative they will help me live a finer life and be a grand citizen after the war. There is no finer physical conditioner than the Army. The basic element of most worldly success, of successful economic enterprise, or a successful society, global in scope, composed of nations—so different, but so one by nature—is taught here in the Army. This element is cooperation, one with another. To break down the old idea of "me for me and don't worry about any else," the Army has installed the "buddy system." In this system every man is a buddy with another. Each must watch out for the other. All through our training here this principle has been instilled into us by our officers.

I say that this thirteen-week period is *fast* drawing to a close because it is. The two-wk. bivouac went very fast—when I look back on it. This week coming I have Monday off, thus making it only a five-day week.

Tuesday Jan. 11.

Well, I said time passes fast, and the length of time taken to write just this one letter proves it. Here it is—Tuesday night already—almost the middle of the week.

Oh well, some news about the march home. We left the bivouac area at 0700. It was very wet out and the roads were covered by about four inches of slush. Since we're on EWT here, it doesn't grow light until about 0815. The whole battalion was going to march in, and the 4th Pl. of the 8th Co. was to be the point in the advance guard and to be the leading element. At 0700 we were already five minutes late. Capt. William P. Baker, or Wild Bill, as we call him, told the Major we would make it up in the first hour. So Wild Bill set a pretty fast pace for the first forty-five minutes. But because of all the running we've done, trying to keep up with him at other times, we of the 4th were more than equal to it.

Now the point of an advance guard is always about 300 yds. ahead of the support, which in turn is about 400 yds. ahead of the reserve. Then comes the main body, which were the three other companies. Well, the pace was so fast and furious that the point was way ahead of the support, and at the end of two hours the battalion was a column some three miles in depth. For every hundred yards that the other bodies fell behind, a connecting file was sent out. Now it's up to the main body to be able to move as fast as the advance guard. But after three hours, a runner came up from behind and told Capt. Baker that we had lost contact with the 7th Co. Well, Wild Bill said that was tough, but if his men could march at that pace, the other companies could too.

A few minutes later, the Major asked Capt. Baker how long he thought we could hold the pace. Capt. Baker said he wanted to see. At that time we were going at 130 steps a minute. A few minutes later a jeep came driving up. A Sergeant dropped out. "Capt. Baker, Capt. Lowe of the 6th says for you to either cut the step or send back the ambulance." Capt. Baker immediately sent back the ambulance. The length of the march was fifteen miles plus. We left bivouac at 0700 and rejoined our regiment at 1100. We were two hours ahead of schedule and entered the regimental area with every one of our original men. We had three "breaks" on the road in, the first of 15 minutes, the second & third of 10 each in duration. So out of the 240 minutes it took us to get in, we only marched 205 minutes, or 3 hours and 25 minutes. Thus, we averaged over 4 mph.

We had Monday off, and had fights almost every time we met some guys from the other Cos. But our outfit is the best of the bunch, and my platoon is the best in the 8th Co. So that rates us pretty high in this regiment of 3,000.

I spent a rather nice day Monday in Columbus. It was only the second time I have ever been there. I have some postcards I shall send home to all the smaller kids. They're very beautiful. Well, to get back to Monday. I got up at 0800 and ate breakfast. I shall say what I ate now. Ahem.

eight eggs, sunny side up
two french frys of potatoes
1 qt. & a half of milk
1 pt. of coffee
1/2 grapefruit
box of Post cereals
4 buttered toasts

This was aw reet? Yeah man. I then went to town. Spent the day seeing the buildings—going through them—the 1st Nat'l Bank, the federal courthouse & post office—the Columbus Savings Bank, the Ralston Hotel (275 rooms). The latter was a really beautiful place with a dining room similar to Kolb's. Then the fellows and I went to the two USOs. These are really swell places here. They have their own gyms—camera clubs, pool & ping-pong tables, etc. Well, I spent a good bit of time here. I then went on a tour of the department stores and dime stores. I bought a half-dozen khaki handkerchiefs and the colored postcards.

I had bought a box of Hershey's chocolate bars at the USO—the only place in town where you can get them. Well, I proceeded on to the post office with some of the fellows, the box of candy in plain view. In front of the post office I noticed two small girls with a cocker spaniel trailing, following me. Finally one said hello. "Hello," I returned, and started to enter the P.O.

"Uh-uh," one stammered.

"Well, young lady, what can I do for you?" I said, stooping to pet her spaniel.

"Will ya'll sell me a candy bar?" she prayed, handing me a nickel.

"Yes, me too," added the other.

"We haven't been able to get any in a long time. Where did you get all those candy bars?" the first drawled in amazement.

"Well, I got them at the USO," I said.

"Will you please sell us just one?" from the second.

"Well," I drawled, "I tell you what I'm gonna do. Since you can't get it, I'll give you two bars apiece. How's that?"

"Will ya'll really do that?" they asked, eyes shining in excited anticipation.

"Here."

"Oh, *thank* ya'll *very* much." And with a jerk on the dog's leash and a "Come on, dog!" they walked proudly, chattering, down the street.

I next went to a tailor & got my blouse taken in. I still have to get my pants altered.

Then I was finally back here and spent about 1½ hours trying to get to a phone in order to phone you.

Well, give my love to all. I got a letter from Aunt Ogie & Aunt Winnie today telling of holiday festivities.

Your loving son,
Morris

United States Army
Fort Benning, Georgia
January 13, 1944

Dear Mom & Dad,

It is already Thursday night and this interim is almost over. This week has gone pretty fast, as have all the preceding ones, when you look back on them. I don't like to look ahead anymore. There are too many rumors in the old grapevine's circulatory system. There are too many threats concerning our future. When you scan a past period, especially a period which has brought forth so much good, you are much happier than when looking into the future, unstable and uncertain.

However, it is pretty definite that I will go to school. Where I will be sent is information still in Washington. When I will be sent is pretty well known. Probably around the seventh of February. I might be home sometime in Feb., this fact depending on several factors.

This morning we spent a very interesting four hours going through a "Combat Reaction Course." The problem was this: I was a soldier lost or separated from my company behind enemy lines. This course presented 12 situations that usually occur in combat. The object is to test the soldier's ability to cope with the circumstance in which he finds himself. It was run by coach-and-pupil method—one fellow, a coach, who had the solution to the present problem, and the other, the pupil who was running the course. The problem was presented, the pupil would react, and the coach would correct him if the need be.

Tomorrow night we will have a night problem. I guess that this is to get us in practice for the next bivouac.

Esther asked in her letter if this next bivouac would be like the first. The answer is emphatically negative. The last bivouac was like a vacation compared to the next one. The next one will be strictly tactical. After sundown there will be no talking, no smoking, and no lights or fires of any sort. We will have with us only the clothes and blankets we can carry on our backs. No newspapers or packages will be delivered. Instead of eating the C rations only once in a while, we'll have them for two out of every three meals. The night shall be our working time instead of the day. It will be pretty rugged, as Luke used to say. Which reminds me—I haven't written lately, and will you ask William to write him immediately and tell him the score. His address is:

Pvt. L.F.B.
AST United 1892
Arkansas State College
Jonesboro, Ark.

We've been living on sulfathiazole pills lately. There's all kinds of sickness around here, and I pray every night that I won't fall before I finish here.

Well, that's all the news for now. I close and I remain

Your loving son,
Morris

* * * * *

USO

January 14, 1944

Dear Mom & Dad,

This is some of the stationery I picked up at the USO last week-end. I carry it in my mess kit and try to write a few lines during breaks.

So far the life hasn't been too hard. The first night I didn't sleep a wink, although I went to bed at eight o'clock and we didn't have to start work until eight the next morning. I don't go to breakfast because first, it isn't worth the trouble, and second, I'd rather remain in the pup tent and get all the rest I can.

This tactical business is stuff for the birds. You live 20 yds. from the next bivouac tent, 15 yds. between men in line, 15 paces between men while eating meals. Most of our work so far has just been digging foxholes & camouflaging them, going out on night problems, digging minefields, working problems in the daytime. It's very interesting and it's pretty good so far. Of course, the weather is fine now, but you can't count on it.

It gets below freezing here every night, but at noon (the present) it's like a beautiful spring day.

We eat breakfast at 6 in the dark and supper at 8 at night (in the dark), except when we have night problems, when we eat at midnight.

I had diarrhea, or the "GI trots" as the Army calls it, for a day. It's not so bad, but when you have to stand over a little trench it becomes pitiful. One guy was straddling the trench when one of the sides caved in. He certainly got out of his shoes fast.

Well, I'll write tomorrow, I hope.

That's all the news for now. I hope all are well. Give my love to all. Tell William to tell Lolita I'll write as soon as I get a chance. I got her letter at the start of the week but you all are the only ones I have found time to write to.

Your loving son,
Morris

* * * * *

Fort Benning, Georgia
January 15, 1944

Dear Aunt Winnie,

I would like to beg pardon for not having answered sooner. But due to extenuating circumstances, I couldn't afford, or even find, the time to write. Things around here are pretty fast and furious at present. We haven't fully recovered from the last bivouac and are at present embarking on another. Only this time is the last time! We have only three more weeks to go, two of which will be tactical bivouac, the other, a week of tests, classification, and waiting.

This tactical bivouac will really be the stuff. It really ought to knock out a good many of us. Especially if this weather we're having keeps up. It's very cold, rainy, and miserable. Of course, on the last bivouac we had closed tents, cots, and fresh-cooked meals. However, on these maneuvers we'll sleep in the very small pup tents, on the very cold ground, and eat those very delicious C rations. Instead of working in the daytime, we'll sleep. Our eight-hour day will begin at eight P.M. and end at four A.M. After sundown, no smoking, talking, or lights of any kind will be permissible, since the situation is tactical. But every one of us is up to it.

On Friday night we had a four-hour night problem. When we started out it was raining cats and dogs. Consequently, the mud roads of Georgia became knee-deep slush. It was cold as usual, and as dark as the inside of a pitch barrel. We wore white armbands in order to keep from getting separated while marching through the woods. However, even at a distance of about four feet, the heavy darkness was impenetrable and the white armbands were useless.

To top it off, a "gas attack" was sounded on a whistle. I had to take my glasses off to get the mask on. Well, I did this all right, but I could no longer see—I was blind. I heard the columns moving up ahead, so I started after them. I ran into an object which I thought was a soldier in the column. As it was, it turned out to be a tree. Disgusted, I removed the mask and tried to see where I was. I finally stumbled into a fellow who led me, like I was a blind beggar, back to the column.

We walked through the shallow rivers of the Upatoi up its slippery banks and through the inky woods. For four hours we did this. I was a wreck at the end. But it was funny while it lasted. No one knew which step might be his last.

At about two in the morning after we had returned to camp, a searching party was sent out to bring in some 20 or 30 stragglers separated from their units.

Well, these next two weeks will be the hardest. So pray for me and I ever remain

Your loving nephew,
Morris

* * * * *

Fort Benning, Georgia
January 16, 1944

Dear Mom & Dad,

This is a short note. I told you most of the news over the phone. However, there was one thing I forgot to mention. Saturday afternoon we had competitive drill on a piece of high ground that wasn't too wet. The gold cup for the drill was awarded to our platoon. If we win the next contest, we'll be tied for first. The platoon that finally wins it will be guests of the other platoons at a banquet paid for by them. Not that I care so much for the banquet, but I would like to see our platoon win it for our Lieutenant and Sergeant.

Here is a picture of the expert medal with the rifle and machine-gun bars attached, which I merited.

Jan. 18 - I sent home my letters. Please save. There are two of my co. pics in there.

Received letters & pics.

Loving son,
Morris

P.S. Will write tomorrow.

Fort Benning, Georgia
January 16, 1944

Miss Ogie Joyce
1905 Calhoun
New Orleans, Louisiana

Dear Ogie,

Well, here it is, Sunday—the start of our eleventh week of Basic. I am sorry that I didn't write sooner, but I just never found the time. At the present we're all set to go on this second bivouac. It's really going to be a lulu. But it signals the coming of the end of our Basic here at Benning.

About a week ago in Columbus when I was getting my clothes altered, the old seamstress asked how I liked the Army. I replied that I liked it well enough. "Sorta like the Boy Scouts, isn't it?" Well, I almost exploded, but being charitable, replied, "Yes, a good deal. Only more so."

After these next two weeks, it'll all be over but the shouting. The last week will be one of tests, classification, and anxious waiting.

Before I forget, tell Gissie Burton hello for me. I thought it was very nice of her to send me the card.

Well, that's all for now. Give my love to the Stuarts and Aunt Lala.

With love,
Morris

* * * * *

Fort Benning, Georgia
January 21, 1944
7:30 P.M.

Dear Mom & Dad,

Tempus fugit! This is certainly true, especially on this bivouac. I am writing this while waiting for the chow truck to come. It probably won't show up till after dark. Last night we had another problem and underwent another gas attack—tear gas. I got my mask on pretty fast but I still shed a few tears.

We didn't have to fall out until 2 this afternoon, so I had all morning off. I spent this time writing letters to Lolita and Charlie Brennan. This evening I heard from Ogie, Luke, & Lt. Mouledoux. I don't know when I'll answer these.

This afternoon my platoon began the platoon defense fortifications for a demonstration in the near future.

The work is pretty interesting and the good weather makes everything pleasant. It continues cold at night and warm in the day.

Next week we have plenty of night problems and lots of free time in the day. So I'll try to write to everybody.

This week has been well spent in training for anti-mechanized defense. We've thrown Molotov cocktails and what-not. We are still digging foxholes all over the place, but I like it.

It's too dark to write anymore, so I'll say good-bye.

Your loving son,
Morris

* * * * *

Fort Benning, Georgia
Sunday, January 23, 1944

Dear Mom and Dad,

This past week was certainly wonderful with regards to weather. God was certainly kind.

Bivouac has been hard in some respects, but the bad has been outweighed by the wealth of interesting things and problems that come up every day.

On all of the problems a bit of realism is added by the use of blanks, dummies for bayonet work, foxholes, camouflage, etc. If I were Ralph's or Ronnie's age, I would be having a grand time, but as always there remains in the back of one's mind the threat that the failure to play the game here can mean death on the battlefield. So in all of these maneuvers this consideration brings out the best that is in us. We've worked out all types of problems. We have supposed all kinds of situations. And in all of these the officers have had as good time as we.

Yesterday afternoon we finished our scheduled work at 4 P.M., thus leaving us two hours of "open time." Well, I had been looking for the chance to get down to the Upatoi River to wash, and I was glad when the Corporal said we were going in if we could stand it. Well, we all took off our clothes and went in "in the raw." Believe me, we were even more raw when we came out. I swam all the way across to the other side and came ashore on a sandy beach. The current is pretty strong and the river itself is something like, and the size of, the Tangipahoa River near Ponchatoula. After the first ten seconds you could appreciate the water, because after that time you were numb. The river has a big sandbar in the middle which makes fording by tanks possible. The rest of the bed is of gravel, which at the low temperature is hard on the feet.

Well, there's nothing more of note. So remember me to the Fonsecas, the Kellys, the Stuarts, the Sellers, the Joyces, and the Redmanns.

The 4th War Loan Drive has started here, so today I bought a $25 bond and took out an allotment for $12.50 a month in bonds.

Well, that's all the news for now. I remain as ever

Your loving son,
Morris

* * * * *

Fort Benning, Georgia
January 30, 1944

Dear Mom and Dad,

Well, the Battle of Benning is almost won. We have returned victorious from the swamps and hills of the field of maneuvers. From the home of the rattler, the snake, the skunk, and the mosquito. From a jungle of vines, reeds, and brush, a land composed of some hard ground and some muck and mire, we have returned singing. However, I must say I have no complaint. Somehow or other, in the darker moments there has always been some "sad sack" who pulled off some dumb trick that brought a laugh.

This last week was really rough. On Monday and Tuesday we had four-hour night problems; on Wednesday and Thursday, we had eight-hour problems. The one on Thursday lasted from 7 o'clock until 5 the next morning. This was the one I told Daddy about. It was really something. It was the attack. In combat a company marches at rout march (regular marching column) until it comes under artillery and long-range machine-gun fire. When this occurs, it takes up the approach march. The company continues in this formation until it comes under the small-arms fire of the enemy. Then it goes out in a skirmish line paralleling the enemy's line.

The next move, of course, is the attack. In this move there is some preparation. The objectives are pointed out on aerial photos, scouts make their reports on the position of guns, the men are given their last hot meal, they are issued two bandoliers of ammunition (which is about 96 rounds), they drop their packs, and then they're ready to go. So the attack begins. The troops take off from the line of departure, and from then on the battle is on. They keep advancing until they meet the outguard of the enemy, which is in front of the enemy's main line of resistance. Then it's pretty rough. There's an old saying in the Army that there are two kinds of men on the battlefield: "The Quick and the Dead." After that night of last week I can well believe it.

In that problem it must have cost the U.S. at least $1,000 for all of the ammunition and material expended. There were about fifty parachute flares that are shot from guns and that drift down attached to a parachute. The light given off lights up the whole countryside, thus giving the enemy opportunity to see and shoot anything to their front. When one of the flares goes off, you either hit the ground or freeze in your steps with your face held down. Then there were pound sticks of dynamite or TNT tied on the tops of trees and exploded to let us know what artillery shelling was like when you were in the woods, and to give the effect of tree bursts. Some charges were planted in the ground, too. One would go off on the right and you'd jerk your head to the left, only to be met with another blast on the left that shook you from head to toes. Then there were many "dago" bombs, too, and cannon crackers all around you set off by the non-commissioned officers around you. Then when you meet the enemy's full line, you lie low with bayonets fixed, awaiting the order to charge. Here's where you rush the foxholes, stab occupants, or grapple hand to hand until they retreat or are overcome. If they are driven out, we must dig foxholes and solidify our newwon positions, get new ammunition, bandoliers, and await a counterattack.

Yeah, it was fun. The only difference between these maneuvers and combat was there were no corpses and no real bullets. Ho hum! Civilian life is so dull. But BOY OH BOY, HOW I WISH I WAS ONE!

Sincerely, very sincerely,
Your loving son,
Morris

Fort Benning, Georgia
[Postmarked January 31, 1944]

Miss Ogie Joyce
1905 Calhoun
New Orleans, Louisiana

Dear Ogie,

I feel ashamed for not writing sooner, but I never got a chance. The last week of bivouac was really hectic. We were in the field day and night executing maneuvers. On many nights we worked till five in the morning and then slept—or rather, rested—until only eleven in the daytime. Of course, we're supposed to have free time in situations like that. But free time seems to be the Army's time. You know that old song: "Your time is my time." Special for the Army.

I am writing this in the Columbus Grill while waiting for breakfast. We marched back to camp Friday night and Saturday morning. And this was really a march. The pack we carried weighed close to 70 or 80 pounds. Of course, we had tent and tent pegs, rope, raincoat, shaving equip., overcoat, two woolen blankets, one comfort [heavy bed spread], extra pairs of pants, underwear, etc. We marched from 10 P.M. 'til 6:30 A.M. and covered some twenty-five miles. Some of the weaker souls were passing out as we marched. I know I almost did. My eyes are still bloodshot from the strain. No kidding. You never saw a wilder-looking bunch. Most of them didn't shave in the two weeks, so they needed a good landscape job. The sight was really something. Down at the latrine where there was plenty of light, we looked at each other. There they were, bloodshot eyes rolling back into their heads, hair that would become a fuzzy-wuzzy, beards from two weeks of not shaving, dirty and torn clothes, with faces and skin to match, sagging knees and shaking legs. They looked like seasoned veterans fresh from a long campaign. But they were just boys finishing the toughest part of any training ever given anywhere. I'm glad it's over. I'm glad I went thru it. But I'd hate very much to have to do it again. And this I mean. Amen.

Well, Ogie, I can't tell you anymore because stories stretch over some pages. However, I hope all are well. Give my regards to the Stuarts and Aunt Lala. I hope to be home soon so I can see all the grand people I know, and in the meantime I remain

Your loving nephew,
Morris Jr.

Le Fort Benning
le 3 février 1944

Ma chère Esther,

Maintenant les jours de la semaine sont longs. Le temps fait froid et mal. Cependant la fin est proche. Nous n'avons que deux jours encore de Basic. Alors, il y aura la "graduation." Quand je tourne les pages de mon livre de memoirs, il ne me semble qu'un temps bref. Mais je peux rappeler des minutes qui me semblent des heures.

Aujourd'hui, le capitaine nous a dit que nous sommes maintenant des soldats. Il a loué notre esprit. Notre capitaine est un grand soldat et nous le respectons beaucoup. Il est un grand guide, maître, et entraîneur des hommes. Les exercices qu'il nous a donné nous ont fait puissants.

Dîtes à la petite Winnie de m'écrire en français, et lui dîtes que je lui écrirai dès que possible.

Dîtes "hello" à tout le monde, et je reste,

Votre frère,
Morris

* * * * *

Fort Benning, Georgia
Thursday, February 3, 1944

Dear Mom and Dad,

Lo! The Prodigal Son returns! I haven't written in a long time, for which I am very, very sorry. However, I intend to make up for it in this letter and I promise to try, from here on out, to write every day.

Today I am on "sick call," confined to quarters, as a result of the very strenuous work we have done in the past few days. I had wanted to go on sick call yesterday, but refrained from doing so because we were scheduled to perform our physical fitness tests in the afternoon. I am not sorry I didn't go, because I have finished, now, the hardest of it all. However, I didn't know what I was doing half the time. But I got up this morning feeling worse than before, so I decided to go. My kidneys hurt, my limbs ached, my feet were shot, and what-not. And well should they be. For yesterday was one of the most grueling days I have ever spent. The first two hours of the morning we had dismounted drill. For the second two hours we had inspection. (I didn't pass the rifle inspection.) Then came lunch. The first two hours of the afternoon were again devoted to dismounted drill. In the second hour we had the platoon competition. Then the physical fitness tests began. The first part was the 300-yd. run in forty-five seconds. The second was 33 push-ups. The third was 11 "burpees" in 20 seconds. The fourth was the 75-yd. piggyback run. The fifth was a zigzag course in which we ran, crept, crawled, jumped, etc., for about 100 yds. The climax was the sixth station—the four-mile run. So you can easily see that after marching 28 miles on Tuesday and after doing all of the aforementioned stuff on Wednesday, I was pretty dead on Thursday.

The doctor here now is really a swell fellow. He's a Major in the medical corps and a real doctor. The last one we had was a butcher in every sense of the word. He was from Brooklyn, and acted as if he had been brought up in a grandstand, yelling at umpires. He was young and loud. This MD is very quiet, sympathetic, a very grand opposite of the New Yorker.

So, today I'm going to try to answer some letters. It's cold, rainy, and miserable outside, and I certainly pity the rest of the fellows who have to be out in it. But there's only two more days before graduation and there's nothing important going on. Tomorrow, Friday, we have more drill and another inspection. On Saturday we have a big parade on the drill field with band and colors, and then graduation. We'll be around for about two extra weeks, however, since most of the terms don't start until the 1st of March. On Wednesday of next, we'll have our company party at one of the USOs in town, or perhaps at one of the rest camps in the fort.

Some of us will be here until the 20th. I might be here that long; I expect to. I don't know when I'll be home. But if I do get home, I think Luke will be in, too. He wrote and mentioned his having a furlough at the end of the current term. Of course, as always, the rumors are flying thick and fast. Some say we're going to go to Ga. Tech. When asked where you heard that rumor, one might reply "Latrine, third bowl on the left." That's about all you ever get here is latrine rumors. No one knows any more than the next fellow, yet all profess to have "inside dope" and other such authority for every statement they make.

To tell the truth, I don't know even where I might be sent. In reality, I don't care as long as I can get home for a few days.

Well, I hope to see you soon.

Your loving son,
Morris

Fort Benning, Georgia
February 5, 1944

Dear Mom and Dad,

With the blaring of the brass and the thunderous booming of the big bass drum, there ended our basic training. As I marched in the battalion parade, in dress uniform, with rifle, belt, and bayonet, I looked back over the thirteen tortuous weeks of very rigid training. In my ears, above the "tinny" blasts and dull booms of the military band, there rang a thousand commands, different in tones, some demanding, some pleading, others furious in their delivery, but now, just memories. I smiled. And before me, instead of the bobbing, khaki-covered heads and shining rifle muzzles, protruding over strong and broad shoulders, I saw a moving picture. It was a vivid, week by week, description of the past thirteen weeks of my life. Weeks filled with awful worry over simple, petty things. Then there came in magic colors the things accomplished. It was then I felt like a little boy who had been afraid to go into a darkened room but who, after being shown that there was nothing there to hurt him, beamed with a newfound confidence in himself.

And so the picture ran, reel after reel, through the weeks of bayonet fighting, hand-to-hand combat, nights of infiltration, days of physical exercise, and the obstacle course, hours which I thought would never end, and minutes, so long in my imagination. All of these have left their imprint in the sands which no wind ever stirs. In one of his letters Uncle Billy predicted that "experiences are varied. Some pleasant and some not so pleasant. But over a period of time they blend to make a pretty picture." And as I look back I become convinced that he is right. I am repeating when I say that it has been a grand experience. I have enjoyed it for the most part. The other times I just kept smiling, and usually found that every cloud does have a silver lining. The gray days have been few but not always far between. But now it's over.

I'll be here for two more weeks, I guess. We'll still have calisthenics, the obstacle course, and marches. Don't worry. We won't be loafing.

My greatest worry now is when and where. Rumors are rank. You can't believe the Corporals. One says most of us are going to Ga. Tech and another says that all but fifteen are going to California. I never was very gullible until I got into the Army. Now I don't know what to believe. But wherever it is, I hope I get a chance to come home for a while—to sit on the sofa and cut up with the kids, and raise sand in the library if there are rainy days. I won't be home long, five days at the most, depending on where I'm sent.

I'm in Columbus now, just fooling around here at the USO. I'll go to dinner in a few minutes and then to a show.

I started a letter to you yesterday while being a sanitation engineer, or more familiar to you, a latrine orderly. Boy, what an easy day I spent. I read every article in the *Reader's Digest,* including the Book Section. Then I started to write you but was yanked out of the boiler room around 4:30 P.M. to go to a "make-up" lecture on street fighting. So I didn't finish it. So I started over today.

Things in the past two days have slowed down. I've read some Shakespeare and brushed up a little on the French. I wrote to Esther "en français," as you know by now. I got your letter with its "customary," and I got Daddy's; one from Esther, too.

How are the Fonsecas? Mr. F., is he home yet? How are all the kids? How are they doing in school? Esther seems to be doing pretty well. But keep after that William.

Well, give my regards to all.

Your loving son,
Morris

P.S. I am sending home two booklets that deal with our battalion and its training.

* * * * *

Mr. and Mrs. C. J. Kelly

Fort Benning, Georgia
Sunday, February 6, 1944

Dear Aunt and Uncle,

I received your most welcomed letter in yesterday's mail. I brought it into town with me so that I could answer it today. I got your address from Mother when I made my customary Sunday call. I also had the pleasure of speaking with Miss Winnie. I tried to persuade her to write me a letter in French. This is a good way of learning the subject and it is usually very interesting. I asked her also to ask Claude Jr. to write me. I would enjoy hearing from them.

Well, yesterday, amidst the blaring brass and thunderous booming of a military band, came the end of basic training. Now, I'm supposed to be a soldier. There is no supposition about it. I am a soldier, I must think and act as if I were the best soldier. Thus, I become the best soldier.

The true measure of morale is given in the story of Private Smith. This certain private was told by this Lieutenant that he was the best man in his squad. So that night in the barracks the pvt. said, "By golly, I'm the best soldier in the squad." Then he thought a little, and added, "You know, my squad is the best squad in the platoon." Then he thought a little more. "By golly, my platoon is the best in the company. I've heard the Captain say that." About here his chest began to expand and his posture became erect. And he thought a little more. His mouth dropped open and he mused to himself, "Well, I'll be darned if my company isn't the best in the battalion." So by this time he was feeling pretty good. "Doggone, if my battalion isn't the best in the regiment. And my regiment is the best regiment in the division, and it's the best in this man's Army. Well, I'll be d——d if I'm not the best soldier in the whole Army!"

Well, when you can figure this way, your morale *is* pretty high.

You mentioned in your letter a card from Aunt Hy with some money. I never got it. It's a good policy always to let me know when you send something, what it is, by a different letter. This way I could always check.

I hope you and Uncle Claude enjoy yourselves very much in Chicago and thanking you for the cookies, I remain

Your loving nephew,
Morris

* * * * *

Fort Benning, Georgia
February 7, 1944

Postcards

Dear Ralph,

Mother tells me that you are really a whiz in arithmetic. Keep studying hard. You have to know a lot of arithmetic to fly one of these ships because everything in flying is based on mathematics. Tell Sr. Kevin hello for me.

Morris

Dear Robbie,

How are you, young man? Since you haven't started school yet, what do you do with yourself while all your brothers are at school? I suppose you and David must get along pretty well. I want you to tell the mailman, the iceman, and the milkman hello for me.

Morris

Dear Kerry,

This is a training plane used to train pilots for the Air Corps. It doesn't have any guns on it because aerial gunnery is taught by other means. This plane is just to help teach men to fly. How are the Blue Jays getting along?

Morris

Dear David,

How is my big boy getting along? I enjoy reading your letters that Mother helps you write. But when you go to school next year, you will learn to write for yourself. I hope you are feeling well and that you are a good boy.

Morris

Dear Esther,

I was glad to see that you are doing so well in school. I wrote you in French the other day. Repondez en la même, s'il vous plait. If Winnie is staying at the house, let her write me in French too.

Morris

Dear Will,

I was glad to have the opportunity of speaking with you and Esther the other night on the phone. There were some things I should have asked you, but I forgot most of them. I had wanted to ask how Loyola was doing on the hardwood and who was who at school. Is Marion Schlosser still the editor of the *Maroon*? If so, tell her I would appreciate a copy of the paper even if I have to send a self-addressed stamped envelope. Tell her hello anyway. Remember me to Fr. Soniat.

Morris

Dear Jerome,

I knew how much you liked parachutes, so I picked this card for you. It shows paratroopers landing with their equipment. When these boys land, they're all ready to fight.

Morris

Dear Rich,

Well, how are you? I hope you are doing well in school, and that you are well. Study your Latin very hard. You can make good marks. This is a picture of a tank destroyer with its 105 millimeter gun. You can't see all of it, but it looks like a tank itself.

Morris

Dear Ronnie,

Well, how are you and your friends, the Fonsecas? Do you still play "soldiers" with the other kids in the neighborhood? How would you like to shoot a gun like this? This gun is used to knock down enemy airplanes.

Morris

* * * * *

Fort Benning, Georgia
February 8, 1944

Dear Richard,

This is just a very short note to wish you a very Happy Birthday and many more. You're thirteen now and getting to be a big man, day by day. But remember as you grow in age, you must also grow in wisdom and knowledge. So study your books and make good marks. I know I shall certainly study hard when I go back to school because I shall have some incentive to study. Enclosed find my present to you on this, your 13th birthday.

Morris

Fort Benning, Georgia
February 8, 1944

Dear Mom and Dad,

There isn't much that's new around here, but I shall briefly tell you what's going on. I received your letter today and I thank you for the buck. I thank you also for the list of birthdays. I know I won't be home for Richard's, but I most certainly hope that I am in town for the others.

On yesterday, Monday, we took that four-mile "forced march" over again. This time all but two made it in the allotted time of fifty minutes, and there were no stragglers. Because we did look good, the Colonel, who watches over us like a strict but loving mother, gave us the rest of the day to recuperate. It wasn't as hard this time as it was the last time we took it.

Today we took another march—one of eleven miles in three hours. For every hour we're supposed to march we get ten minutes off. So you only march fifty minutes while resting ten minutes. So, in two hours and thirty minutes, we came in ten minutes ahead of schedule, and we marched the eleven miles with full field equipment. Well, that's going pretty strong.

While in town Sunday, I wrote the Kellys at the Palmer House. I also answered one of Peggy Mc's letters. Yesterday I got a beautiful box of cookies from the Solaris. Thanks to the Kellys. Tell Winnie hello for me. Give my love to all.

Your loving son,
Morris

* * * * *

Fort Benning, Georgia
February 11, 1944

Dear Mom and Dad,

I am sorry I neglected to write, but since Basic has been over we've been working pretty hard. So I hope you didn't worry too much. I have been to the show almost every night with the fellows to relieve the strain. Wednesday night our company held its party; $100 of it came out of the Company Fund, and the rest was made up by contributions from the members of the company. I must say that it was the best time I have had since I can remember. The scene was the Student Training Rest Camp. This is a big, beautiful building on top of a pine tree–studded hill that overlooks Victory Lake. The outside is finished in pine logs and the inside is all veneer, just like our library. The chandeliers were made of old wagon wheels hung in a parallel plane with the floor. The lights were placed evenly around the rims. In the huge ballroom there were two big stone fireplaces, one at each end, and a very fine bar. There were full-length double doors that circled this room, opening onto the porch that faced the lake. Out on the porch were many chairs, tables, davenports, etc. This was really some brawl. There was one pound of chicken per man, one-half case of civilian beer per man, ham, potato salad, cheese, olives, pickles, cigarettes, cigars, pretzels, potato chips, milk, Coca-Cola—everything we could have wanted. It started at 6:30 and went on 'til 11:30. There was grand entertainment furnished by comedians and musicians from our own company.

Of course, the morning after was fiendish. At eight-thirty we started on a fifteen-mile march that had to be done in four hours. But almost everybody made it.

Since January 1st I have bought $23.75 worth of war bonds. I'll be darned if I buy any more outside of my $12.50 per month allotment. I had to shell out a buck for the party, too. I may have to borrow some money from you if I can ever come home. I think I may be going way out to UCLA or to Southern Cal, in which event I would have a hard time getting home. Don't tell this to anybody, even the kids. I'm not sure it's true, and then if it is, it has to be kept secret. However, at any rate, I won't be leaving until the twentieth.

I got a nice letter from Aunt Jeanne and one from Ogie and Kerry, too. I shall try to answer these as soon as possible.

We had inspection this afternoon at two o'clock and have been "free" since. Tonight I'll go to the show to see Spencer Tracy and Irene Dunn in *A Guy Named Joe*. It's pretty good as seen in the previews. The other night I saw *The Desert Song,* a beautiful musical with music by Sigmund Romberg, and featuring Dennis Morgan and Irene Manning.

Well, I don't know anymore to write, so I say "good-bye," while remaining,

Your loving son,
Morris

Fort Benning, Georgia
Sunday, February 13, 1944

Miss Ogie Joyce
1905 Calhoun St.
New Orleans, Louisiana

Dear Ogie,

Today being Sunday I find opportunity of writing and thanking you for the good candy you sent. Such thanks are late, I know, but I couldn't find time for writing.

Today I spent all day writing letters, some due months ago. But I'm almost caught up now. I probably won't get another chance to write until next Sunday because this week will be another rush one.

I can't think of much to say because there hasn't been much happening except marches, marches, and more marches. There's nothing much that happens on a march. It's just another walk. Of course, I could describe the beautiful steep hills that we have to walk up; the shaky rustic bridges over, or rather under, the streams—most have sunk in the soft riverbed until they now rest three inches below stream level—the beautiful white sand so hard to walk through, and the brilliance of the red and yellow clay, so sticky that a fast pace is impossible. But since such description makes me tremble, I won't.

I've been thinking of home and all the folks a lot lately. I've learned a lot in the Army, and one of the things I have learned is how dear, how prized, is man's love for home and the memories strung upon its sacred walls.

The one complaint that American Generals have in regard to us is that we are the most homesick soldiers in the world. Perhaps it is because American homes and American families are the finest in the world, and therefore the most missed.

Sincerely,
Morris

* * * * *

Fort Benning, Georgia
February 17, 1944

Dear Mom and Dad,

This is just a short note because there hasn't been much happening. There is absolutely no news at all from this quarter. A list of colleges was read and the closest to home was Arkansas—next, Kansas. There are only two colleges on the east of the Mississippi—one in Maine, the other in Mass. But there are many on the West Coast. So my chances are for the West or Midwest. Grapevine has it that we will leave here around the 21st, 2nd, or 3rd of March.

We had final inspection of rifles and other equipment, which was then turned in to the supply room. I was really happy to get rid of this rifle. We don't have to carry it anymore. All of this seems to point to our leaving in the beginning of the week.

Well, that's about all the news I have. If the *Times-Pic* hasn't been stopped, please suspend it until I get to college, so as to avoid their piling up here.

Give my regards to all around.

I remain,

Your loving son,
Morris

* * * * *

Fort Benning, Georgia
February 18, 1944

Dear Mom and Dad,

Today is the fourth monthly anniversary of my entrance into the Army. Even though I've been in the Army here at Benning for sixteen weeks and will not leave for another week, I will not get paid for a long time. Perhaps not for two months. Since I will be here until the twenty-fourth, I think you had better lend me some money—about twenty-five dollars—until my next pay. I think you had better wire it to me at this same address. I guess that's the quickest way. I know where I'm going, but I can't tell anybody. I don't know if I'll get a furlough. Such prospects are pretty dark. But now I have at last some peace of mind. I know where I'm going and so I won't be "sweating out" my next assignment anymore. I have a swell bunch going with me to the land of oil and Indians. I'm satisfied, I guess. Beggars can't be choosers.

Enclosed find $10 worth of stamps. Put them in my book, or in any of the kids' books that need them.

That's all the news for now.

Your loving son,
Morris

P.S. Dad, you could never come see me—it's a dry state.

Aunt Lala would not part with the following letter. When asked, she told Dad that he could have it on her passing, but not before. After her death, this beautiful letter from her eighteen-year-old nephew was found in her "important papers," in an envelope addressed to Dad.

United States Army
Fort Benning, Georgia
February 19, 1944

Miss Lala Joyce
1905 Calhoun St.
New Orleans, Louisiana

Dear Aunt Lala,

This is the first time in many years that I will miss your birthday celebration. So, I write to wish you a Happy Birthday, and to express the hope that you enjoy good health and that you shall see many more years.

Of course I'm grown up now. In time of war everyone grows older. But the passage of years hasn't yet—and I hope, never will—sweep from the pages of my memory the happy thoughts stored there of the many hours spent with you. And I am sure I shall remain ever grateful for the kindly care and interest you took in me as a child.

I can remember the Carnival Balls of peacetime when Mother and Dad, dressed in their best, and smelling of powder, perfume, and what-not, would leave in a rush to attend the party. I can also remember with what loving care you saw my smaller brothers tucked in bed, and saw that they got their warm bottles while Mother and Dad were away. I remember, too, the times when Kerry, Ralph, and Ronald would act like demons, jumping off of the higher pieces of furniture and onto the bed. I still can plainly see what a hard time you had making all of us behave. And to this day I wonder why Aunt Lala stood for all she did from us kids.

I guess, too, that if you look back, you can remember us as we were many years ago—with our long Buster Brown haircuts, our shiny, patent-leather shoes, our sagging stockings, our dirty faces, punctured with "all-day suckers."

Thus, on your celebration of the passage of another year of your rich life, I wish to extend to you, Aunt Lala, my best wishes and many happy returns of the day.

Sincerely, your loving nephew,
Morris

Fort Benning, Georgia
Sunday, February 20, 1944

Dear Mom and Dad,

Can you keep a secret? Well, I'm going to tell you on the phone in a few minutes anyway. So here's the dope. I'm going to the University of Oklahoma at Norman, Oklahoma. No, you can't find it on the map. I looked. However, it's a small town of about 11,000, and right in the middle of the state, sixty miles outside of the capital. I will leave here by troop train on the 24th, 5th, or 6th, which means I will not get there until the end of the month at least. Then I'll be there for a few days of orientation. Then, if I'm lucky, I might get a chance to come home. In which case Luke will be in, too. He's in neighboring Arkansas.

If he comes in on the fifth, I guess I'll be in too around that time. Some of my good buddies are going with me, so I'm satisfied. I guess it'll take a day to get home from Oklahoma and a day to get back. If I get a seven-day furlough, I'll be home for five days.

But legislation in Congress is fast doing away with the ASTP. On April 1st, 110,000 students will be sent right overseas. Of course, it's not probable, only possible, that I will be one of these—but don't worry. Even when you go overseas, you've got a long time before anything happens. However, I guess I'll be in the States for some time yet. So that's the story. I have received letters from William, Kerry, and Ronald lately. I appreciate them, and shall write soon.

They say you've been having rain lately. Well, well, what do you know! Georgia at this time of the year is rain and knee-deep mud. I don't bother to wash clothes anymore. I just go stand out in the rain.

By the way, if *Standing Room Only* shows in N.O., please go see it. It is really funny. It is a satire on the administration and life in Washington and the help situation.

That's all for now.

Your loving son,
Morris

* * * * *

Fort Benning, Georgia
February 20, 1944

Dear Mother,

It was certainly some shock to receive the news of Gregory's death in the Pacific. But I used the newspaper with his picture and article in it, unknowingly, to start a fire in the stove. Therefore, I am lacking in details.

I have had a feeling for some time that his number was up. I have thought about him constantly and it worried me so much that, if you remember, I asked how he was in one of our conversations.

When you first told me this morning, I couldn't believe my ears. But then in an instant the days spent with him at the mouth of the river, the times years ago when he and I climbed in the shed behind his house, and the Loyola dances at which he and I had such good times, all flashed before me. The day he joined the Marines I was with him, and we went to S.A.K.'s formal dance at the Grand Ballroom of the Roosevelt Hotel that night.

This afternoon right after I spoke with you, I left the USO and went to the Holy Family Church. I spent about half an hour there, praying for the repose of his soul. I thanked God, too, that he was killed immediately and that he wasn't captured by the Japs. The pictures of the battle were shown here in a restricted film. The Battle of Tarawa was perhaps the most costly for us in this war. Tarawa was probably the heaviest fortified spot in the Pacific—the fortifications stretching out into the sea. In the sea were cement posts every few feet with railroad track pieces sharpened to a point and sticking out at an oblique angle upward. These steel prongs stuck every landing barge that tried to reach the beach. After this there were rows and rows of barbed wire set underwater to entrap any soldier that might have outlived the bath of fire given the stricken landing barges by shore guns. Then right on the shore were terrific concrete pillboxes. A heroic attempt by a marine to blast a hole in one resulted in the killing of the occupants. This marine dragged barrel after barrel of oil up to the pillbox. Since there was a tunnel connecting the some hundred pillboxes, the oil flowed freely into the whole fortification. Soon, a pump was set up and oil in great quantity was poured in. The marine then set fire to the oil and crawled back down the ditch to the beach. He cremated four thousand of those dirty yellow devils in a few minutes. This is said to be the man who won Tarawa. If he hadn't done what he did, every marine would have been wiped out.

I am deeply moved by Gregory's death. Yet he died fighting for an ideal—the American Way of Living. He died so that the squealing babies I saw baptized in church this afternoon may live in peace, speak their free mind, and worship God in the true religion. Not a few have died thus in the past years of confusion, hate, and intolerance. Their country was their creed, and they are their country's pride.

Gregory should be remembered from Guadalcanal. He will be remembered for his work, his duty done, his death at Tarawa.

If you would, Mother, please express my deepest sympathy to the family—or should I write a note myself?

Relying on a hasty answer, including a clipping from the paper, I remain,

Your loving son,
Morris

* * * * *

Fort Benning, Georgia
Wednesday, February 23, 1944

Dear Mom and Dad,

The situation here is as muddled up as it could be. I think we're going to college and then again I often think we're not. We might go any number of places besides a college campus. For instance, we could go to an infantry replacement center, or to the Air Corps, or to a Port of Embarkation. The latter is highly improbable. No one here knows where we are going or what is going to be done with us. The Major admitted that himself. Our orders sending us to college have not been canceled as yet. But even as I write, perhaps, cancellation of all orders could be taking place.

Latrine rumors are, as always, the only information that we have. This Lt. still with us volunteers all sorts of information—never pleasant—none of which is acceptable as true. He starts the worst rumors just to make us worry. He has done this all through Basic, and continues it every time he gets a chance to get us alone to talk to us.

"He never went to college
But he got him a degree
I reckon he's the model
Of a perfect SOB."

He's always telling us about how he worked in the FBI. Well, one of the wise guys who chanced to be Charge of Quarters looked up his record. He wasn't anything before he got into the Army. How he got to be a Lieutenant, I'll never know.

I don't think I'll get a furlough for a long time. That's something else that has come up in the last few days. But Lt. Tyler (my-y-y boy) (HA) told us we definitely wouldn't, so we might.

Today I'm a dishwasher. I went on at 0730 and have just gotten off at 1015. I go on again after lunch and then again after supper.

Last night I thought I'd go to the show. So I went. *Jane Eyre* was playing with Orson Welles and Joan Fontaine. It was really a marvelous picture—very much out of the ordinary and heavy with oppression and drama. The photography was one of the most outstanding things in the film. Orson Welles seems to have followed his habit of having terrific settings with odd lighting effects to add to the psychological effect on the audience. As a rule I don't go for the serious, heavy stuff, but I must say I enjoyed this picture.

I received Dad's telegram and money order. I haven't cashed it as of today because I haven't needed it yet. I don't think I will need it unless I ship out. I hope to get out of this mud hole. It has been raining every day, and I'm afraid the buildings will sink out of sight if it don't stop.

Today being Wednesday, we will get a swell meal at noontime. Ice cream as dessert. Good eats. I'll eat once with the co. and then again with the KPs. Ah, what a life. I'm reconsidering an offer from the Mess Sergeant to be a cook here until we leave. Some of our cooks have shipped out already, leaving the Mess Sergeant shorthanded. That's like the old sad story:

> *Sergeant: Any of you guys know anything about shorthand?*
> *Anxious Pvt.: Yes, Sergeant, I do. (3 times).*
> *Sergeant: Well, they're shorthanded in the kitchen. So report to the Mess Sergeant.*

Well, that's all the news for now. I remain, *still* hoping to see you soon,

Your loving son,
Morris

* * * * *

Fort Benning, Georgia
February 26, 1944
USO

Dear Mom and Dad,

Of the many experiences in Army life, the most unforgettable is the "GIing" of the mess hall. It takes plenty of GI soap, GI brushes, and about twenty GI "goldbricks," or, more commonly, privates. The holder of such a job has it, not through reason of merit, not as reward, but because of some mistake he made in the presence of a Sergeant. Therefore, the kitchen detail is made up of those few, picked men, best suited for the job.

Around eight o'clock of the night of the job—which is every night—the Sergeant starts making the rounds of the huts, picking guys that either have nothing to do or who are not doing what they should be doing. Well, this Sergeant usually carries a flashlight in order to look under the beds for such characters that think that's a good place to hide. He usually walks up the street with the light lighting the way. Well, as even the most ignorant GI knows, this is the signal for all men wishing to remain free to take off in any direction, for any place that offers cover and concealment. So everybody grabs clothes, hat, writing paper, or whatever one might need to look like he is presently being employed elsewhere for something very important.

However, it is my luck, and mine good friend Schonefeld's, too, that we are in our birthday suits, having just lately returned from shave, showering, and shampooing.

When the alarm is given, I am already thinking of what I say to the Sergeant so that he lets me off. However, when I see who he is, I don't say nothing because I am not having any truck with him who can put the arm on you in a moment's notice. So, regretfully I put on my clothes and follow authority and march to the mess hall. Here I see many other characters like myself who were caught trying to clean up or wash in their off hours. Among these is Willie "The Creep" Steinburg, a character from up in Brooklyn. He is very small with the frightened expression of one who has just opened a sack of potatoes, supposedly, to find a pair of size-eleven shoes come out first on the feet of one of the boys from a Bronx mob, who offended a Brooklyn boss. Then there are others who look like the cops have put the sleeve on them at one time or another. Still others, those unmistakable characters from Virginia, Tennessee, and Caintucky. Then as I sit down I see "Liver Lip" Louie Lippel, who comes from over the states in Los Angeles, California. He is a cinch to loaf on any job at any time unless it was putting out a fire in the seat of his pants.

Since it is now getting to be 8:15, the Mess Sergeant—whom many would like to put the arm on in a dark alley—calls us together. As soon as he calls, there is a general rush by one and all to be the last one to get up to him. But finally the soap, brushes, and water are passed out and the night's work begins.

I am naturally one of the first to reach a good broom and mop that Schonefeld and I can lean on. It is in these leaning moments that most of us look like we are working hardest.

But already the scrubbing of the tables has begun, and I see Russo and Raczykowski turning one of the twelve-man tables on its side and starting to scrub it on the undersides. Meanwhile, Max Negri is earnestly trying to interest some of the more sporting like of us in a crap game in the storeroom. Another character, P. P. Rich from Phillie, is offering 6-1 odds that we are through and blown by eleven-thirty. But since most of us are convinced that we are here for the night, there are not many takers, and P. P. Rich has to go back to scrubbing tables.

Well, about halfway through the tables, the Sergeant asks us if we have done the ceiling and the rafters. Of course he knew we hadn't, and when we complained, pleading ignorance, Sgt. Glenn Finley from County Cork, Ireland, formerly, and now from Chicago's East Side, told us politely what we had to do before getting to bed. Well, it turns out that Chicago Roberts gets "Liver Lip" Louie, Dynamite Dan, and a few others organized to get up in the rafters and scrub them and the ceiling. After I see this done I start over on the tables. About this time Negri has taken "Killer" Kellher to the cleaners in the storeroom, and "Killer" comes out to look for work, and Negri for some more sportsmen.

By and by, all the tables are scrubbed clean and wiped off, and the walls and floor are then scrubbed, and then everything is sprayed with a hose. Hoseman Willie "The Creep" looks like a big-time gunman scragging some Bronx sidewalk and rubbing out some of the city's inhabitants. Then we get some oversized windshield wipers, which are stolen from the next mess hall, and proceed to wipe dry the wooden floor. After the Sergeant inspects everything, he tells us to get our jackets and scram. As I walk into the storeroom I see "Rough" Ruffrano, Christian name Robert, stuffing apples by the dozen into his loose-fitting clothes, and I am wondering why he does not let some of the apples there and walk out with the hamper they were in. But I suppose he might be forced to kick to "Killer" Kellher if seen with apples in such great quantity.

As we walk back to the hut, P. P. Rich is happy that no one covered him at 6-1 since it is now close to 0100 in the A.M. Louie Lippel is completely worn out, since it is the first time he has ever worked so hard in his life. But he would have been worn out just from being awake, since I see him always asleep whenever he can.

But, me, I am pretty tired too, so I go to bed.

Your loving son,
Morris

In the following letter, Morris tells of his not going to advanced engineering school at the University of Oklahoma in Norman, Oklahoma. The U.S. Congress has rescinded the program, and he will be sent to an Infantry outfit. He tries to veil his disappointment in his letter to his parents, and accepts his new assignment without a murmur.

Sunday, February 27, 1944
USO

Dear Mom and Dad,

I am now in the Infantry. Unofficially, of course, because I have not yet been assigned to an Infantry replacement center where the real soldier is molded and tempered until he becomes a highly efficient member of a great fighting organization.

Little is ever said of the Infantry soldier except perhaps that he is often called a sucker for being in the Infantry. There is to outside eyes no flash of brilliance, no shining glory, no romance to the Infantry organizations fighting throughout the world. They are such an old part of the Amy that they are synonymous with it. But behind every personal victory, every single engagement, every battle won, there is the background of effort, sacrifice, and hard work given in the months of training. There are the hours of strenuous exercise given to the development of strong minds and bodies; the days in the field where each waking minute taught new rules of life, because obedience of the old rules would no longer serve the purpose; the hours of marching in the sun until there wasn't a piece of dry clothes on you; the days on the dry-firing line, practicing positions from which you can fire a target most effectively, all while lying on the sopping ground with the rain pelting you on the face until the water runs in a steady stream off the tip of your nose; peeping through the sights until the targets swim before your tired eyes; the painful hours of bayonet practice that promotes proficiency in the use of that dangerous weapon; sleeping and living in foxholes, and crawling through the pest-infected swamps in order to learn a new way of life so necessary to self-preservation; going for days on end, eating only out of cans and canteens; half running, half marching for hours and hours until your aching bones and dry throat tell you you couldn't go any further; finding out that some bit of self-respect, some strength of heart kept you going long after your tired limbs said you had to stop; slow hours spent quietly behind a log or bush in the marsh, waiting, learning patience the hard way;

not moving a muscle lest you disturb the tall grass around it, or you. All of this and much more goes into the making of an Infantry soldier.

The Infantry is the greatest branch of this man's Army. You walk a lot, you fight a lot, and you've got to be plenty rough and tough. To some it is romantic to see giant birds wafted skyward into the evening light, bomb Berlin, and then return for early chow. But no Air Force has ever captured a single foot of ground. The Infantry will get to Berlin, too, and stay for chow until ordered home. When the giant General Grants and Shermans bog down in the soft earth, the Infantry will move ahead. None other than the hard and valiant Infantryman will receive the vanquished sword. No spot of ground was ever won without the Infantry. None was ever held without the Infantry. And thus she's called the "Queen of Battles." So wherever I go, I know I'll be in a good outfit, one in which I will be proud to serve.

Things here are as indefinite as ever. I took my overseas physical on Saturday afternoon. The only defect is my eyes. My vision is 20/400 in both eyes. Sometime this week I will go over to the Main Post and be issued two pair of GI glasses.

There isn't much other news except that I will be here about three more weeks. Schedules have been made up for the next two weeks. During one of these weeks we shall study the Browning Automatic Rifle, or as it is commonly known, the BAR. We shall also get the chance to fire it on the range. It is really some gun, firing about 750 rounds a minute.

Well, that's about all the news I have now, so I'll say good-bye.

Your loving son,
Morris

* * * * *

Fort Benning, Georgia
March 1, 1944

Dear Mom and Dad,

Starting on Monday coming, we will take up advanced infantry training. This training will last four weeks. After that, many of us will go to P.O.E. (Port of Emb'k't'n). I have given up all hope of seeing home until after it's all over, but I guess I'll like it all the more then. We shall go out into the field on Monday for two weeks' bivouac and night jungle fighting.

Because of the new training I'm going to stop being a cook and go back to work as a trainee. I won't need the cooking experience, but I will need the other.

School isn't ever mentioned anymore. Plenty of the fellows are very bitter, which is rather a childish attitude to take. Most of the "brainier" guys are all busted up. Their dreams are shattered. These are the boys that never thought they'd see combat. It was rather a rude surprise. Oh! But life is full of tricks.

"As toads to wanton boys
are we to the Gods.
They worry us for their pleasure."

"Gods" meaning the Washington jokers who started the whole business.

Before I go any further, don't send money by wire anymore. It's too much trouble to cash. Send it, if I need it, by postal money orders not exceeding $15, or cash. I won't get paid until April 1, and this Western Union money order is cashable only in town, and I don't know when I'll get in again.

Oh, well, I can't think of anything else except that I hope Dad & Uncle Kelly had a good birthday party.

Your loving son,
Morris

* * * * *

Fort Benning, Georgia
March 4, 1944

Dear Mom and Dad,

The company was reorganized today into three rifle platoons and one heavy-weapons platoon. I am in the heavy-weapons platoon, but I'm neither on the machine-gun section or the mortars. I'm attached to headquarters. I would have really liked to have been on the mortar squad because those are some weapons. I fired the mortar on the range and it's really a good infantry weapon. A good mortar squad can go into action in thirty seconds and have fired a target. Our Platoon Sergeant, Sgt. Barnero, could get into action in 25 seconds. The 60 mm. mortar weighs only 48 pounds and is worth its weight in gold. A newer mortar—the 4.2 inch—is bigger, and is mounted on a jeep. The shell is about 2.5 feet and weighs 25 pounds. It is very maneuverable and can fire as fast as it can be loaded. It's really the daddy of them all. Reports have come back saying that it can hit a moving tank. One report tells of a gunner who called his shot as the turret of an enemy tank. He got it on the first shot.

I learned today that the chaplain on board Gregory's troopship gave conditional absolution to all the Catholics on board over the PA system and had all say an Act of Contrition. So I guess he's received his eternal reward "in the garden of his Father's Palace."

As I told you over the phone, I thought I might be shipping soon. Well, I don't know. I don't know. Everything seems to point that way, and yet it's hard to believe that we are moving out. Some men from the other regiments are being sent to divisions now encamped in Louisiana. I wish I could get back "home" like that.

The war news is encouraging these days. A close examination of smaller bits of news seems to reveal a plan of larger-scale operations. A third member of the Allied High Command in Asia visited President Roosevelt in the same week as two of his fellow warriors. This would seem to indicate that something is about to break in the Pacific. Our fighting Admiral Bill Halsey is also now in the States. His successful operations have done much to reduce the size of the Jap Army of 8,000 in Burma, and lays wide the path for an Allied advance in the CBI Theatre (China, Burma, India).

The Navy in throwing its Sunday punches at a stubborn opponent's outer defenses has decreased the distance between the American flag and the flag that flies over Tokyo. In the invasion of the Admiralties we have pocketed 50,000 Jap troops doomed to certain annihilation at the hands of our veteran marines and soldiers.

The fact that our bombers bombed Berlin against no opposition would indicate that Herr Hitler has thrown his dwindling Air Force against a greater menace—either the Russians, now well into Estonia, or the advancing Americans fresh from their Mount Cassino and Anzio Beachhead victories.

I read a typical German communiqué the other day in a *Reader's Digest.*

Last night huge formations of American bombers, numbering hundreds and thousands, attempted to bomb Germany. Our gallant and courageous fliers of the Luftwaffe took to their planes and guns and shot down two hundred of the attacking planes. All of our pilots returned safely. One of our cities is missing.

That's all the news for now.

I remain,
Your ever loving son,
Morris Jr.

PART THREE

CAMP MCCAIN, MISSISSIPPI

MARCH 9, 1944–AUGUST 4, 1944

Morris finally receives his orders—leaving Fort Benning, Georgia, on March 8, 1944, and going by train to his new destination, Camp McCain, Mississippi, and the 94th Infantry Division. He writes his parents in the following letter, reflecting an upbeat attitude. But that was always his style.

Camp McCain, Mississippi
March 9, 1944

Dear Mom and Dad,

Yesterday was the day. We packed our bags in the morning, and at ten of one began the two-mile march down Wood Road to the troop train. The regimental band was there to see us off, and they provided some pretty good music. After taking our last look at Benning, the train pulled out. I must say that I have *never* been on a finer train than the one we came here on. It had Pullman accommodations for all. Yes sir, we really traveled in style.

We arrived here at ten this morning. It is now about 1:30 in the afternoon. My new outfit is the 94th Division. It's an infantry division and a real live outfit. I haven't much to say yet. We have had one meal here so far and it was swell—served out of dishes, home style. There are barracks here, too, instead of huts. So far I'm pretty well satisfied with it, and I think I'll like it here.

Camp McCain isn't a very old camp. It is situated about 100 miles below Memphis, Tenn. The nearest town is Grenada, which is 20 miles from Winona, which is 271.14 miles from N.O. So I'm up in the northern half of Miss. and still a long way from home. Don't think I'll ever get home now. We've got plenty of work to do.

I'll write again as soon as I get my full address. Tell all hello.

Your loving son,
Morris

* * * * *

Camp McCain, Mississippi
Friday, March 10, 1944

Dear Mom and Dad,

On our way over here on the train, I read for the most part, but at times my attention was distracted by different things that were taking place out in the countryside. The day was very bright and the first touches of spring were beginning to appear in the Infantry Woods. All along the way the peach trees were in bloom, and many different types of wild-flowers were pushing their bright faces through the dead grass. It seemed like one of those pleasant June days full of color and sunshine and cool breezes, quite a contrast to the bleak, dreary day that saw our arrival at Benning. The hours flew by fast, and soon the sun was casting its last shadows over the green pastures and grazing cattle that made up the countryside. Past small towns and villages. Past shabby, faded houses where happy farmers' children danced and waved to us while, stopped, we waited for clearance up ahead. As I watched the happy children, I remembered much of home, much of the cheerful days, the happy hours. Here was a large group of kids, brothers and sisters, all having a grand time by their home, just like we used to. Soon the train gave a sharp jerk, squealed a little, and then smoothly picked up speed in its initial direction. Then I continued with Agatha Christie's *Unknown Adversary.*

In the distance the lights of some big city began to be reflected in the sky. We went rolling on until finally I asked a porter where we were. "We gwan ter stop in Muntgum'ry in few minutes." The lights I had seen earlier were the huge neon signs and bright streetlights of the main stem of this southern city. And in a few minutes the train was pulling into the Montgomery station. It jerked to a halt, and immediately other civilian travelers and the curious stared at all the soldier boys seated in their troop train.

Then through the crowd a red cross flashed, then another and another, until finally a great number of the red crosses were below our windows, passing in cigarettes, candy, coffee, cakes, magazines, etc. The food came in handy because a meal on a troop train isn't much. This was certainly a great booster for our morale, and I will never regret that I ever gave anything to the Red Cross—the greatest mother in the world.

But soon we were rolling along again. The lights of the Jeff Davis Hotel began to fade, and another Orleanian remarked, seeking an argument, of course, that Jeff Davis, as the 16th president, was one of the best we had ever had. Argumentation did result, but it faded almost as soon as the lights. Then I went back, reading as we rolled along. Then another stop. But soon a slow start, and we crept past legendary, fabulous Maxwell Field with its long rows of lights that mark the runways. Then came a very nice sight—that of seeing the big Mitchell bombers shoot in just over our train and down onto the long runways. One after another they came, huge sky dreadnoughts with their landing lights on, seeing their way safely home. Soon everything faded and I was asleep.

The next morning we were awakened at the usual hour of six. We got up, dressed, and then washed. By the time we came back to our seats, the porter had the berths up and the curtains down. So we sat and waited for breakfast. Almost immediately after the paper cups and plates and wooden spoons and forks had been passed out, the KPs came through and dished out the scanty rations. We had eggs and bacon, bread, butter, preserves, and coffee. So much for breakfast. Or in truth, so little for breakfast.

After breakfast we "policed" the car, getting all the paper gathered up, and sweeping. Then we settled back to reading, or cards, or talking. The train rolled on through Winona and Duck Hill and Grenada. Then into Camp McCain. We had arrived.

Somewhere among the black, tar-papered buildings with their yellow slats was home. Home—not for too long, just for a while. Here, sprawled out in front of us, was the 94th Division which *is* Camp McCain.

And, as it had the first time I saw Benning, the old lump rose in my throat and I waited to hear the calls of "Hey, Rookie! Oh you yardbird!" True, I felt like a rookie, and I felt that as long as I was ever in the Army, I'd still be a rookie. But the actions of the non-coms and the officers—their spirit of fellowship toward us in the first few minutes of our acquaintance—made me feel that no matter what their rank, they wanted us to be at home in the 94th, and to be their buddies and true brothers-in-arms. For the first time my spirit changed. I was then a soldier in a live outfit. I was a soldier. I now had a regimental emblem to wear on my hat and on my lapels, and a division patch, plain and drab, of silver and black, to wear on my arm. I was no longer just another soldier, unattached and unassigned.

Thus I must admit that I am well satisfied with this new post. I am proud of my outfit. It's a pretty good outfit because some of it is now in Italy. But even if it was the worst in the Army, I'd still be proud of it because it's my outfit.

Give my love to all.

Your loving son,
Morris

* * * * *

Camp McCain, Mississippi
Saturday, March 11, 1944

Dear Mom & Dad,

I'm in the Fourth Army, Twenty-first Corps, Ninety-fourth Division, Three hundred seventy-sixth Infantry, Third Battalion, Company L. Boy, what a mouthful! This outfit has just returned from three months' maneuvers up in Tennessee. As the old Colonel told us, "We're a pretty hot outfit." *Hot* meaning that they'll be sending us over soon.

The few days we've been here, we've attended lectures by the Colonel, training films—one, the technicolor version of the Battle of Tarawa—and played football and baseball. This afternoon I'm going to try out for the company's basketball team, which is at present tied for the Battalion Championship. If I can make the team and if the team would win the Regimental Championship, our Sergeant said that some three-day passes might be given out.

The food here is really swell. Every meal I've eaten here is better than the best at Benning. Besides plenty of the solid food, such extras as doughnuts and hard candies (jawbreakers) are placed in mounds on the tables. These same-sized tables that held twelve at Benning hold only eight here, which gives much more elbow room for the "lefty-louies."

My barracks is in an ideal situation here. Within a 150-yard radius there is the War Department Theatre, the day room with pool tables, Ping-Pong, radio, and reading material, the Post Exchange, the gymnasium, the public telephones, and the chapel. Last night I went to see Donald O'Connor in *A Chip off the Old Block*. It was pretty funny. In one scene, adolescent Mr. O'Connor (Kerry's type) sticks his head into an outer office where a pretty brunette sec't'y is typing.

"I'm looking for a little blonde with whom I'm supposed to go to dinner. Have you seen her around?"

"No, I haven't. But I'm not eating dinner tonight," said the sec't'y seeking an invitation.

"Well," said O'Connor, withdrawing his head and disappearing from view, "You'll be awful hungry in the morning."

By now, Luke Bruno must be in a live outfit someplace. Would you find out his correct address for me from his family? Give them my regards.

I have just received your card and a letter from Ogie.

That's all the news for now, and I remain

Your loving son,
Morris

P.S. Have just been classified to company H.2 of the 1st platoon.

* * * * *

Camp McCain, Mississippi
March 12, 1944

Dear Mom and Dad,

This morning I got up at 0715, got dressed, washed, and then walked over to the Chapel to attend Mass. I had thought Mass was at eight o'clock, but after waiting a few minutes and seeing no one else arrive, I went out into the vestibule and tried to read the bulletin board. Sure enough, I was wrong. Mass wasn't until 0930, so I went back to the barracks. A good many of the fellows were really sawing wood even at this hour. Then one of the cooks came through shaking all the sleepers, giving them an oral menu and telling them that chow was "in fifteen minutes." Most of them got up, but a few expressed their thanks and rolled over and went back to sleep. So at 0815 I was eating my two fried eggs, hot buttered toast, cereal, marmalade, and drinking coffee and milk. It was a good meal. I also got a big red apple.

After breakfast I went over to the day room and read my Jackson paper and tuned in on WWL. At 0845 I went over to the latrine and shaved. Then I got my prayer book—the one that the H.N.S. gave me through Fr. Castel when I left—and went over to the Chapel.

The Chaplain is a swell fellow who looks something like Humphrey Bogart and who gives a very good sermon. I was very much impressed with his sermon, based on a phrase of today's Gospel—"A house divided against itself shall come to desolation." He pointed out how everybody has the law of the soul or the intellect, or of one's intelligence to go by, and then another law with its laxity and animal qualities; how there is always the inward conflict between the urge to do right and the urge to do wrong. He cautioned us that the only way to avoid the conflict, and, hence, the division, was by prayer and sacrifice. He really gave a swell sermon. Each pew is equipped with six Sunday Missals—something I had never seen yet in any GI chapel. Then too there was an organ and a choir and participation in the singing by the congregation. When the singing started at the beginning of the Mass, there was only one soldier singing and he was sitting next to me. When the priest had finished the prayers at the foot of the altar, he turned and walked to the altar rail and asked all to join in. He sang the first verse to get it started, and then turned and walked up to read the Introit.

After Mass was over I went over to some of the other barracks to look up some of my other friends from Benning. I found a few of them already up and getting dressed to attend their Protestant services at 10:30. I must admit, and they admitted it too, that this was the first time in twenty-one weeks that they had attended their services. I used to always kid them, especially during our arguments on religion, about attending their services. But now for the first time, they must have realized that they'd better start getting on the good side of God. So I waited until they returned from church and then with them came up here to the Service Club to have dinner and phone home.

We had a pretty good meal of fried chicken, creamed potatoes, green peas, peaches, milk, and hot buns with butter. It was pretty good, all right, especially when I found out how cheap it was to get a good meal here.

Enclosed you will find a drawing showing how regimental emblems are worn. Our shield is blue in the top third; red in the center, with a gold flash of lightning thru it, and gold in the lower third, with a coiled rattlesnake in it.

This is the 94th Division insignia. It is silver and black, the inked-out portion being the black. It is worn on the left sleeve, 1 inch below the arm and shoulder seam.

Well, that's about all the news & "views" I have, so I say good-bye.

Your loving son,
Morris

P.S. Will you have William find out Warren Mouledoux's address for me from his family.

Camp McCain, Mississippi
March 14, 1944

Dear Mom and Dad,

On Monday we started out at 0745. We marched out about five miles into the hills for the day's work. Here, we had a lecture on patrol work at night and on squad tactics. The problem to be run during the daytime was the driving of the enemy from the top of a big hill. Since only one platoon worked the problem at a time, we spent the extra hours of waiting at playing football or baseball on one of the flat plains between the surrounding hills. We played a pretty rough game of tackle. At twelve we had chow, eating out of our mess kits. After chow we continued with our game until two o'clock, when the platoon got ready to move out. From the heavy-weapons platoon we had some mortars—81's, they were. Our platoon was equipped with a "walkie-talkie" radio which is a very handy instrument for field communication. Every soldier learns how to use it. It isn't much more than the ear and mouthpiece of a French telephone, with a 3-foot aerial on it. Well, we worked the problem. The Lieutenant, in his critique, said that our platoon had done the best job on the problem.

Last night, and until about 0430 this morning, we were out on night patrol problems. It proved very interesting and exciting. It took us eight hours to get through the enemy lines and back, with the information of a road junction a mile or so behind the lines, without being discovered. Patience is very necessary, and stealth and quiet are essential for the successful completion of such an operation. For this reason steel helmets are not worn, because if you should brush against some leaves of a low branch, there would be a lot of extra noise. Even little noises—such as the cracking of a twig—have to be avoided, because such sounds as these are heard at great distances at night. In night warfare you don't shoot at what you see, you shoot at what you hear. So does the enemy. But I had a good time playing and sneaking along streambeds and through draws and ravines. I get a kick out of seeing how quiet I can be. Last night I got so close to the "enemy" that I could hear the Lieutenant's conversation over the walkie-talkie. Once we had to lay still in a ditch for 45 minutes while some enemy patrol was going about the vicinity. But we finished the problem having reported our information on the road junction without ever being discovered.

This morning I went through the tear gas chamber again, and then thru the chlorine gas chamber. The concentration in here was so great that gold buckles and other pieces of metal on our clothes and equipment turned black. We were told afterwards that in that lethal chamber was enough gas to kill sixty of us in ten minutes. Even though we had been instructed on the use of the gas mask, there were several stretcher cases—the results of inattention and carelessness in the use of the mask. Mine worked perfectly all the way through.

I didn't make the basketball team—too much competition. But we really have a swell team. At 1530 today, L Co. played M Co. and ran right through them to the tune of 65 to 14. If this keeps up, the regimental championship is in the bag.

Well, that's all the news for now. I have KP tomorrow and I'd better get some sleep.

Your loving son,
Morris

P.S. Received money order. Thanks. Also Ogie's and Aunt Eleanor's.

* * * * *

Camp McCain, Mississippi
Tuesday, March 14, 1944

Dear Aunt Eleanor,

Here at Camp McCain is the home of the 94th Division. Camp McCain is America's most modern "Theatre of Operations Camp" and was activated on Oct. 10, 1942. It embraces about 41,000 acres, or about 65 square miles. It is recognized as having outstanding facilities for the training of combat troops, having very favorable terrain, location, and climatic conditions. So much for the camp itself.

The food here is pretty good—better than what we got at Benning—and living conditions are much better. Here we live in barracks. My barracks are in a very good place as regards nearness to other buildings and places frequently used.

You asked what kind of work I am doing. Well, I was with Hdqtrs., but am now back in the first platoon, 2nd squad. I am a scout—the worst job in the whole infantry. Scouts are always way out in front of the main body and their function is to draw the enemy's fire and make them give away their positions.

Last night we were out all night on a reconnaissance problem. It was a lot of fun and very exciting. There were minefields and "enemy patrols" and everything just as in combat. We spent eight hours getting thru the lines and reaching a road junction 1 mi. behind them. Night work is such an important part of modern warfare that sixteen hours a week are spent on it, and shall continue to be spent for as long as we are in the country. We are going out again Wednesday night, but I don't know what kind of problems are in store for us.

I am very happy that Paul Jr. is now an officer, and I wish him all the luck in the world. He won't be an ensign long, tho'; he's got too much "stuff on the ball." He'll move up fast.

Well, I haven't any more to say except thanks for the money and for your prayers. Give my regards to Uncle Paul and Paul Jr.

Your loving nephew,
Morris

* * * * *

Camp McCain, Mississippi
Thursday, March 16, 1944

Miss Ogie Joyce
1905 Calhoun St.
New Orleans, Louisiana

Dear Ogie,

I tried to answer your letter the other night, but just got off one to Aunt Eleanor and Mother & Dad before I got so sleepy I couldn't see. This week has been rather rough, but it's almost over. Wednesday I got up at 0430 for 0500 KP. I was on all day until I was relieved at 1900. At 1920 I put on my helmet and pack and went out with the company on another night problem. This one was infiltration through enemy lines. We used a map and a compass to get through. We must have walked ten miles all through the night because I was certainly tired at five this morning when we ate breakfast. But we had good luck. We got through the lines, captured a command post, an enemy Colonel, took a jeep, and raided the regimental C.P. The funny thing was that we thought we were lost and that we hadn't even reached the enemy lines yet when we stumbled upon a command post and its sleeping personnel. From them we found out that we were way behind their lines. Sgt. Vastola, our squad leader, then took the jeep we'd captured and with half of us in it and half following on foot started raising the roof behind the lines. We all had a good time, but I was glad to eat breakfast and go to bed.

Tomorrow we have a 25-mile hike. If I go on it I'll have a chance at getting the Expert Infantryman badge.

Thanks a lot for the "buck." I can certainly use it.

Well, I'll say so long. I can't think of anything else to write.

Your loving nephew,
Morris

* * * * *

Camp McCain, Mississippi
March 19, 1944

Dear Mom and Dad,

I am sending you the bond I bought at the beginning of the 4th War Loan Drive. I had kept it as protection against the high-pressure tactics of bond salesmen, but now I'm afraid I might lose it. So you all can put it away someplace.

This letter won't be too long because I can't tell you too much about our training, because we're not allowed to tell everything we do. Therefore, from now on I guess my letters will be kind of shallow.

I asked over the phone that you send me some pictures of the family. I would like some of Dad and Mother in them, too. Also, if ever you take any more pictures or if anybody in the whole family takes pictures, please send me some copies. Everybody here has pictures of their families and relatives and I would like to have some too.

Well, I said this one would be short. So this is it.

Your loving son,
Morris

* * * * *

Camp McCain, Mississippi
March 19, 1944

Dear Aunt Winnie,

I am sorry that I did not write you sooner, but we have been working pretty hard here, night and day. Besides, I lost my good stationery and had to resort to this.

We get up at 0600 every morning, stand reveille at 0630, eat at 0645, and begin our day's work at 0730. On a regular day we come in at 1130 for chow and go out again at 1230. We usually come in by

1700 get dressed in our ODs and stand retreat at 1730. After retreat we have chow, and then are free until reveille the next day. However, lights are out by 2200.

On Monday we hiked five miles out into the reservation and played football for two hours. We ate at 1130 after which we began to work on tactical problems. We did practical work the rest of the day and then marched in at 1730. We ate dinner and then dressed warmly, for there was an eight-hour night problem that night. We started out at 2000 and didn't finish until 0400 on Tuesday morning. It was a beautiful night for a problem—a full moon and plenty of stars. I had a good time running around out there, sneaking along the banks of the numerous streams and trying to keep concealed in the shadows, crawling across the open ground and stepping carefully through the woods.

Tuesday I was rudely awakened at 0900, after only four hours of sleep, and told that I should get dressed and wear a gas mask. I asked, why the mask. "You'll find out in thirty minutes" was the reply. I did. We went through tear gas and then an extra strong concentration of chlorine. If one doesn't get panicky and can hold one's breath there is absolutely nothing to worry about, even though the chlorine was strong enough to kill everyone in minutes. But, in spite of all the instruction, the commanded precautions, there were still gas victims carried out of the area and over to the dispensary.

What they learned the hard way we got the easy way. Their experience provided the example of the effects of the gas. Although they had only a few breaths of it, they were coughing and vomiting for hours afterwards. One fellow held his breath until he turned white because he took too long to get his mask on.

Tuesday afternoon my company played another company basketball. We won and have kept on winning.

Wednesday I got up at 0430 for 0500 KP. I was on until 1900 that evening when I got relieved. At 1930 I fell out with the company to go out on another night problem.

Friday we got up at three o'clock, rolled our packs, and then ate breakfast. At 0400 we started a twenty-five mile march which we completed in eight hours. In the afternoon we rested. Not much else we could do.

Saturday we had a full-field inspection and rifle inspection, after which we went over to the battalion drill field to hear our Bn. Commander, Col. Bennet, bid farewell to his command. He has left for a secret assignment. In the afternoon we had a physical examination and then were free for the week-end.

This briefly is the story of a long week. This one was really a lulu. We—that is, my squad—were to infiltrate through the enemy lines and to destroy command posts and to capture personnel. We were pretty lucky, I must admit, but we destroyed an outpost, captured a jeep, a Colonel, and destroyed regt'l headquarters. Then, going back, we surrounded some enemy and they started running. Some of them we tackled and started fighting with. One guy ran off a cliff and fell into a river.

Thursday we had off and I slept until twelve; played ball in the evening.

I have prayed that Claude Jr. would win the oratorical contest. That speech of Patrick Henry's is classic among rhetorical selections. I remember when Roy Guste gave it and won the gold medal. I hope Claude will do the same.

Well, I wish you all luck and I hope that all are well.

Your loving nephew,
Morris Jr.

* * * * *

Camp McCain, Mississippi
Thursday night, March 22, 1944

Dear Mom and Dad,

Well, work around here is fast and furious. That's the reason I haven't written since Sunday. This past week we were out on the range to fire known distance ranges and transition courses with the M-1 rifle. We've been out in the field every day. We eat and live out there in fair weather and foul. Lately it's been pretty foul. These broad, flat plains catch a lot of rain, and it rains a lot around here. The roads are impassable to all except the mud-slogging infantryman. The mud is knee-deep, and big GI rubber boots had to be issued.

Our Company L basketball team won the regt'l championship and the first game in the divisional play-off. It was a very thrilling game. With two minutes to go we were losing 29–28. But the final score was 37–29, our favor. It was a whirlwind finish all right.

I am glad Esther did so well, but I had hoped that she would win. I don't know the reason for Ogie's gift either. I wish you would thank her for me now. I don't have any time to write anymore, but will try to get a letter out to her this week-end. (We were out today from 7 'til 7.)

There are rumors that the division will move to another camp for amphibious training or for more maneuvers. If it's for maneuvers, there's a chance of going to Louisiana, since they were in Tennessee last time. But rumors are rumors and that's all. If we're still around I'll get a furlough around June—only 2 more mos.

Thanks for the buck.

Loving Son,
Morris

* * * * *

Camp McCain, Mississippi
Sunday, March 25, 1944

Dear Mom and Dad,

The past week was rather rough, I must admit. One of our Sergeants declared that it had been the hardest he had ever worked since he had been in the Army. There were twenty-five-mile marches, forced marches of nine miles in two hours, battle inoculation courses, and finally, on Friday, not one, but two infiltration courses. The first was in the daytime. The place was a wide, flat, muddy field studded with barbed-wire fences and land mines which were marked off by tape. These mines were deep in the slush and when one went off, there was a geyser of dirty water and huge hunks of wet mud that splattered everybody when it fell to earth again. Everything was a mess. I was wringing wet from head to foot and covered all over with slush. But I grinned and bore it. After everybody went through it we marched back to camp. Then we washed and dressed in our ODs and went to chow.

After chow the Captain requisitioned some trucks and the whole company piled in and went over to the 302 Regt. where our company was playing for the championship of the 94th Division. Boy, what an affair. Colonels giving buck privates fists full of cabbage to bet for them on their separate regt'l teams, Lieutenants stepping outside to make a bet, and the chaplain holding numerous monies. I believe that the Sergeants and non-commissioned officers bet close to $500 on our team. Then they were sweating the rest of the evening because the other team started out like a flash and made eight points right away. It wasn't until the last few minutes of play that we were finally safe. The score stood at 44–37 at the end of the game.

Then we piled into our trucks, raced back to our barracks, changed into our muddy clothes, and marched out into the night for the night infiltration. This was really an experience. Tracer bullets were used. They were going right over our heads and the Lt. wasn't lying when he said that they would be only three feet off the ground. They lit the way though, and a burst of a land mine could give one a glimpse of the land toward the front. In the brief half-second flash, one could see all the other fellows blindly feeling their way forward through the slush and barbed wire. Yes, it was quite a time.

We're well on our way in the "Expert Infantryman" tests. We have completed all of the physical work. Sometime this week, however, we'll be out for forty-eight hours running a platoon problem. This is to test our ability as a fighting team.

On April 10 we're going out for a bivouac up in Holly Springs. Keep the letters coming.

Your loving son,
Morris

* * * * *

Camp McCain, Mississippi
Sunday March 26, 1944

Miss Ogie Joyce
1905 Calhoun St.
New Orleans, Louisiana

Dear Ogie,

The Infantry, the Infantry with dirt behind their ears,
The Infantry, the Infantry, they drink up all the beers.
But the Artillery, the Cavalry, and a Corps of Engineers
Couldn't lick the Infantry in a hundred thousand years.
From the Army's Pocket Book of Songs

The past week was a rough one. We had every opportunity of getting dirt behind our ears in the past few days of work. I should add "nights" too, because we work in the night as in the day. It's been rainy out and the roads are knee-deep slush, as are the open fields on which we work. But we don't care anymore. We've learned to laugh at things like that. And it is funny when you're crawling along with tracers going over your head and nitrostarch going off and throwing up huge pieces of slush and geysers of water up into the air. It's even funnier when you pull your face out of the mud to look across at another buddy crawling alongside of you, sweating and swearing. You grin and ask how he's making out. He comes out with a loud "Oh baby!" accompanied by a shake of his head. Then some of the nitro goes off and he looks up to see how high the debris will go. Just as he looks, some of the flying mud splatters in his face and he lets loose with some profanity. You laugh, but even as you do, the shower of mud and water begins to fall around you and on you, and you stick your face back in the mud and keep crawling. It's all in a day's work. You really earn your board and keep around here. That's a fact.

But as ever there's a lot of play. We have plenty of football and baseball games. We're all brothers. Our basketball team won the championship of the division the other night in a very thrilling game between my company (L) and Company A of the 302 Regt. This made our Captain pretty happy, I guess. At the same time we were declared as being the best co. in the regiment.

Mother tells me you gave her a $25 war bond for me. I thank you very much. You're really too kind.

Well, Ogie, I haven't anything else to say, so I say good-bye.

Your loving nephew,
Morris

* * * * *

Camp McCain, Mississippi
Tuesday, March 28, 1944

Dear Aunt Winnie,

There isn't much to write about these days except the weather. I have never seen such terrible weather in all my life. Ordinarily I wouldn't mind the rain. But rain here means mud, and the mud is awful. It has been raining a steady downpour since Sunday night. The drill fields and recreation grounds are underwater, and the giant drainage ditches are filled to their capacities. Everywhere is water, water, water. Then too there is plenty of lightning and thunder going on. The lights around have gone off about four or five times a day during these electrical barrages. I don't have any clean clothes except the ones I have coming home from the laundry. It was during the height of the rain last week that we had to crawl through the deep mud while machine-gun bullets popped overhead and land mines went off around us. This was the fourth time I've had people shooting above me. The day before infiltration I had sat in a foxhole for eight hours while bullets skimmed all around, digging up the mud and showering me with dirt. Ah me, what a life.

I guess there are plenty of changes about town. Things like the different lakefront would make a visit home interesting. Of course, the biggest change will be in people's faces. I wonder if I'll remember everybody. I wonder what my younger brothers will look like and how tall Winnsey and Claude are, and if everybody looks and is healthy. I have written Mother for some pictures. I would like to have some of all the relatives, but Mother says films are hard to get. So if you do have any of the Kellys, old ones even, I would appreciate a print more than anything else. I still have all the Christmas presents you sent. I never got a chance to use them, so if you feel like sending anything I think I could use the money best. The day after Easter we move out for some maneuvers, so I couldn't really appreciate any cakes or something like that.

Well, it's getting near Taps and I must say good-bye. Give my regards to Uncle Claude and to Winnie & Claude.

Your loving nephew,
Morris

* * * * *

Camp McCain, Mississippi
Wednesday morn., March 29, 1944

Dear Mom and Dad,

Although I had told you that Sunday had been a beautiful day, it didn't necessarily follow that this was the beginning of a beautiful, sunshiny week. Far from it. I got up this morning to the third straight day of continuous rain. Everything except the blacktop roads are underwater. The drill fields and recreation grounds form the bottom of a gigantic pool. The large ditches and draws are swollen almost to rivers, and it is still raining. And we are still working.

And with the falling rain has come cold weather. We don't usually mind the rain, but when you have to go, wringing wet and numb with cold, then you begin to complain. But funny to say, I don't even have a cold or any aches or pains. I guess the good food here really builds up our resistance to the cold diseases.

This morning we had pancakes about ten inches in diameter, with hot syrup and bacon. Then we had hot coffee, milk, cornflakes, and apples. For our other meals during the day we have meat dishes, not much potatoes, and lots of vegetables. Always we have pie or cake or ice cream for dessert.

Well, that's all for now. We're ready to fall out.

Your loving son,
Morris

Morris wrote the following letter to his mother on her birthday. He had forgotten that April 2 was her "special day," but upon realizing it, he composed a beautiful poem for her and included it in his letter.

Camp McCain, Mississippi
Sunday, April 2, 1944

Dear Mother and Dad,

This past week has been pretty rough. We have done a lot of work and most of it has been in the rain and mud. And to-day, Palm Sunday, it is still raining.

The work is still very interesting. The night problems are very good. Lately we've had jobs of a type using explosives. This makes for a lot of noise. A few nights ago we had a job of blowing up a house on top of a hill. It took us four hours to get our squad through the woods without making any noise. At about midnight we arrived at the road that led past the hill. Here we had to lay low until the moon went down. So I lay down in a dark spot and went to sleep until about two, when we prepared to move out. Evidently we had passed the line of resistance because there was nobody there. Well, we planted the explosives under the foundation and ran like the wind. In thirty-five seconds it blew, and we immediately organized and moved out. These sorts of problems in which you actually do something are lots more fun.

The other day there was a very good problem out in the hills. I was part of the enemy detail and I had all kinds of stuff to blow off. I used smoke grenades and land mines and I fired about sixty rounds of blanks before I was ruled out of action by the umpire.

I have some souvenirs that I will send home one of these days. They include a piece of shrapnel from a mortar shell, the safety pin and spring handle from a grenade, and some blanks.

Mother, I am truly sorry that I didn't know about your birthday, or else I would have done something about it. However, now I can only wish you many, many more, and also that I might be home for the next one.

I miss the gentle touch and loving smile,
I miss the pleasant voice so sweet and soft
That at my efforts never, never scoffed
But always urged the very best within me;

The familiar form that in my dreams I see;
The words of her who makes it all worthwhile;
The loving care and ever-fond caress
Of her that beats so strong within my breast
With face so fair, so cool and calm,
The heart of hearts beating ever warm,
The sweetest girl in all the world—
My only girl—my sweet, my lovely mother.

To my mother—done today, her birthday.

Your loving son,
Morris

* * * * *

Camp McCain, Mississippi
Monday, April 3, 1944

Dear Mom and Dad,

Today I started mine school. It will last about a week. In this time we will learn all about our land mines. These are of two types: anti-personnel and anti-mechanized. Today we spent our time playing with booby traps. It was very interesting. In the morning we had two movies on booby traps. Then we marched out into the field for some practical work. Out there we set traps and disguised them. Instead of using TNT, though, we used big cannon crackers. Then we changed over with each other and disarmed the traps by finding them and putting safety pins in the pin holes. It sounds simple, but it's far from it. These devices are very ingenious and they are as tricky as they come. However, it's good to know about these kinds of traps because the Germans use them a lot.

Later on we shall study the different types of enemy mines. We shall also use our mine detector, which picks out metal objects under the ground.

Well, it's getting time to fall out for a problem, so I'll say

Good night,
Morris

Camp McCain, Mississippi
Tuesday, April 4, 1944

Dear Mom and Dad,

I am sorry that I haven't written more often in the past few days, but I haven't had any time to spare. It's very hard to get in eight hours of sleep around here. Lately we've been working day and night. We've fired combat ranges, and yesterday I fired the automatic rifle for my service record. I fired from 7 in the morning until about 6:30 in the evening, continuously, and I estimate that I must have fired close to 700 rounds of ammunition. The rifle has a fast cyclic rate of 550 shots a minute, but this is hardly ever used except for 25 seconds of sustained fire. Usually you fire single shots (this is on the range), or bursts of two or three.

The weather was beautiful yesterday, but today we have overcast skies, and I think it will rain. We had a 25-mile march last night, and this morning some of us, incl. me, are going to walk out to the range to fire the carbine familiarization course. So you can see that I don't have any time to waste and every extra minute is spent sleeping.

I didn't get to go to Mass on Holy Thursday and receive Holy Communion, but I read the Mass this morning from my missal. I think I'll carry my missal with me out into the field in case we have any time off.

To-night we have a night problem which will include our course at mine school. This has been a terrible week. I hope the next one is easier.

On Monday morning we're moving out to Holly Springs for two weeks' bivouac. I don't know how things will be out there. I don't know if I'll get a chance to write or not. I assure you that I will every chance I'll get.

If you have any more pictures, don't send them until I get back, because out there they'll just get ruined.

Tell everybody hello and Happy Easter. I hope that you and the children are well and I remain

Your loving son,
Morris Jr.

* * * * *

Camp McCain, Mississippi
Easter Sunday
April 9, 1944

Dear Folks,

I would like to thank all of you for your letters and Easter greetings. I would like to have Mother thank Aunt Winnie for the money she sent, and tell Aunt Ogie I'll write again in a couple of weeks. I'll try to write in any off time I might get while on these maneuvers. However, we'll be moving quite a bit, as these problems will last for six days at a time. We won't have any cooked meals for the first week or so. We'll eat C and K rations.

This past week was pretty rough. However I added two more bars to my expert medal. I fired expert in the BAR—the Browning Automatic Rifle—and in the carbine. I fired 95 out of a hundred in this. I guess I fired about 800 rounds of ammunition in the past week with the combat range and the other ranges on the schedule.

When I come back from these maneuvers, I'll have to send home all clothes other than those issued me. I wish you would keep them someplace handy in case I write for them.

I certainly appreciate your letters. I received William's and Kerry's. The latter I got in this afternoon's mail. With it were some pictures of the house. It was really nice to get. I have offered my Mass and Communion for all of you and for all the relatives. I know that you will remember me in all your prayers. It is my fervent wish that all the blessings of the glorious Easter season will descend upon your heads and that soon the peace of the Risen Christ will descend upon the whole of mankind. *Resurrexit tertia die secundum scripturas.*

Remember me to Fr. Castel and to the Murphys (rf. Kerry).

Your loving son,
Morris

* * * * *

Morris wrote the following journal entries during the Holly Springs bivouac (April 10 through April 19, 1944). He wrote them in a notebook, which was discovered later among his personal effects. These entries provide a glimpse into Morris's experiences during the two weeks he spent at Holly Springs.

Journal Entries April 10–19, 1944

Monday, April 10

Left camp at about 1200. Arrived at Holly Springs 1900. We rode in an open truck apart from the long convoy numbering hundreds of trucks.

Morris Redmann Reported Killed In Action In Germany

By MADELINE MILLER

Pfc. Morris B. Redmann Jr., 1943 Arts and Sciences graduate, has been reported killed in action in Germany. With the 94th division of the 3rd army, he had previously been wounded in France.

Redmann was at one time chairman of the activity heads committee, president of Le Cercle Francais, the French club, president of Thespians, day school dramatic club, and an artist on the Wolf. He was a member of Beggars, social fraternity, Pegasus, poetry society, and the Edward Douglass White Debating society.

In 1941-42, he received a student council citation for extracurricular activities. He won the first place trophy in an oratorical contest sponsored by the College Sodality union. The A. J. Bonomo award for the best individual acting was given him in 1943 for his leading role in "King Lear."

Having received his A. B. degree in 1943 at the age of 18, Redmann entered the Law school, and was drafted shortly after. In all his letters from overseas, he was always inquiring about Loyola activities and asking to be remembered to his former teachers, all of whom he genuinely admired.

* * *

MORRIS REDMANN

Loyola *Maroon*—University Newspaper

The ten children, July 1941. Ronald, David, Kerry, Esther, Ralph, Morris Jr., Robert, Jerome, William, and Richard.

Mother and Morris, Jr.

PFC Edward Thomas Moore, Jr. was seriously wounded in action in Germany on January 26, 1945.

PFC Morris B. Redmann, Jr., and PFC Vincent A. DeMase of Albany, NY. At barracks in Camp McCain, MS, May 1944.

Morris B. Redmann, Jr., at the ole swimming hole at Camp McCain, Missouri, 1944.

Daddy and Morris, Jr.

Men and vehicles coming ashore from landing craft.

Men walking up to the beach with their gear.

Sherman Tank emerging from LCT on beach.

Ever on the "ready" in Hedgerow Country in France.

Field Marshal Rommel (left) inspecting coastal defenses.

Village of Cerisy-la-Salle, Normandy. The little girl—one of the few survivors—is being comforted by two GI's.

American tanks and infantry advance through St. Fromand, Normandy.

Men of the 94th Inf. Div. attending Mass. Christmas, 1944.

Christmas 1944—Men of the 94th Infantry Division dry out in a "manger."

A welcome pause from the fighting and the dying.

American Mortar Group near St. Vith, January 1945.

American soldiers take cover in a ditch to avoid German shelling during the Battle of the Bulge.

On lookout for any German movement near Ardennes Forest, January 1945.

Bombed-out city of Metz, France, 1944.

Battle of the Bulge. German infantry advancing past destroyed American military vehicles.

Captured German officers wait along the Autobahn near Giessen, Germany, watching vehicles of the U.S. 6th Armored Division moving up to the front March 1945.

An American soldier waits out a German artillery barrage—the coldest January in fifty years.

Chow time in the Hurtgen Forest, January 1945.

German spirits were high on this second day of the Ardennes Forest offensive—as indicated in this captured German photograph. Soon the Tide of Battle would change this fleeting face of temporary glory.

Soldiers scope out the ruins of a bombed church.

Oberleuken . . . a shattered, desolate ruin where the odor of death hung heavy in the air.

A captured panzerfaust—equivalent to an American bazooka.

Near Grundstadt, ME-262s (German jet-propelled planes) strafe and bomb elements of the 12th Armored Division in the zone of the 94th, setting fire to several ammunition vehicles.

Medics at work in a combat area.

American GIs in a foxhole, pointing toward the enemy. One GI is taking a much needed break for K-rations.

Three high ranking officers of the 94th Infantry Division confer near Nennig, Germany. From left to right: Brig. Gen. Henry B. Cheadle, Maj. Gen. Harry J. Maloney, division commander, and Col. Roy N. Hagerty. (National Archives)

German prisoners marching west to their POW camp after Americans crossed the Rhine River, fighting their way into Germany, March 1945.

Ancient city of Aachen almost totally destroyed.

Pointe du Hoc, Normandy, September 2000.

Kerry Redmann and brother Ralph at Morris' grave, September 20, 2000, accompanied by Ronald J. Drez.

View of the Luxembourg American Military Cemetery and Memorial.

The grave of Morris B. Redmann, Jr. today.

We passed through many little country towns and cities, the biggest of which was Oxford, the University City. On the way over I saw for the first time certain phases of social life in the country. We passed a carnival which was getting ready for an early show. A little further on we rode past a stock farm where an auction was going on.

The towns we passed through presented a pleasant picture to the eye accustomed to seeing only the dull, drab buildings of an Army reservation. It was good to see so many civilians again carrying on in the old "business as usual" style. But what I enjoyed most was waving to almost every kid we passed on the streets.

We stopped once for a break and enjoyed beer and sandwiches. Here too I ate one of the candy bars that I had brought with me. (I was carrying 31 of them.) After a few minutes we left the little country store and were on our way again.

Up and down. Up and down. Over the hills of northern Mississippi we rode, until we were only some 40 miles below the big city of Memphis.

It is now 7:30 P.M. and only a few minutes of daylight remain. I have not yet joined my company and am waiting to eat chow with the Service Co. After chow we'll move down the hill and catch a truck that will take us out to our battalion area. By that time it'll be dark, and we'll have to pitch a tent in the dark.

Huge black clouds are everywhere, giving promise of rain.

Thus ends the day. But I found out later that the day didn't end until one got to sleep. I write this paragraph at about 7:30 on Tuesday morning. It had taken me seven hours to get to my company, and it wasn't until three o'clock of the eleventh of April that I finally lay down on top of some C rations and called it a day.

Tuesday, April 11

Got up at 0605 in time for breakfast, which was a very good meal. At 0745 we started out with an orientation lecture and then moved out to our areas. Remained as a flank security man until problem started at 9:30. I sat on the edge of a brook that ran thru a swamp, trying to observe what was going on over on the enemy side. There was no action over there, and we waded the brook to take up positions in the hills.

However, as soon as we had gotten up the opposite bank, a machine gun situated at the base of the hills opened fire. We were forced to get back down into the creek itself and take cover.

Finally, by firing and maneuvering, we took our objective.

In the afternoon we had another problem that took us out into the countryside. While on this problem we passed thru a farm, and a couple of the sergeants bought a couple of chickens. After our meal of Army beans tonight, we are presently preparing for a chicken dinner à la Sgts. Dugan and Claybaugh.

The sun has set and numerous campfires have begun to dot the bivouac area, silhouetting the campers and casting a red glow upon the tall pines and birches. C'est tout pour la jour.

Wednesday, April 12

Awoke to a cool gray morning that seemed to hint of an early rain. Had C rations for breakfast and for every meal throughout the day. Worked a little in the morning and had the afternoon off to clean our rifles and equipment, in preparation for the six-day problem starting on Thursday.

Thursday, April 13

Walked and fought from 7 'til 8. Slept in the woods at night. During this long day our platoon had about twelve engagements with the enemy. We had breakfast at 5:40. At 6:10 we were in the trucks and off for the line of departure. Arrived at line of departure at 0710. Here we were issued ammunition in preparation for the problem ahead.

We ate lunch out of cans down in one of the numerous valleys that divide the countryside. Opposition, from lunchtime on, was mostly snipers. Ate cold beans for supper, but had hot chocolate to drink. At this time too we received our rations for the next day—six cans of food and one quart of water. Had a little more opposition after supper further up the road. Then bivouacked for the night. From one of the natives we procured a pint of "white lightning" and then hit the hay.

Friday, April 14

Got up at 0620, rolled up our equipment, and started out again. Ate breakfast from C rations and washed in creek around 0800. Started out again cross-country at about 0900. It's really rough.

Marched until about 1200. Ate lunch in a little clearing on the edge of a swamp. After lunch entered the swamp and walked through it until about four o'clock, when we reached a small river. It was about 30 yds. wide at the most, and had a pretty good current. We shed our clothes and swam across. Our equipment was floated over on rafts made of branches and shelter-halves or tents. All men across at 1715. Went two miles more and stopped for the day. Pitched tents and got ready for a bad night. The sky was gray and some rain had fallen. Promise of more. At 2030 we moved out under cover of darkness.

Saturday, April 15

Got up at about seven. Cautiously moved out, and after a few hundred yards left the road and entered the woods seeking some free-flowing stream at which we could get water. Got the water, and the Lieutenant poured some purifying element into it. We then set out again over hills and through entangled woods and vines, and then through some more swamp. After going through the swamp awhile, we crossed several small streams that had fallen trees for bridges. At noon we reached our objective for the day and here set up a defensive position to await an enemy attack. While waiting in the dense underbrush, a large water moccasin passed within a few feet of my position. I got up to shoot it with a blank from my gun, but did not for fear the enemy detail would learn of our position. Everyone left their position to see the snake that was by this time surrounded by men armed with clubs, guns, and canteens. A well-placed shot with an empty canteen crushed the head and killed the snake. After getting a good look at it, we went back to our positions and awaited the enemy's attack. Attack never came. Just before dark we received our rations for the next day and some mail. I got two letters, one from Mom and one from Aunt Ogie. We moved to our bivouac area and settled down for the night. It began to thunder and the Lieutenants sent out scouts to find some suitable shelter. Moved out at 2000 and spent the night in an abandoned farmhouse.

Sunday, April 16

Got up at about 0630. Set off cross-country for our next objective. We were to proceed on an azimuth of 260° in a westerly direction. We went cross-country for about two and a half miles until we hit the railroad. When we hit the tracks we blew up a trestle, and then proceeded up the tracks until we were hit by the enemy. After disposing of them we took to a road and moved to Point K, where we bivouacked for the night. Cold.

Monday, April 17

Got up early, around 0545, rolled our packs, and after having camouflaged the rolls, set out with only combat packs, rifles, belts, and steel helmets. This was some day. We started out looking for water very early in the morning. We marched all over the country looking for a stream, a well, or a spring. Finally, an old Negro took us up to the top of a hill where there was a well, and here most of the platoon got water. However, when it came my squad's turn to get water, the water became muddy and we couldn't use it. We were told that it would clear in a few minutes and I was appointed to remain there and fill the remaining canteens. While waiting, I bought two dog biscuits and three jars of jelly and jam from a Negro farmer. They were really good, too. Well, I waited for about 45 minutes and the water never did clear, so I went back to where the platoon was eating breakfast. After breakfast we set out again cross-country. After an hour or so, and still no water, we hit the big highway 78. We marched on it and the sun was beating down on us. Everybody was thirsty. Then a strange thing happened. As we marched past a cut along the route, a new spring came spouting up along the side of the road. Here we watered and washed. Then we marched on. Covered maybe 20 miles in the day and about 15 miles at night. Feet were killing me. Pitched shelter, not tent, for the night, and of course it rained like hell and the blankets got wet and we got wet and everything else got wet.

Tuesday, April 18

Problem over. Got up at 0530 and moved to another point where truck picked us up around 0900. Got back to area at 1100. Cleaned up. Cleaned rifle, and at 11:30 ate breakfast. Slept. Had supper at 1730 and went immediately to bed.

Wednesday, April 19

Got up at about 0700. Ate. Moved out at 0845. Marched about 7 miles to a stream. Practiced different methods of crossing a stream—over a fallen tree, on a raft, and hand over hand on a rope. Marched back about an hour after lunch.

Got into Bn. A about 1630. Ate chow at 1730. Am now getting ready to go to bed.

* * * * *

Morris's first "pass" since arriving at Camp McCain, Mississippi, March 9, 1944, from Fort Benning, Georgia, came on the weekend of April 22 and 23, 1944. He decided to come home to New Orleans even though it was a short weekend. He couldn't leave camp until after formation and roll call on the 22nd, which meant he had to get into Grenada, Mississippi, late Saturday afternoon and then wait for the train to New Orleans that departed Grenada at 1:55 AM *Sunday, arriving in New Orleans at 9:35* AM. *Thus, he only had Sunday at home before having to return to Camp McCain.*

His mother was very surprised, as his pass came through at the last minute. She called the family and some of his friends and arranged an impromptu party for him that Sunday afternoon—one that I'm sure he never forgot. His memory of it is captured in his following letter, dated April 25, 1944.

Tuesday, April 25, 1944

Dear Mom and Dad,

The pleasant memories of a few hours at home on a big Sunday remain as one of the best pictures ever imprinted on my mind. I was certainly glad to see home once more, to see its plaster walls and oaken ceilings that hold forever within their substance the echo of familiar voices, the reflection of the bright lights and happy faces of many joyous Christmastides, the record of a grand family life.

I shall remember forever the warm welcome given to the son by the surprised mother. I promise I shall be home again at the first opportunity. Perhaps I shall come in Sunday. If I do, I shall arrive at 9:35 A.M. at the Carrollton Station. This is a new schedule. I catch the train at Grenada at 1:55 A.M. and arrive in N.O. at 9:35 at Carrollton. It is better to waste two hours by coming in at a later hour, but is worth it because I could get some sleep on the way down.

I appreciated the party in the afternoon and I would like you to thank everybody for coming up, and also for the money that everyone gave me. It was really swell.

Well, that's about all. There's a great day coming.

Your loving son,
Morris

* * * * *

United States Army
Camp McCain, Mississippi
Dimanche, le 30 avril 1944

Ma soeur Esther,

J'écris cette lettre pour découvrir ce que vous savez de l'histoire française. J'ai lu le livre *Une Semaine à Paris* et je l'ai trouvé très intéressant. Alors, je poserai des questions sur l'histoire et des monuments de la belle France.

Il faut que vous sachiez quelque chose de la grande ville de Paris, la capitale de France, pour apprécier la langue elle-même.

Voici les questions:

Est-ce que Paris est la plus grande ville du monde?

Qu'est-ce que c'est la population de Paris?

Quand était commencée la tour Eiffel?

Vous savez que de la tour on peut voir très distinctement tous les grands bâtiments et les monuments de la ville. On peut voir l'Arc de Triomphe de l'Etoile, l'église Russe, l'église St. Augustin, la gare St. Lazare, la gare du Nord, les Buttes-Chaumont. Et par télescope on peut voir le Louvre, l'église Notre Dame, le Panthéon; et plus près de nous, l'hôtel des Invalides où se trouve le tombeau de Napoléon.

Quel est l'usage du grand bâtiment, le Trocadero?

Pourquoi était-il changé le nom d'avenue d'Eylan à l'avenue Victor Hugo?

Qui était le gardien de l'Arc de Triomphe, qui s'est distingué pendant la guerre de 1870 et était décoré de la croix de la Légion d'Honneur?

Alors, voilà les questions que je vous pose.

J'espère venir chez nous bientôt, peut-être le 10 mai.

Eh bien, répondez bientôt, s'il vous plaît.

Affectueusement,
Morris

Camp McCain, Mississippi
Sunday, April 30, 1944

Dear Mom and Dad,

I would have much rather spent this Sunday at home with you, but at the eleventh hour I turned from the trip, feeling sick and tired from the hard work of the week-end. On Friday we had bayonet combat with gas masks on, and on Friday night they sprung a twenty-five-mile march on us. I got to bed from this at twenty to four on Sat. morning, and at five-thirty of the same, was gotten up to run the close combat course. Well, I griped and griped and griped, and I said I wasn't going to go (I had run it once before), but I went, only because I didn't want anything to hold me back on the week-end.

So it was, with only one hour and about fifty minutes of sleep that I started out for the week-end. I packed my little bag and with my friend, John Randall, went into Grenada. We got into town at about six-thirty and went to the USO and checked our bags. From here we went over to church, and thence to the train station to check on the schedule. While there, the Panama pulled in on its way to Chicago. The train to N.O., we found, wasn't until 1:55. I thought it would be a good idea to get a room at the hotel and go to sleep until about one o'clock, but in every hotel we received the same answer: "No rooms left."

Well, I tried my best to sleep in one of the USOs but soon gave up. Finally, at eleven o'clock I called it quits and with a couple of other fellows went back to the barracks.

I slept until nine-fifteen this morning, got up and dressed and hurried over to the nine-thirty Mass. I received Holy Communion and remembered everybody in my prayers.

I hope that Dad isn't going to Philadelphia in the near future. I have worked into position for a furlough sometime in May, perhaps the tenth. I certainly hope so. I could use a rest.

This Sunday, as has been every Sunday, is rainy. I hope that you're having good weather in New Orleans, and I pray that if and when I get there it'll be beautiful spring weather.

Well, give my regards to all. I hope to see you soon and I remain

Your loving son,
Morris

Camp McCain, Mississippi
Tuesday, May 2, 1944

Dear Mom and Dad,

I have the rest of the day off due to the fact that we had a battalion problem that started Monday morning and lasted until six-forty-five this morning.

The chaplain is away at present and will not be back until Wednesday evening. I shall try to see him then. Of course, he can merely make suggestions and has nothing whatsoever to do with the administration. However, I shall speak with him, get his advice, and as much information upon future possibilities as I can.

You must understand that time is short; that this is a hot outfit; that application for transfer is turned down on divisional order. All the records are gone over daily so that everything is ready in case of call. In the process of P.O.M. (Preparation for Overseas Movement), all records of training, equipment, clothing, and physical condition must be carefully checked. Thus, only the fittest men are sent overseas. The men unfit for combat duty are transferred sooner or later into some 4-F outfit to sit out the rest of the war.

From what I have read in memorandums sent down from divisional hdqtrs. from time to time, the only OCS that I could go to from this outfit would be the Infantry School at Benning. This is for Infantry OCS—the toughest of all. But you have to be combat material these days to get the appointment, because the Army is interested only in combat officers for the Infantry.

No amount of courtesy or friendliness can get you any place in a line outfit. They don't care who your people are or what they are. One of my friends here, a very fine fellow, is no more than I am, even though his father is a Brigadier General. His name is Werrell.

At the beginning of the war commissions and ratings were cheap; they were given away to anyone who made application for them. But the present Army is tough. It's three years older now and has in this time made many officers, turning them out like Ford turns out trucks. But officers don't wear out as fast as trucks. Thus, there has been a drop in their production. Today, in order to get into OCS, you have to hold the rank of at least a Corporal. Thus, possibilities of my ever becoming an officer are nil. I am not too interested anyway, but will find out all I can about what kind of work I could get into and in general, just what the future offers.

I am going over to regiment tonight with my friend Roth and will find out as much as possible what my status is.

Well, I am writing this some hours later. The longed-for day has arrived. We got our notice at four o'clock this evening. I don't know how much longer I can write to you. One thing is possible—that's the furlough. I may still get home on the tenth. Well, I'll say good-bye.

Lots of love—give my regards to all. Pray for me.

Your loving son,
Morris

P.S. Keep last confidential.

* * * * *

Camp McCain, Mississippi
Thursday, May 4, 1944

Dear Ogie,

I hope that you have not taken offense at my not writing but I, as has everybody else around here, have been very busy for some time now. From now on I don't know if I can write at all. You see, the "magic word" has come down from Washington. Everybody took their final physicals last night. It may be a matter of weeks or even months. The final process is a long one. It involves the requisition of millions of dollars of new equipment, and this includes all new clothes and guns. It involves the replacement of those men unfit for combat service. So it will be, perhaps, some time before anything does happen. But we are on our way.

Thanks a lot for the ties. They will come in handy. They go fine with my sun-tans. By the way, I think I'll get home on furlough this month. I surely hope so.

Well, Ogie, tell everybody hello for me—Aunt Lala, Uncle Paul, Aunt Eleanor; and remember me to Paul Jr. in your next letter. Will he be home at any time within the next two weeks? If so, I'll get a chance to see him, I believe.

That's all the news I have. Don't know when I can write again. Time is scarce.

Your loving nephew,
Morris

Camp McCain, Mississippi
Friday, May 5, 1944

Dear Mom and Dad,

I still expect to be home sometime this month, either around the tenth or the seventeenth. There are two trains daily, one at 1:55 A.M. that arrives in N.O. at 9:35, and the other at 12:30 P.M. that arrives in N.O. around eight o'clock at night. There is only one bus that I know of, and that leaves here at 4:40 P.M. and doesn't get into the Canal Street station until 7:10 A.M. the next day.

Another schedule I have checked is plane service to N.O. from Jackson. There are planes leaving Jackson for New Orleans at 5:58 P.M. and at 11:08 P.M. and arriving at 7:05 P.M. and 12:15 A.M. respectively. This is pretty fast considering the fact that the same distance by bus takes eight hours.

The reason I investigated the various schedules is due to the fact that the furlough papers don't come down until around three o'clock of the first day of the furlough. (That's 3:00 P.M.) I don't know what the reason could possibly be, but it necessitates my waiting until the next day for a train or my taking a slow bus at 4:40 in the afternoon. The 4:40 bus gets into Jackson at 7:53 P.M. This would enable me to catch the 11:08 plane for N.O. and save me about nine hours at the most. But before I do anything I'm going to find out if I can't get those papers early enough to get the 12:30 train. If I can't, I'm going to phone for reservations on the "Cotton King" at 11:08 P.M.

Well, enough about schedules. A couple of nights ago we took overseas physicals and got some more shots. I told you that we had gotten our notice here. However, nothing will happen for a good while, as it takes a lot of time to re-equip a whole division with all new guns, trucks, and equipment.

So don't worry. They'll probably transfer me out anyway. Well, I hope to see all of you soon.

Your loving son,
Morris

* * * * *

The following letter of May 7, 1944, was in reply to his mother's letter of May 4, 1944, wherein she mentioned if he did get the 10-day furlough (his first), his brothers William and Kerry would move to other quarters in the house so he could have the large bedroom to himself and sleep as late as he liked. The following is an excerpt from his mother's letter:

"We do not nor have we ever prayed for promotions or honors for you. Our first concern is your goodness; and the second, your safety. There is no happiness in this world, or hope for it in the next, without goodness. So that's why we put it first in our prayers and your safety second. At times like this we must put all our trust in God, and expect from Him only in the same measure as we have given. Whenever any of you children were sick, I used to remind God that I had taken all He had ever sent and gladly. But still I'd have to add, 'Thy will be done.' And so I do now."

* * * * *

Camp McCain, Mississippi
Sunday, May 7, 1944

Dear Mom and Dad,

As I told you this morning, I don't know when I'm coming home. Up to the present, and it's about 1615 right now, no furlough list has been published. I do not expect to be on it because it's just not my luck. However, I should be on the one for the seventeenth, as this will be the last of the furloughs. All furloughs and passes are cancelled for after June 1.

When I do come home, I don't want you to go to the trouble of moving Kerry and William to "other quarters." I don't think that I'll be sleeping too late in the morning because I think that is now impossible. Besides, I probably wouldn't be able to become accustomed to sleeping in such a soft bed in such a short time. I'll probably be up cooking breakfast for you all every morning. I guess I'd like to be doing that all right!

Some night while I'm home I would like to have one of those big family affairs. I used to enjoy those a lot, with the ice-cold beer and the rye and cheese sandwiches and the ham, etc.

Thanks for the offer, but I don't need any more money. I got paid Saturday, and with some other money I have more than sixty dollars.

I thank all of you for your prayers and I remain, in hopes of seeing you soon,

Your loving son,
Morris

TELEGRAM

CAMP MCCAIN, MISSISSIPPI
1944 MAY 10 PM 958

MR. AND MRS. M. B. REDMANN
7017 BROAD PLACE NRLNS

DEAR MOM & DAD ARRIVE MUNICIPAL AIRPORT 12:15 AM THURSDAY LOVE MORRIS

* * * * *

The following letter was written after Morris's first ten-day furlough since he entered the Army. He had taken a 4:40 PM *bus from Grenada that got into Jackson at 7:53* PM. *He flew home from Jackson, Mississippi, on the 11:08* PM *flight Wednesday evening, May 10, 1944, and arrived in New Orleans at Municipal Airport at 15 minutes after midnight.*

Camp McCain, Mississippi
May 20, 1944

Dear Mom and Dad,

Well, here I am back soldiering again. I'm a fire orderly in the officers' latrine.

I enjoyed a wonderful trip up here on the Panama. I enjoyed quite a few hours of it with a gentleman from New Orleans who is the father of one of the Lieutenants of Co. M of my battalion. His name is Mr. Richard Jones, either the president or general manager of the Jackson Brewing Co. I asked him about Mr. Ludwig Eisemann, knowing darn well that he must have known him. He spoke very highly of Ludwig, calling him by his first name. We recalled other people, many of whose names were familiar to us both. He told me that Mr. Ralph Schwarz was the one that had engineered the contract between Jax and the Grain & Feed Co. He had said that he was sorry to have heard of the death of Mr. Schwarz, adding that Daddy had lost a grand partner at Schwarz's demise. I added also—one of his (Daddy's) best friends. Mr. Jones met me in the diner. Our conversation started when he noticed the 94th Division patch on my shoulder. He asked me if I knew Lt. Jones from N.O. I replied that I had heard of him and volunteered his regiment, battalion, but was wrong on his co. Well, he began to talk about his son Dick. When I went to pay my bill, which was very close to $2.00, he insisted that he pay it, and then invited me to visit with him in his compartment. I replied that it would be a pleasure. I excused myself and went to wash up and returned to his compartment in a few minutes.

We then had a chat that lasted about two hours and fifteen minutes. I finally brought it to an end when I said that it was necessary that I go to get my stuff together in order to get off the train. We shook hands. I asked that he tell Mr. Eisemann "hello" for me when he returned to N.O. He said that he would be only too glad to do it, and extended to me an invitation to visit him the next time I was home in N.O. I thanked him again for his generosity and bowed out of the compartment. This had indeed been a very pleasant trip.

Tomorrow, Sunday, I won't call until late in the evening because we (the whole company), are going over to Calhoun City for a beer, chicken-fry, and swimming party. It ought to be a good time. It had been promised us for a long time.

I now have a foot locker—thank goodness. The Swede and Rubenstein were shipped out to Washington State while I was gone. No indication, however, of what's going on.

Well, I've got to get over homesickness again, but I guess it gets easier every time. I got Daddy's letter. It was mailed on the eighth, but wasn't rec'd here until the eleventh. Please thank Miss Winnie for that swell meal again, and Mr. Kelly for the present at the station.That's all for now.

With lots of love,
Morris

P.S. I left George's address home. Please send it to me; it was on the dresser.

Camp McCain, Mississippi
Sunday, May 21, 1944

Dear Aunt Winnie,

I am writing to thank you once again for the swell dinner you had for Mother, Dad, and me. I will remember your kindness towards me always, no matter where I go.

Now I'm back at soldiering again, and although I hated to leave home, I am, in a strange way, content with being back here. After all, this is my job for a period of time, which no one knows the length. However, since I've had a furlough I have a peace of mind and an attitude that would permit me to be sent anywhere without a drop in morale. Having had the pleasure of being home, I am now prepared for the work that lies ahead.

Today everybody is going up to Calhoun City for a big company party. Transportation will be furnished by regimental headquarters. The beer and the food, which is being prepared for us by an American Legion Women's Auxiliary, will be paid for out of the Company Fund. This fund is a deposit of credit in the McCain Bank built up by the monies made from the sale of Coca-Colas in the co.'s day room, from the small fees charged per game of pool, and from a percentage of the profits from the Post Exchange. We ought to have a swell time. I know I will. I can't remember a party when I didn't have a good time. We're supposed to go swimming. Although I don't have a suit, I'll probably go in. Sgt. Dugan has offered me a suit for my own use. He's got two.

By the way—ask Uncle Claude if he, by any chance, knows Mr. Dick Jones of the Jackson Brewing Company. He lives out in Metairie. I met the gentleman on the train. He is the father of one of the Lieutenants in my battalion.

Well, I hope you are all well. Give my love to all.

Your loving nephew,
Morris

* * * * *

Camp McCain, Mississippi
Monday, May 22, 1944

Dear Mom and Dad,

Today I had the unique experience of being actually buried alive. We got up at six o'clock this morning to a very gray day. We ate hurriedly and were hustled out to the regimental drill area. Here we were issued engineering tools (big shovel and picks), and told to dig foxholes. This was the start of a strenuous six weeks of training with tanks. The first lesson was to show us that we need not fear a tank should it run over us in the foxhole. Well, to make assurance doubly sure, I dug a hole that was more than six feet deep. And when the tank got ready to start its run, I crouched as low as I could in such a position as to be able to push my way up through any loose dirt that may have been shoved in by the big tank. The tank was the famed General Sherman and weighed about thirty-four tons. It is a medium tank.

Just before I had gotten into the hole it had begun to rain. But now there was a steady downpour which was making everybody's job harder. As I dropped into the hole, the tank driver gunned his engine, and the big Mark IV moved ahead. I hastily took up this squatting position, at the same time saying an Act of Contrition and a Hail Mary. Then I waited. The sound of the big motors grew nearer, the earth shook a little, and then there was darkness. The tank passed on and left me on the bottom with about two hundred pounds of dirt piled on top of me. My helmet had been knocked over my face and thus some air was trapped, enabling me to breathe fairly easily. However, I was helpless. I tried once to push my way through the mud but found it in vain. I could hear the excited voices of the officers and men up above. I heard one of my Sergeants asking me if I was all right. I yelled that I was, and added laughingly that they had better hurry up and get me the hell outa there. They were digging, I knew, for there was more mud falling down into my little air space inside my helmet. I then yelled for them to take it easy lest they stick me in the back with a shovel. Finally, I tried pushing again and this time broke through the dirt. About ten hands reached down to pull me out. Soon I was shaking the dirt out of my hair and letting the rain wash the big lumps of dirt off the rest of me. Thus ended another thrilling chapter of my life in the Army. Although I was buried for only a very few minutes, it had seemed like years.

Afterwards I got a ride around the regimental drill field and sat in the tank commander's seat up in the turret. I looked through the periscope, but the vision is very limited. The noise is heavy and I guess a lot worse when the 75 gun it carries starts off. There is absolutely no room in those tanks for anything but what belongs in them.

Well, that's all the news for now. I hope that all are well and I remain

Your loving son,
Morris

Camp McCain, Mississippi
Wednesday, May 24, 1944

Dear Mom and Dad,

I am writing this not knowing when I'll finish it. We've been up since three-forty-five this morning. We were supposed to run a full-scale assault on a fortified position. However, it has been raining all night and the order has come down that we'd have a rainy day schedule, i.e., lectures in the barracks. So it is now a few minutes after six and everybody is sitting around either writing letters or listening to the strains of some popular dance band on the radio.

The training is rough and rugged. We're having the full-scale business. We run all our attack problems with everything we'd ordinarily have in combat. Yesterday we attacked a dug-in position on a little knoll. First, our bazookas knocked out some resistance that was penned up in a house. Then the fire and movement of us, the infantry, started, and we moved forward until we were pinned down by machine-gun fire.

Our platoon leader found that we couldn't move ahead, so he requested a rolling barrage that would roll right up the hill, with us just behind it. The barrage started and we moved forward. Up ahead of us, scarcely more than 75 yards, could be seen other artillery bursts. Finally, when we were only 125 yds. from the base of the little knoll, we hugged the ground and let the artillery pour it in. We then fired all the ammunition we had and fixed bayonets for an all-out assault. Upon the word, we all rushed forward, whooping and yelling, and made the charge up the hill. This brought to an end a pretty good problem. And I was really worn out. Boy oh boy!

Enclosed you will find a snapshot of me standing on the front steps of the barracks. I have some others that I will send later after I get some prints made.

Well, I'll say good-bye. I won't phone 'til Sunday, so don't worry about me. I didn't phone this Sunday past because we were late in coming back from the party up at Calhoun City.

Give love to all,

Your loving son,
Morris

* * * * *

The following letter from Morris's mother, dated May 24, 1944, to Major General Harry J. Malony, Commanding General of the 94th Infantry Division, was prompted by General Malony's thoughtful Mother's Day greeting card of May 14, 1944, to the mothers of all personnel under his command.

May 24, 1944

Major General Harry J. Malony
Commanding 94th Infantry Division
Camp McCain, Mississippi

My dear General Malony,

Your thoughtfulness in sending Mother's Day greetings of a Division Commander to the mothers of personnel is characteristic of our fine way of life.

Morris Jr. (38499577) was as pleased as I was with your consideration. We have just had the happiness of having him home with his eight younger brothers and sister.

Should you visit our city, it would be a distinct pleasure to extend to you our hospitality and to be of any assistance in making your stay enjoyable.

Cordially,
Esther Joyce Redmann

* * * * *

Camp McCain, Mississippi
Wednesday, May 24, 1944

Dear Aunt Ogie,

I had wanted to write sooner and tell you how glad I was to have been home and to have seen all of you once again. However, I haven't had much time for writing since I've been back. They're working us pretty hard now. We have, facing us, six weeks of training with tanks, which would include attacks on fortified positions. It has been pretty interesting even though my experiences include being buried alive during a tank attack that crumbled the walls of my foxhole and put me under a darn good bit of dirt. I was some minutes down there before they finally dug me out with shovels and picks. One of the factors that led to the cave-in was the pouring rain that weakened the top mud. However, I am none the worse for it and have gained a lot by the experience.

I finally got my glasses. They're really fine. I couldn't have gotten a better fit or a more accurate prescription from anybody.

The weather here is unbearably hot. I have been sweating off a lot more weight. I guess the next time you see me I shall be as skinny as a rail. I hope so. The more weight I lose, the faster I am on my feet.

Well, Ogie, I hope you are well. Give my regards to all, and tell Aunt Eleanor and Hyie that I will write them in a day or so. I was going to write Thursday night, but we'll be out all day and night running raids.

Your loving nephew,
Morris

* * * * *

Camp McCain, Mississippi
Thursday, May 26, 1944

Dear Mom and Dad,

I got the pictures about a day ago. I certainly enjoyed receiving them. You, Mom, are looking very well. I thought while I was home that you looked much better than when I had left. I thought Dad looked well too.

Saturday the division is having the inspection to end all inspections. I'm not kidding! The Secretary of War, the Undersecretary, about forty Generals and Senators, and almost every brass hat in Washington will be down here for this inspection. Our battalion was chosen as the one that would be inspected. Thus, we have a lot of work to do cleaning up equipment and what-not.

I don't know if I'll be able to phone Sunday because we're supposed to be out in the field.

I would like, if it is not too much trouble, another box of food.

Well, that's all for now.

Your loving son,
Morris

P.S. Please get William to find out Charlie Brennan's, Warren Mouledoux's, and George Reinecke's addresses.

Camp McCain, Mississippi
Monday, May 29, 1944

Dear Mom and Dad,

I am learning now that I had never had a full appreciation of the term "hot weather." The hottest day of July or August had nothing on a "Spring Day" in May over here in Mississippi. The air is close. One's breath comes in short gasps. There is no cloud up in the sky. In fact, there is no blue sky. There is only a big, white-hot ball of fire that permeates the whole ether, parches the earth, and burns and melts the human beings who unfortunately have to work through the day. The heat was so terrific at nine o'clock this morning that I couldn't even write or read. The guardhouse was like an oven, and still is. I am writing this over in the big recreation hall, which is somewhat cooler. During the while I stayed in the guardhouse I lay down to sleep. I got up an hour ago and found myself wringing wet. At present I am wondering how on earth we can ever live through the summer down here.

Enclosed you will find a newspaper clipping. One of the staff cars that were present at the parade flew from its flagstaff the red flag of a General, and on it were sewn the four stars of Gen. George C. Marshall, Chief of Staff. Also in the long procession of staff cars were many red flags of two- and one-star Generals. It was quite a show.

I received a letter from William today. I hope he is better, and I hope that at his second time at bat up at school, he'll hit a home run as did the Hero of Mudville after having struck out with the bases loaded the game before.

Well, that's all the news for now.

Your loving son,
Morris

P.S. How about those addresses?

* * * * *

Camp McCain, Mississippi
May 30, 1944

Dear Mom and Dad,

I am sending you what I think is a good article written on the Army weekly, *Yank*. It is a nonprofit magazine published by and for the enlisted men. This article appeared in the June issue of *Coronet.* In the same issue are beautiful color pictures of the musical *Oklahoma.*

I have subscribed to *Yank.* It cost $1.00 per six months, or five cents per copy.

Your loving son,
Morris

* * * * *

The following is a poem Morris composed at a time of uncertainty. It was at a time when his division, the 94th, was having its "inspection to end all inspections" with the Secretary of War, Henry L. Stimson, the Undersecretary, many Generals and U.S. Senators, and included the Chief of Staff, four-star General, George C. Marshall. It was an ominous time with rumors and guesses flying.

Thoughts of a Different Time and Place

Were that we all were transported to another happier realm,
to a place whose evening star is The Pilot at the Helm.

Here would see but as a comet, this groaning globe, this race of men,
free from all this earthly carnage hav'n gained accord again.

Nations free from world distress, filled with majesty and power,
sharing all the earthly fruits, planning peace within the tower.

Warless worlds and happy people, educated, healthy, free,
such a dream is only stardust, such a dream is as to me.

You that hold the key to power, educated through and through,
face the world with favoured brightness, look upon a dawning new.

Education, right, and power, cords to bind a happy land,
for today but breeds tomorrow when the pen is in the hand,

Treaties, made by man and broken, through the passage of the years,
stand as dreary monuments of a nation's hopes and fears.

Treaties, made by man and broken, hence they have not stood the test,
the covenant of a heavenly realm is a constitution blest.

Men may think that they are real, but the flight of time belays their words,
as the blaring, brilliant sunlight turns the finest milk to curds,

Forward is the hourly cry, forward through the worlds unknown,
forward through uncertain darkness over fields that were unsown.

Science guards the human life from the worst of all diseases,
gives the world luxurious comforts, gives it all that e'er it pleases.

But men are more than matter merely, within their walls there lurks a soul,
that remains forever living though the frame decay and mould.

In the final count there lingers no mention of our earthly goods,
as a man deals in lumber sees not the leaves but only woods.

The mouths so filled with good intentions that rarely ever purpose well,
spend themselves on deafened ears as no striker in a bell.

Though the note is writ on paper, there is no sound upon the ear,
till the chord is stricken softly and the music doth appear.

—Morris B. Redmann Jr.
Camp McCain, Mississippi
May, 1944

* * * * *

Camp McCain, Mississippi
Sunday, June 4, 1944

Dear Mom and Dad,

Today presents the first opportunity I have had in some days of writing you. It's been a rugged week. And I mean rugged. We've been out in the field most of the week running problems with tanks and airplanes. We went on a two-day march during which we were under constant attack by strafing "enemy" planes. Every time they came over, we had to leave the road and lie low in the fields or take concealment in the woods. There was some novelty to it, so we didn't mind it too much at first. The planes would swoop down along the road, flying low at a height of about ten feet. However, when the temperature is up in the hundreds and you're covered with dust and sweat and grime, and the planes make you hit the dirt every few minutes, it gets to be trying. The first night we bivouacked on the side of a big hill that rises some hundreds of feet above the level Mississippi plains. The snakes and insects were awful. One of the worst of the insects is what is called here the "chigger." It digs into your skin, makes a lump, and itches like a mosquito bite, dies, and then festers out. The itch and annoyance of the chigger stays with you for several days.

Yesterday was payday. I received $36.85 from the government and collected twelve dollars from the fellows that owed me, so I now have about fifty dollars. I am going to make an earnest attempt to buy a fifty-dollar bond this month. I don't think I'm going to have much opportunity to spend any money for awhile, as we're supposed to go up below Memphis for three weeks of maneuvers with tanks. All of a sudden I've had the urge to save money. I don't know why, unless the "postwar era" isn't far off.

I went to Mass at 9:30 this morning, and afterwards washed out my underwear, socks, and other clothes.

I'm going to try to write William, Aunt Eleanor, and Aunt Hy as soon as I can. These days we don't have much time to do anything but work. Often we are allowed only eight hours a day for sleep. The other sixteen we're on the move. Always on the move. Sometimes I wish I'd go overseas. It can't be much rougher than this. My eyes are much better. We get a lot of carrots and other vegetables that help you regain, or keep up, good sight.

I guess I told you many a time that the training constituted the roughest days of my life. Well, each day it gets rougher and I get tougher.

If you are buying any bonds this month, send me the money and let me get them. The soldier in each co. buying the most number of bonds in amount of dollars and cents gets a three-day pass. I'm tenth in line for a pass now, but the three weeks at Holly Springs will kick that out the window.

We are going someplace, that's for sure. It may be either Louisiana for maneuvers or Fort Breckenridge in Kentucky, or to P.O.E. in New York. I am sure that something's up, because the officers and men have been told to send their wives home.

If we go overseas I'll get $10 a month more. If Ernie Pyle's bill in Congress goes through, Congress will give an increase of 50% in pay to all Infantry soldiers on the front lines. Not that 50% increase in pay means anything to someone who risks his life every second. Money is perhaps the furthest thing from his mind. Perhaps the bill presents further tribute in a small sort of way to the best branch of this man's Army—the Infantry.

Well, that's all the news for now.

Your loving son,
Morris

* * * * *

Camp McCain, Mississippi
Sunday, June 4, 1944

Dear Will,

There isn't much that I can write to you about. I don't know anything much about happenings at home or school, and so I can't discuss the latest gossip. But perhaps I can describe our recent attack on fortified positions. It is an example of the tactics that make our infantry squads a winning team. Such an operation necessitates not so much the execution of the right thing at the right time, but rather the action and position of the right men at the right time. The most essential element is timing. One action must immediately follow the preceding one. Each man must do his part and take up his exact position. Here's where the right man in the right position at the right time is of utmost importance.

The pillboxes of any fortified wall are always covered by fire from the other boxes of the wall. The boxes are staggered back and may cover an area tens of thousands of yards in depth. The first obstacle is the rolls of barbed wire, often called protective wire. This is to slow down or hold up the infantrymen. It is, however, one of the easiest obstacles to get through. The next is the traps and obstacles designed to halt the advance of mechanized vehicles such as tanks, half-tracks, or gun-carriers. These, however, can be breached by concentrated fire, or by explosive charges. Then comes a minefield primarily to halt the advance of the Infantry. These mines are of the anti-personnel type. They are very troublesome and hard to detect. Once through this field we face the final barbed wire that surrounds the pillbox. This wire is set up about 75 yards from the pillbox.

During the whole operation the artillery has been blasting the boxes with everything they have. Now the assault squad of an Infantry platoon moves up under the heavy fire of the artillery to assault and knock out the box. This squad is made up of five men who are on the wire detail, two who are the flame throwers, three who are on the demolitions, and two who fire the bazooka. This team means a lot of trouble for anybody.

First, the wire detail—consisting of three riflemen and two automatic riflemen who carry wire clippers and bangalore torpedoes—creep up to the wire. The bangalores are laid underneath and perpendicular to the wire. This detail takes up a tactical position, a term which means that they merely withdraw to safer ground. As soon as the wire is blown up, these men rush through it and fan out on the other side and concentrate their fire on the openings of the box. Immediately after the wire detail has started their concentration of fire, the flame throwers rush through the gap in the wire and hit the embrasures with a burst of liquid fire. Before I go on, there is one important detail I forgot: As soon as the wire was cut, the squad leader had the artillery lifted by signal from a berry pistol. This left it safe for the flame throwers to move past the wire. The flame throwers exhaust their fuel and withdraw to a tactical position just as the demolitions men rush up and shove pole charges through the windows to wipe out anything that may have been left alive inside. These demolitions men then take up a tactical position so the explosion won't get them too. As soon as the pole charges go off, the whole assault squad rushes up again and surrounds the pillbox. The men face in all directions to prevent counterattack by enemy foot troops. As this squad spreads out as a sort of security, the rest of the platoon, which is called the support squad, rushes up and enters the broken box.

The same procedure is followed in the knocking out of the other pillboxes of the fortified wall. It's a rough business, but in a strange way, I like it. I would always advise that anybody coming into the Army do their best to keep out of the Infantry. However, I have grown to respect, admire, and love my Infantry outfit. There's nobody in the world that can say anything against the Infantry in front of me. When the Infantry wins, everybody wins. When it loses, everybody loses. The Infantry is the Queen of Battles—the ace in the hole of any General's hand. The tactics discussed above show that its battles are not brainless operations but a series of individual operations executed by the individual soldiers related in time and position that form a winning combination.

In the Air Corps, victory is determined by the ratio of enemy planes destroyed—there, machine against machine; in the tank corps, again—machine and armament against machine and armament; in the Navy, ship against ship. However in the Infantry, victory is bought only by the successful matching of men against men, bayonet against bayonet, rifle against rifle. In such an engagement, survival depends not upon the quality, quantity, or superiority of machine, but upon the resourcefulness of the individual soldier.

Victory goes to the unit that wins the greater amount of small engagements.

Take it easy. Watch your health. Tell all the fathers hello for me.

Dein Bruder,
Morris

* * * * *

Camp McCain, Mississippi
Tuesday, June 6, 1944

Dear Mom and Dad,

The fall of Rome, the eternal city, seems as though it was the signal for the start of the invasion of Hitler's "Festung Europa." In operations set as the greatest of all time, the Allied armies have had initial success. In fact, the success has surprised us, I believe, as much as it has the Germans.

The strategy of Gen. Eisenhower—literally the Iron Striker—shows a daring plan, if one can believe the various commentators that have voiced their views in this first day of the Invasion. One such commentator, a French Colonel, described the section of the coast struck by the Allies as the best-fortified part of the Channel coast. The same section of Normandy is only one hundred and fifty miles from that nation's once gay capital—Paris. If Paris were to be reoccupied by Allied troops within a short time, let us say a month and a half, the psychological impact would shatter any remaining belief in the defensive power of the German Army. Such a blow would, I believe, water the budding despair embedded deep in the hearts of Germans who have felt the shaking blows of American and British air power.

There are, in relation to the Allies' initial successes, many questions as to the strength of Germans in Western Europe. It has been necessary that the German High Command—to keep most of its power along the Eastern front—face the Russian menace that makes for a front of some twelve hundred miles, stretching from the Arctic ice of Finland to the oil fields of Roumania. The High Command has also deployed its armies against the American, French, British, and Polish troops threatening its soft underbelly in Italy.

However, the fall of Rome left only the fleeing, shattered, disorganized armies of Germany in Italy, to be reckoned with in the battle for the Italian peninsula. Now the great adventure of the invasion on the fields of Normandy has begun, and Herr Hitler must now face the enemy on three fronts. Certainly no hint was given as to where the heaviest blow would fall. There arises then the speculation as to the size, strength, and mobility of Field Marshal Erwin Rommel's "mobile Army."

Without a doubt, Gen. Spaatz's Army Air Force has knocked out the possibility of any success on the part of German Gen'l Kesserling's Luftwaffe to keep the Allies from landing. For we have landed. Where was the great firepower of the German coastal batteries? Were these big guns only a myth? Or was the element of surprise so great that the Germans were caught napping? True, some batteries opened up. But these were quickly silenced by the six hundred and forty naval guns of our capital ships that escorted the giant armada across the sixty-some-odd miles of channel that separates southern England from the northern coast of Normandy. These 640 guns ranged from four inches to the gigantic sixteen inches of our largest line ships.

The invasion got off to a grand start with four thousand troop-carrying ships and several thousand smaller craft. There were eleven thousand aircraft employed in the first operations. Four airborne divisions were landed behind the enemy lines by parachute and glider. The new front stretches from Calais to the Cherbourg peninsula. Many divisions are now engaged in mortal combat with the enemy along the 240-mile front. The Germans have stated that they expect another larger invasion for the French coast before Wednesday morning.

But so much depends upon the success of this invasion that strength of arms alone is not enough to bring to the world peace which the world alone cannot give. In the words of Jesus Christ to his Apostles, *Pacem relinquo vobis, pacem meam do vobis. Ne respicias peccata mea, sed fidem Ecclesiam tuam.* "Peace I leave you, my Peace I give you." And in the prayer of the Mass we add, "Look not upon our sins, but upon the faith of thy Church."

There must be prayer on every lip and hope in every heart. There must be strength in every arm and faith in every mind. Faith in God, in our leaders, in our strength of arms. But above all there must be charity and love and forgiveness in our hearts if we are to win the peace.

The philosophies that have governed the actions of the national governments of Europe must be shattered, not as the lightning rents the darkened skies, but as the sun breaks through the darkness of the night, bringing a new day. A bright day wherein all may live and work and pray in any manner they please. A new day bringing a new hope and joy for mankind with the promise that the nations will once again walk together hand in hand in majesty and power.

We must all repeat and act *Panem caelestiam accipiam et nomen Domine Invocabo*. I will take the bread of Salvation and call upon the name of the Lord.

So much for so many by so few.

Your loving son,
Morris

* * * * *

7017 Broad Place
New Orleans, Louisiana
June 6, 1944 (D-Day)

Dear Morris,

As you will notice, my secretary [Morris's brother Will] is typing this letter to you. It is four o'clock in the afternoon and I am just starting to go to market, down to Stassi's. I will drop this letter at the branch post office.

This morning at six o'clock I got up and got ready for 6:30 Mass. Dad got up at 6:20 and made it with me on time. You can imagine my surprise when upon entering the church I saw the Blessed Sacrament exposed. I knew immediately the invasion had begun. However, it was only after we were out of church that Dad got it by my explaining. There was a photographer in the church to take pictures, but Dad didn't see any reason why he should be there, except maybe because of some special thing about which he knew nothing. I don't think he was finally convinced until we reached the front porch and he picked up the morning newspaper and read the headlines. Thereafter he kept listening to the radio until after 9:00.

I have listened to the radio off and on all day. I am wondering if you have had the chance to listen. I know you will eat up every word of this.

Nine members of this household went to Mass this morning, and almost all of them received Communion, and offered up prayers for the success of this great undertaking. Ralph and Ronald spent from ten to eleven in Adoration. I am going for a while after I come home from market, and Dad and the big fellows have certain hours during the night. There was a write-up in the "Extra" paper today about the early worshippers at St. Rita's Church. Some half-a-dozen were reported there from 4:00 on.

Will went back to Loyola today. He had seen the doctor yesterday, and was told that his jaundice will have to wear itself out. My chief problem now is to nourish him up.

I must run along now, so, "So long."

Lovingly,
Mom

P.S. Dad will send you money for you to get a $100 bond.
Everyone is well.

* * * * *

Camp McCain, Mississippi
June 10, 1944

Dear Dad,

We, as have our sources of information—the newspapers and the radio—concerned ourselves with the invasion of France. Although this is good news and commands our attention, there is nevertheless the remaining importance of continued success in the Italian Campaign. Upon the successful efforts of our Allied Armies hinge many possibilities that cannot be ignored when a hasty conclusion of this conflict is to be considered. The exact position of our forces above Rome is not known. For the last few days there has been no contact between the fleeing Germans and our main body. We have captured an average of 1,000 vehicles a day since the fall of Rome. We have seized enough equipment to outfit several divisions. This would indicate that the German 14th Army is pretty well chewed up. The strategic possibilities depend on the occupation of the Italian city of Florence. This is still some miles up the coast, but it is not believed that the Germans will put up much of a defense before this city. The capture of Florence would give us a free sea between the Italian coast and the big islands of Corsica and Sardinia. The importance of these islands cannot be overlooked if we are to make use of every advantage afforded us to enter Hitler's Festung Europa at another point. In all probability we have considerable supplies and men based on Corsica. From Corsica could spring a sizeable invasion armada to strike at southern France. This would indeed be the other point of a giant pincers designed to divide France through the middle. The fall of Florence would enable our fighter planes to protect an invasion fleet from enemy bombers. From Corsica could flow supplies of great amount to speed the advance of our troops.

Affairs of today seem to weave a web of steel around Germany. Other possibilities to be considered are landings on the eastern Adriatic Coast and a concerted drive with Marshal Tito to join the advancing Russians. who are cutting through the middle of Roumania. Such a meeting of forces would isolate, or force the evacuation of, the Germans on the Balkan Peninsula.

Getting back to South France and Corsica. Such a blow would fall only after the whole German mobile Army was occupied with defending Paris and the other important points and cities of northern France. In South France there is no wall that the Germans have ever boasted of. Probably the only opposition that could be offered would be accredited to the terrain.

Such an operation—the British, Americans, and Canadians coming down from Normandy; French, British, Colonials, and Australians coming up from the southern ports—would write "finis" to the European Campaign. It is supposed that Germany will again surrender before she herself suffers herself to become a battlefield.

I would make some conjecture as to our future. I have a considered belief that Paris will fall by this date in July, and that the war in Europe will come to its conclusion by the end of September. So much for a discussion of Allied strategy.

By the time you get this I will be out on a big problem. This is our last week of training starting Monday. It'll be, I guess, the roughest week of all. We have reached the stage when there is no simulation of circumstances. When we request artillery on a hill or mortar fire on dug-in positions, there is no supposition that there was such. One can feel the concussion, hear the shells whistle overhead, and see the bursting shells and their effect. In the last week there have been many hurt by shell-fire, some maimed for life. When we can't move up because of hidden automatic fire, we call for tanks and then we move up behind them and take the position. I'll paint many a good war picture after this is over because I've seen many a splendid operation which used every means we had at hand to make it a success.

We are due to move out anytime after the 17th, but we will probably be here until the 21st of July.

I am writing this to you to extend you the best wishes I hold for a Happy Father's Day. I won't write again until next week (after Father's Day); I say I won't because I know I won't get a chance to write again.

Well, I'll say so long—

Your loving son,
Morris

Camp McCain, Mississippi
Sunday, June 11, 1944

Dear Mom,

Here it is—June again. And with June come four birthdays and Father's Day. I am sorry that I missed Robert's on the second of the month. However, I do not intend to miss the rest. I am enclosing eleven dollars for the several occasions. You can put Robert's two in his Homestead account if you wish. Give Ralph his two on his birthday and Kerry his on the twenty-eighth. Next Sunday is Father's Day. I have enclosed five which should get Dad a nice present.

The training here hasn't slackened any, but it is still interesting. We've been running large-scale problems involving thousands and thousands of men and costing thousands and thousands of dollars in artillery shells. I guess our D-Day is getting near. Perhaps, tho', we'll pull Louisiana maneuvers. Furloughs are out. I believe I'll get a three-day pass sometime in July, perhaps; of course, I can't be sure. This coming week is our last here of this phase of training. After this week we could move out at any time. However a light schedule has been made to carry us through the twenty-first of July.

I got a box of candy from Ogie. I wish you would thank her for me. I probably won't get a chance to write anybody except you all for some time. I got a letter from Esther, little Winnie, and Marie Louise Salatich.

Enclosed also is a clipping of a letter published in our paper, *Attack*. It is self-explanatory. Winnie might be interested to know that her school chum's father is herein commended for his work.

I'll ring next Sunday when we get back into camp here. Give my love to all.

Your loving son,
Morris

* * * * *

Camp McCain, Mississippi
June 20, 1944

Dear Mom and Dad,

I certainly had a swell time at home the past weekend. Monday morning I went in to see the Company Commander. I asked for a three-day pass.

He asked if Saturday, Sunday, and Monday of next week would be all right. I said yes and thanked him. He then told me to come see him on Friday.

However, fate as ever has proved unkind. We've had a change in Company Commanders since then, and also a change in First Sergeants. So I'm really "sweating it out" as they say. Our acting First Sergeant advised me to let it ride, but to try and speak with the former Co. Commander, who is now our executive officer, around Thursday. I intend, if in any way possible, to speak with the latter some day out in the field and ask him exactly what should or can be done. So hope and pray.

Today I went up to the hospital to have X-rays taken of my leg. I hurt it in a baseball game and the doc at the dispensary thought it might be a fracture. The bone is, however, only bruised. By now most of the pain is gone. Outside of this I'm fine. We play football and baseball for the most part. Don't wear shirts during these hours, thus I'm brown as a nut.

Tell Will to tell Fr. O'Conner hello for me. Make that boy study hard. He might be the man of the house some long time from now. Give my love to all. Don't expect me.

Your loving son,
Morris

* * * * *

The following letter to his mother and father, written on his nineteenth birthday, is full of soul-searching and self-evaluation. Morris's developing philosophy of life and his deep love for home and family—remarkable for his age—are expressed in this poignant letter.

June 27, 1944

Dear Mom and Dad,

In the past nineteen years I have accomplished a little more than have most of the fellows of my age. Yet I am conscious of achievements only at times when, with a somewhat egotistical attitude, I recount my physical, mental, and moral value, raised day by day by new lessons learned and decisions made. I daresay that as I write I'm in one of those egotistical moods.

I was born—but this happens to everybody, so it's not much to talk about; but I guess it should be mentioned because it was the first thing that ever happened to me. From what I don't remember I was blessed by the late Pope Pius XI, and I was first dressed in clothes bought in some Paris clothing store "pour petits hommes." I must have been easy on my clothes then, for if I remember correctly my last and youngest brother at one time or another wore the same little French jacket that was my "Sunday best" sixteen years before.

A very few years after I had outgrown my French lace and white diapers, and had lost my brown Buster Brown, I must, as well as I can figure, have started school. To be sure, I considered myself a martyr for a cause—the cause of staying at home and playing with my automobile or riding my three-wheel bike. But I finally capitulated, and yielding to superior numbers, attended not one, but two, mind you, schools at once—St. Rita's Parochial and Lafayette Public.

Around this time, too, I must have been pretty noisy, because I was operated on for my tonsils which kept me quiet for a week or so and gave everybody, I suppose, a well needed rest. I can still remember the rubber ice bag that they had choked me with for some hours after the said tonsillectomy. Also do I remember the grand steamship that made many a trip up and down the hospital bathtub. I don't think I flirted with the nurses because as near as I remember, I didn't have a crush on any girl until I was about ten years old and ready to graduate from grammar school.

I graduated second of the boys, through no fault of my own. I would have probably finished last had it not been for Mother's helping hand. Shortly after, I enrolled, or rather, was drafted, into a place of higher learning called high school. Being pretty young, some of the more generous bookies were offering ten to one against my survival. However, I was running in good form with top weight of two parents, both of whom were teachers. The high-school "prom" rolled around the night of graduation and I had my first date.

As time passed on, I entered college and after three awfully short years I found myself in the category of educated people. I pursued law, but the law turned and pursued me and gave me a new home here in the Army.

Today I celebrate my nineteenth birthday. And I look back over these years as a traveler would look back upon a smooth road that he had just passed over. The years were easy years filled with blessings, with happiness, with ease, with some personal triumph, with some, but very little, responsibility acquired by the election to the highest offices of the trivial college organizations. I have, during two consecutive years, had a few artistic attempts on exhibition at the Delgado Museum. They say that morale is made up of a lot of little things, such as flowers and candy on one's birthday, or the mere remembrance with a card. But I never needed a boost in morale, and all my success added to an inward pride—a pride I must confess that urged me on and made me think that I should run the whole show. But the more I got into it, the more I felt the responsibility of making it all a success. And because success demands the best one has, it taxed this lazy man and made him at the end relieved when he came into the Army and faced nothing but a strict routine wherein he merely followed.

I have known the joys of childhood, hours of happiness and ease. I have known what education was, the comforts that it brings. I have seen some pretty days from rise to set of sun. I have learned a new life, different from the one of perfect ease. I have seen, through the magic of the motion picture, the brutality and the criminal aggression of the common enemy, the object of our common cause. The past few years have been tragic ones—but not for us. We don't know what war is. Surrounded by two oceans, we stand a fortress, blessed by God. The American people have made no sacrifices that can be spoken of. Our dead have merely done their duty. The true measure of sacrifice is found amidst the slaughtered dead, the starving millions, and the twisted, crumbled buildings of China, Greece, Holland, England, Russia, and Poland. These people have fought within their crumbled homes the oppression of a nation who, not satisfied with the destruction of the vanquished armies, sought to crush the heart and spirit of the people. What American city the size of Rotterdam saw thirty thousand men, women, and children killed in ninety minutes of air bombardment that leveled this once-proud city? What group of Americans have seen millions of their countrymen killed in cold blood as have the Chinese? What city in these states could have withstood the horror, terror, and frightful devastation of twenty days' siege as did the city of Warsaw? Shall this nation be maimed by millions of underfed, of crippled, of blind, of deformed? Shall it be faced by years of reconstruction? Shall it weep for bread or milk? Shall it ever see its children with sunken eyes and bloated stomachs, too weak to speak or to even lift a bowl to their drawn mouths? I don't think it will. Ever. They (us) talk about the small restrictions of rationing, the tragedy of buying war bonds. But from this grand picture I have learned that the Americans of today are not the solid brand of people as were those who fought for our Independence, are not the same as those who fought at Valley Forge.

But the biggest lesson I have ever learned is the appreciation of my home. I have learned that one's people are the most beloved by his heart. That it is to them alone his step will ever turn. To them can come the sons with open hearts. From them can come consolation for every affliction. From them can come the strength for great pursuits. And no matter where I go or where I stand, I shall appreciate the lesson learned during these few months away from home.

It has been a happy birthday. Tonight I signed my three-day pass. It remains only to go through Regiment. If successful, I will arrive at Muny Airport at 7:05 Saturday evening.

Your loving son,
Morris

* * * * *

Mrs. Morris B. Redmann
7017 Broad Place
New Orleans, Louisiana
June 27, 1944

Dear Morris,

Nineteen years ago to-day I was made perfectly happy with the arrival of my first baby—you. I can remember it just as though it was yesterday. That big head of yours was smashed quite a bit, and you looked exactly like a Billiken. You were so strong you held your head up and looked all around at everything. I had you lying on my stomach watching your every movement. I'm thinking of how Mrs. Schreder took care of you—how she changed your dresses twelve or thirteen times a day. What a difference now—you with your GI underwear that you wear through mud and slime and what-not! Oh, well, life's like that.

Tomorrow is Kerry's birthday. He'll be fifteen. I recall waiting for his arrival all during the day of your fourth birthday—how we didn't plan a party, but how I finally walked around to Walsdorf's and bought all the small toys they had, then called in some of the children from the neighborhood, and had grab bags and prizes and a party after all. Of course you had your presents that morning, and Bertha had two Sunshine cakes and plenty of ice cream made. The Preston children were here, but long since they have lost both father and mother. However, they were left very well off. Their mother was a wealthy girl. She and her husband and her children lived off the income of her money.

This morning I offered my Mass and Communion for you on your birthday. I hope you haven't had to work too hard to-day, and that you've had a somewhat pleasant time.

There was a cartoon about a soldier's birthday in this morning's paper. I was going to send it to you, but Aunt Winnie said she had mailed it to you this morning along with a check for purchasing war bonds.

We are hoping you'll get that three-day pass.

Right now the kids are hosing in their bathing suits in the side yard. They are squealing and fussing over whose turn it is.

Esther cleared out her closet this afternoon, and she and Ralph carried all her "possessions" up to the library. They arranged all the dolls and bed and carriage and china closet and dishes and doll punch bowl and silverware, etc. to a Queen's taste. Esther says she might as well let the little fellows play with her things.

I'm still putting away winter clothes. They keep coming in from the laundry and the cleaners'. It seems to be an endless job of checking and storing away. And spraying, too.

Well, here's to your day! And may you have the next one home with those who love you and have you ever in their thoughts and prayers.

Lovingly,
Mom

* * * * *

Camp McCain, Mississippi
June 29, 1944

Dear Mom,

I received your beautiful letter of the 27th on the next day. I appreciated it more than any other remembrance that could have been made. I often wonder what happened to all the people that used to live around us—the Thompsons, the Stevens, the Shelbys, Clayton Kruse, and others. Many things have happened to all of them during the course of years, some happy, others tragic.

Well, my well of luck runs dry. All three-day passes were turned down. I had planned so much for this week-end. Dreamed about it day and night. Thought of driving the new car—if you had it yet. Thought of seeing Numa and all the fellows one last time. For this would have been the last time. But by hook or by crook I'll be coming home every Sunday from now on. And there's no power in this Army that could tell me I won't, unless they get me on some job I can't borrow, buy, or steal off. I'll probably be in on that 12:05 plane if I can get a reservation, or else on the 9:35 train Sunday morn. I asked if I could get off at 12:00 noon Saturday. I won't. Shucks, I get so darn disgusted at times. But this latest has really got me mad. When something like that happens you feel like biting everybody. It's not the fault of the CO. It's all due to a stinking personnel officer over in regimental hdqrts. There have been very few officers that I have taken a permanent dislike to. He is one. A very small man and a poor officer.

I believe Charlie Brennan and Luke Bruno might be in town this week end. I had wanted to tell them hello.

How's the car situation? If Daddy's going to get it, I hope he'd get it so I could drive it once before we leave here.

Well, this is M. B. Redmann reporting to you from Camp McCain and reminding you that "Troubles ne'er come single spoused but in battalions," and that what they shouldn't be some Lieutenants are.

Lovingly,
Morris

P.S. I'll bring the bonds with me.

* * * * *

UNITED STATES ARMY
Camp McCain, Mississippi
July 4, 1944

Dear Mom and Dad,

Well, I think my train ride Sunday was "Casey's last ride." I don't think I'll be home for a long, long time. I had the same thought when I told you all good-bye at the station. I mean, I really felt homesick again. But I had a pretty nice trip up. I met Fr. Emmett Bienvenue, S.J., freshly ordained. He was my old Greek teacher out at Jesuit Hi. A very fine fellow too. We had dinner together, for which I paid. After dinner we had a long chat and recalled the good old days back at the alma mater—the Greek newspapers and the Greek Club picnics. By accident the high school sent his invitation to his first Mass to William (by, or rather,) instead of me.

I got the results of the exam I took. I made 140 out of 150. But my friend Roth didn't quite make it. However, it was to no avail. A physical report was supposed to go in on Monday, so they found out later, and I wasn't there. But at least I am assured of one thing—I have the mental ability. Does Daddy have any friends among the congressmen from Louisiana to whom he could ask whether there would be anything that could be done about it? I don't want him to obligate himself to anybody, but if perhaps someone owes him a favor he could explain that I have made a high score of 140 on my Army General Classification Test, which is way above average. One needs only 110 to get into OCS. Also, that I have just turned 19, have a college degree, and have had a few courses of mathematics during my years at school. Also, that I have had about nine months' military service in the Army. This is just, shall we say, a suggestion? I know that Daddy doesn't like to ask for anything from anybody, even when they owe him something. Not that any Democratic congressman from the Solid South owes Daddy anything. But if anything can be done, well, I guess now's a good time to get it done. I will still ask my CO about OCS. Maybe I'll get somewhere. Pray for me. I know you do, and always will.

Your loving son,
Morris

* * * * *

Camp McCain, Mississippi
Wednesday, July 12, 1944

Dear Mom & Dad,

Just a short note to let you know I'm still around. Monday we had a division review at which the Expert Infantry pennants and badges were given out. The 376th, 301st, and 302nd regiments of our division were the first in the Army to attain the title Expert Infantry Reg't. However, the 376th was the first of these, having qualified every company in the regt. as an Expert Infantry Co. This is a darn good showing.

The weather here has been pretty warm. A few drops of rain have fallen on the two preceding evenings. That's the way it is—fair all day long, then cool and windy in the evening, sometimes with dark clouds.

If I am able to get a pass this week-end, I'll be in on the 9:35 Sunday morning. I'll wire. Love to all.

Morris Jr.

Camp McCain, Mississippi
Friday morning, July 14, 1944

Dear Mom,

I am sending home by the same mail the General Order by which I was made an Expert Infantryman. I wish you would keep this for me.

I've been on detail a lot lately, voluntarily. On a detail one can usually "goldbrick," as there is no one to watch you. In a way you're on your own. Yesterday I was on a detail of ten men to build a bridge across a big drainage ditch. We had a good time, but spent the better part of the day horsing around while building this twenty-foot bridge.

From the little war news we get, I draw that the Germans are fast crumbling. If we don't hurry up we're liable to miss the show. I saw that the Germans have begun a general retreat from all the Baltic states, and that the Russians were now only 30 miles from German East Prussia. Perhaps the war will end over there in '44. Japan will take longer. But as our General said, "We shall not fail."

Lovingly,
Morris

* * * * *

Camp McCain, Mississippi
Monday, July 17, 1944

Dear Mom and Dad,

I guess it'll be some time before I see you again. But everybody will always remain in my thoughts.

Today hasn't been too hard. We had some exercise this morning which wasn't hard at all. I slept pretty well last night and was well rested when the day's work started. Shelby and I went to sleep right after we left the station—didn't even make our customary trip to the club car for sandwiches and beer. However, we both woke, and with Dupre, a friend of ours, who like Trice, has been with us all the way, ate Dupre's fried chicken and drank orange juice. The chicken was very good, and with it we had plenty of buttered bread and fresh tomatoes. It got kind of messy when we started on the tomatoes, but from the looks on the other people's faces, we were a very envied threesome. This was during a thirty-minute layover in Jackson. Right after we pulled out, the three of us were back sawing wood again. It wasn't until passing through camp that we awoke. We moved as far to the front of the train as possible so that we could reach the cabs first. We got a cab and got out to camp in about fifteen minutes. By about twenty to five I was sound asleep again. Slept 'til six.

I received your letter this morning telling about Jerome's afternoon fevers. Would you ask Dad about that ticket refund from the tri-state bus lines?

Well, I'm on guard duty from 5 today until 5 to-morrow, and I've got to get over to the guardhouse, so good-bye.

Lovingly,
Morris

* * * * *

Camp McCain, Mississippi
Tuesday, July 18, 1944

Dear Mom and Dad,

Well, I definitely will not be home this Saturday. I kinda felt that way when I said good-bye at the station. That's why I was jumpy and nervous, I guess. That's why I went to sleep right away on the train instead of sitting up in the club car and talking half the night. But if time passes as fast as it has passed in the last four months, it won't be too long before I come flying in again. Only then it'll be for good.

There isn't much to write about, and for this reason my letters from now on will be pretty short. It's no longer a pleasure to write. It is a bother, which often makes you feel depressed. I know I should write people—the Kellys, the Stuarts, the Sellers—but there is no inspiration. The thought of writing a letter produces the same effect as does the thought of extremely hard work. For this reason I write very few. However, I am always thinking of everyone.

The days here are the kind you would call beautiful back home. They are everything that a person—who didn't have to be out in them for twelve hours—could want. Plenty of sunshine and blue skies. But they're awful here. There aren't any shade trees on the drill fields, and there aren't any electric fans or cooling drinks at hand's reach that could help you through the dog days. We've been sweating things out right along, but with the heat we now sweat twice as much.

Give everyone my regards. I'll write as often as I can.

Lovingly,
Morris

July 21, 1944

Dear Mom,

The work I've been doing has been mostly pencil pushing, but I certainly don't mind that kind of work. Yesterday we had a pretty bad blow here. The power went off and it was so dark we couldn't even do the work. So we looked out the window and watched the wind and driving rain rip through the camp. Everything was flying past—clothes, newspapers, tar paper from the buildings, garbage can covers, and everything else that could be picked up by a stiff 50-mile wind. The storm blew the windows out of the barracks and the fellows say they had to brace the walls with the double-decker bunks. I don't know if this is true because I was over in the day room, which was shaking like a leaf in the breeze.

Well, there isn't much to write about these days. Everything is dull and uncertain. Rumors are rampant. Possibly Trice's company in the Special Troops won't be restricted and he'll be able to get home. If he does go home I'll have him ring you.

Well, I'll close now. It's almost time to "fall out." So long.

Lovingly,
Morris

P.S. Sept. 1, I'll be saving $47.50 a month. If it lasts a yr. and a half, I'll save $855 dollars. This, plus 400 I have in bonds, will be pretty good.

* * * * *

Morris's last visit home before shipping overseas was a weekend pass for July 22 and 23, 1944. Morris met with his good friends, Numa Bertel, Charlie Brennan, and a few other Tri-Sigs (fraternity brothers) that weekend. It was during this visit that Morris confided in Charlie Brennan that he didn't expect to come back—that he felt he would be killed. Charlie told Morris, "Aw, Morris, don't talk like that." This story was related by Charlie Brennan only recently.

Monday, July 24, 1944

Dear Mom and Dad,

The trip back wasn't too bad. I even got about three hours of sleep in my comfortable chair in that air-conditioned chair car. While not sleeping I was reading the interesting articles in the latest issue of *The Saturday Evening Post.* Commando Kelly's "One Man Army" and "We Avenged Pearl Harbor" and "Marvin Was There on D-Day," the story of the youngest sailor on the USS *Texas,* were about the best. An article on the FCC and its chairman, Mr. Fly, was interesting, but it tries to make a hero out of a tyrannical communications boss who has for years attempted to control the radio networks by nasty looks, words, and raised eyebrows.

When the conductor came through to get the tickets, I asked the time of arrival at Grenada. He told me it was at 4:45. I then asked if the train went through camp slow enough for one to jump off. "You want to get off at Camp McCain?" sez he. "Yes, I do," sez I. "Well, we'll see if I can fix it," sez he. "Thank you," sez I. And so I got off right at camp and signed in on the pass book at ten of five. We, then, didn't do a darn thing and haven't yet. I went to the PX and to the nine o'clock showing of *Sensations of 1945.*

Well, time is short. I'll write again to-night.

Lovingly,
Morris

* * * * *

Tuesday, July 25, 1944

Dear Mom and Dad,

I am still thinking of the past week-end. It was without a doubt the best week-end that I have ever spent since I have been in the Army. Everything was swell. The mackerel was very, very good, as were the beef chops and the wine. I really enjoyed that meal, and I enjoyed having Shelby and Mrs. Trice up for it. All in all, I think it was very pleasant.

On the way back I read Cardinal Newman's "Lead Kindly Light." Happened to find it in a magazine I bought.

Have you had any news from Paul Jr. lately? It seems to me he should get a leave soon. I think the Navy is easy on them.

Give my love to the Kellys, Stuarts, and Sellers. Thank Aunt Winnie for me.

"The night is dark, and I am far from home."—Cardinal Newman.

Lovingly,
Morris

Wednesday, July 26, 1944

Dear Mom and Dad,

I got Esther's letter and yours of the twenty-fifth. I am writing this in hopes that it'll get out in the twelve o'clock mail. I wrote Aunt Winnie this morning, thanking her for the mackerel and the beer. I also told her about how much I enjoyed it.

I'm glad Kerry had a good time at Waveland. That's a swell place to spend a vacation. It'd be good to live over there in the summer.

I guess the kids are all having a swell time during their vacation.

Give Uncle Billy my regards.

Love to all,
Morris

* * * * *

Camp McCain, Mississippi
Wednesday, July 26, 1944

Dear Aunt Winnie,

I would like to take this opportunity of thanking you for the beautiful mackerel you gave me the other night while I was home. It really was delicious.

Right after I got home, my friend Shelby Trice rang me up and I invited him and his wife up to the house to eat dinner with me. We really had a swell time. It was about the best week-end I ever spent. We had the mackerel, some beef chops, cold asparagus spears, and hot bread and butter. To drink, we had beer and wine. I really enjoyed the fish very much.

We didn't finish up until after twelve o'clock. I then drove the guests up to their house.

The next morning I got up for five-thirty Mass, feeling pretty tired. After Mass I ate a very small breakfast. I was still pretty full from the night before. We then talked a while and read the paper. At eight o'clock we moved out to the train station.

The train didn't leave until after nine o'clock. I bid my last farewell and the train pulled out.

I got back into camp at 4:30. I had asked if they could stop at Camp McCain. The conductor said he could. This saved me time and money.

Well, I've got to go, so I'll say good-bye. Give my love to all.

Lovingly,
Morris

* * * * *

Somewhere on the East Coast
July 30, 1944

Dear Mom and Dad,

Our trip over was very fine. It was executed with the grand air of "know-how," and was the best piece of collective action that I have seen since in the Army. No sooner had we gotten on board than we pulled out. We had pretty good accommodations coming over and the meals were very fine—in comparison with other Army chow we've had.

After this trip I am of the opinion that the railroads must consider us good passengers. Certainly there was no need of sending our cars out to the yards to be cleaned as is done after almost every "civilian" trip. The cars, if anything, were cleaner when we got off than when we got on. The reason is this: After each meal, which is served to us in our seats on paper plates and in paper cups, we swept the floor and then mopped it. The brooms and mops are passed on from compartment to compartment on through the car until the job is done. The plates, wooden forks, and paper cups are picked up in a basket and probably burned in the kitchen. Thus, there is no littering of the countryside with all sorts of trash and rubble.

Things are swell here. There are regular beer halls that sell ice-cold beer on tap, and there are Post Exchanges that are combinations of department stores and hot dog stands, with a jewelry counter thrown in. There is a loudspeaker over which comes popular music and the latest news. The first song I heard, however, struck a sour note. Its title—"Welcome Home."

On our way over, I passed through Cleveland. I thought of Paul while going by. So near and yet so far. If Aunt Eleanor will send me his address, I'll try to write him one of these days.

Give my regards to all. Write soon and often. Tell Mrs. Murphy hello.

Lovingly,
Morris

Somewhere on the East Coast
July 31, 1944

Dear Mom and Dad,

The morale situation with me is pretty bad. I have had one letter in a little over a week. That was the one from William with Mother's note enclosed. Perhaps, though, the fault is not with you at all. I am now wondering whether you have received my change-of-address cards. I imagine that it will take some days for the back mail to catch up. I realize that you don't have the time because both of you need all the time you have. But what about my eight brothers and sister? They must be doing something during their vacations. Have them write me. Let them tell me where they go, what they do. I hear often from William, but I am certainly interested in Kerry's progress as a baseball player. So have them write. It's a sacrifice to take time to write, especially during one's vacation, I know. I never wrote a letter until I came into the Army. But, really, don't let the tone of this letter disturb you. I don't really feel bad at all. It's just that if I could get one letter a day from someone at home, I'd be a lot happier. I'm far from home—and will be for a long time. And now a letter means a lot.

I am in the best of health and gaining weight day by day. The meals are tremendous and well done. I have a ferocious appetite, which sometimes makes me feel ashamed. Besides three heavy meals I usually spend a good deal of my $1.66 per day at the PX on ice cream, soft drinks, hot dogs, and other stuff.

I haven't seen Trice since that last week-end but I guess he's all right. I guess he was just born with a golden horseshoe in his pants. I could never pull his tricks and get away with it. However, that week-end was really a good one. I was glad that he and his wife were able to come up. I had known him from the time I took my first draft board physical and I had grown to like him more and more right along. We used to pull all kinds of crazy tricks together, such as putting bunks on the roofs of the huts back at Benning so that our other "buddies" would have one devil of a time getting to bed after a late show or pass. I guess we both remember the time we were in bivouac when it wasn't enough to shake a fellow to wake him up, but it was necessary to rub him to start the circulation. Then, after you knocked the ice off of your feet, you could walk to the chow line. Yes, we'll agree its funny now, tho' it didn't seem so then. Yes, he's a pretty nice fellow. With the job he's got, he'll get through this problem and gain weight doing it. Maybe someday he and his wife and you and I will sit down again to a dinner of mackerel, beef steak, beer, and wine. But let's hope it'll be in the daytime instead of the middle of the night.

How's the bank's case against LSU coming along? Have the judges given any decision? Maybe someday I'll be a lawyer. I liked as much of it as I had. But that's a long ways off.

Give my regards to all.

Lovingly,
Morris

* * * * *

Somewhere on the East Coast
August 2, 1944

Dear Mom and Dad,

We shall probably leave in a very few days. I would advise you to use V-Mail in writing me in the future. It will be some time, in all probability, before you hear from me. That is within the next few letters.

I was on pass to New York. I couldn't phone because the delay was too long. I got around and saw as much of the town as I could during the few hours I was there. I won't get another pass because time won't allow. Write soon. All my letters are censored except this one because I am having someone mail it in town.

All my love,
Morris

* * * * *

Somewhere on the East Coast
August 4, 1944

Dear Mom and Dad,

I got Dad's letter with the enclosure on yesterday, the third. It sure didn't take much time for it to get straightened out. Since the last long letter I wrote I've gotten almost two letters a day. I am very glad to get them. They help a lot.

The other day I had a pass and went in to see what I could of New York. There is so much to see that it is impossible to do so on pass. However, I did get around quite a bit. Saw the Statue of Liberty, and tried a meal at Fraunce's Tavern, as Aunt Winnie had suggested in a letter I got from her a couple or so days back. Then there were other places we went and things we did. I walked up and down Broadway and through and through Times Square, both of which are overrated as to size, brilliance, color, or what-not. Perhaps war has changed this thoroughfare's dress. But it has done so to Canal Street in NO, and Canal Street is in my opinion still the greatest in the world.

There are all kinds of facilities up here for servicemen. In New York City there are huge centers at which one can obtain all the information one wants, and, in some places, all the food one wants. I think a serviceman could spend a furlough in New York without ever spending a dime. Tickets to all of the plays are given free, having been subscribed for, I suppose, by leading organizations and corporations, etc. However, the caliber of modern plays, and especially the ones adopted for the New York stage, are very low. Most of them rely on the vulgar element in human nature for their success. I have read about them but did not go to see any.

One of the great spectacles that I ever hope to see is New York Harbor. And beyond the ships and wooden wharves and stone warehouses, and above the dirty tenements, rise the towers of the greatest city in the world. Still untouched by war, still growing. And seeing all of this, one can thank God. For we have never seen, nor felt, the despair or horror that other cities through the world have in the past five years.

I welcomed Dad's letter. It was the first I had heard from him in a long time. Yet it was a very interesting letter. I was extremely glad to hear that the "firm session" had produced results. This will mean a lot to both of you. And I suppose it's about time. Let me know if there is ever any other change made.

I suppose all the kids are having a grand time during their vacation. But it'll only be one short month 'til the school doors open and they'll all troop back to books and pens. Esther will be a junior or a senior?

Please get Es a very good present for me for her birthday. I have plenty of money and will have for a good time yet. I'll wire it or send a money order. But not for some time.

Also send me Geo. Reinecke's address again. I just can't keep track of it. Keep me informed of all the birthdays and graduations. I have received letters from both Will and Es.

That's all for awhile. Give my love to all.

Your loving son,
Morris

Somewhere on the East Coast
August 4, 1944

Dear Dad,

I received your welcomed letter on yesterday the third. It seems it didn't take long for the postmaster to get my address straightened out. Thanks a lot for the five bucks. I have plenty of money and nothing to do with it. I can't spend it anyplace. I'll probably send it home in a money order in a week or so, or as soon as I can. My pay will continue high until I can get my allotments straightened out. I had intended to have a $7.50 bond taken out and a $40 allotment sent home to be put in my account. However, the latter didn't go through as yet, and I might have to start at it all over again by making another application.

I won't be able to do anything for Esther's birthday, so I have asked Mother to get her a very fine present. I have the money so I wish that after you get it, let me know the cost and I'll send a money order.

The mail situation is fine now. I'm getting an average of two letters a day, which helps a lot. I appreciate all the letters, even though it is impossible for me to answer them. The next letter I write will be to Es, I guess, and then I'll try to write to William. I have gotten letters from both and I would like to answer.

Well, I've got to get this in so it can get out. So long.

Your loving son,
Morris

P.S. Glad to hear that everything got straightened out.

* * * * *

Somewhere on the East Coast
August 16, 1944

Miss Ogie Joyce
1904 Calhoun St.
New Orleans, Louisiana

Dear Aunt Ogie,

Today I got some letters long overdue. Among them I found yours of about the fourth. It takes some time for the mail to catch up with us over here. The situation seems excellent over here. Our troops have hit South France just like I told Dad they would in one of my letters some time back. If the armies of northern France and the armies of South France should meet soon, I think the war here will soon be over.

In re *Going My Way,* I saw that picture some time back while in the States. I thought it was really good. *Home in Indiana* showed also, but I didn't get to see it.

I thank all of you for your prayers.

The boys are fixing their beds for the night and it's getting pretty dark, so I say so long. I've got to spread my blankets yet.

Give my love to all. Remember me to Paul Jr.

Lovingly,
Morris

* * * * *

Somewhere aboard ship
August 22, 1944

Dear Mom and Dad,

This, I am afraid, will be a very short letter. There isn't much to write about for the simple reason that there isn't much I *can* write about.

I am on board ship somewhere, but I have hesitated to write because of the reason stated above. However, I have read many books lately by authors known for their super detective stories. Oppenheim, Christie, and Gardner are about the best.

I sweated out going over and already I have begun to think about getting back. When I do come back, I am sure that I won't mind keeping my nose in the law books for a while.

Went to Confession before Mass on Sunday.

Give my love to all. Write.

Your loving son,
Morris

Somewhere aboard ship
[V-Mail, postmarked August 22, 1944]

Dear Mom and Dad,

We only get two meals a day, one in the morning, one in the evening. But they suffice. The food is pretty good and there is plenty of it. The weather has been fine and there seems to be no forthcoming change. There has been no seasickness because there has been no cause for it. Cards are a great pastime. So are dice, if you only stand and watch. A fellow had just covered a bet of $96 out on deck when a gust of wind blew it overboard. So it's not always the roll of the dice that makes one lose.

How are the kids getting along with their vacation? I guess they're enjoying it as much as ever. Tell everybody that I'll write when I can and ask them to write me.

Your loving son,
Morris

P A R T   F O U R

EUROPEAN THEATER OF OPERATIONS

AUGUST 1944–JANUARY 1945

Wars may be fought with weapons, but they are won by men. It is the spirit of men who follow and of the man who leads that gains the victory.

—*General George S. Patton Jr.*

* * * * *

Somewhere in England
[V-Mail, postmarked August 23, 1944]

Dear Mom and Dad,

I am trying to get this out to send my best wishes to Esther on her birthday. I am someplace in the European Theatre. Our trip over was very nice and we saw some beautiful country on our way to our present location. The land is well cared for and the towns and villages are very neat and clean. When I can I'll write again, and perhaps will be able to say more. Give my love to all.

Loving son,
Morris

* * * * *

Somewhere in England
[V-Mail, postmarked August 23, 1944]

Dear Mom and Dad,

Last night I had the best rest that I have had in a long time. I went to sleep in a position and woke up in the same this morning. Although it's pretty warm during the day, it gets very cold at night. But I slept like a log and didn't feel it (the cold) until a few minutes after I woke up.

The meals aren't too good; that is, they don't taste as good. However, quantity, I suppose, replaces quality. There is plenty to eat.

I received four letters from you all to-day. I think I have received all that you wrote. I got Daddy's letters, and I thought I had written him and thanked him. I heard from Kerry, Esther, and William in today's mail.

My eyes seem to be improving, so don't worry about me. I'm in good health except for a head cold which I caught on the way over. It doesn't even bother me.

The country around here is beautiful, consisting of rolling, cultivated fields and pasturelands.

There are no PXs here, and I guess shows and electric lights are out for the duration.

Your loving son,
Morris

* * * * *

[V-Mail]
ETOUSA,
August 27, 1944

Dear Mom and Dad,

I am writing this to wish you the best of happiness and joy on your twentieth wedding anniversary. I am only sorry that I will not be there to celebrate with you. I don't know if this will reach you in time, but I hope it does. Do not worry because I have not written. I am all right and in the best of health. I couldn't write any sooner than I do because of circumstances.

Today is a very beautiful day. One of few that we have had since over here. The weather is usually gray and damp, and a part of the time cold. When it rains it gets muddy and the mud makes things hard. But today is really grand.

There is a volleyball game going on now. Our CO, our Colonel, some of our officers, and a group of enlisted men make up the teams. I shall try to write again soon. Remember me to all.

Lovingly,
Morris

[V-Mail]
ETOUSA
August 30, 1944

Dear Mom and Dad,

I received your letter of the 23rd. I cannot understand the hold-up in the mail. Certainly in this time you should have started to receive my letters. I wrote rather regularly up 'til about a week ago.

I appreciate all the letters that I have been receiving from all of you. However, it is impossible for me to answer all of them. I hope that no one is offended. I think of everybody. I have Paul Jr.'s address and will, one of these days, write him. By some chance he might wind up around here and I may run into him someday. I would have liked very much to do something for you on your anniversary, but all means of communication, as Dad suggested, are for military purposes only.

All my love.

Lovingly,
Morris

* * * * *

[V-Mail]
ETOUSA
September 1, 1944

Dear Mom and Dad,

The handwriting might not be so good, as the candles don't give too much light. A few days will see the end of the fifth year of the war. Perhaps in a few more days we shall all see the end of this war over here. This will be some cause for celebration. They say that back home most of the people think that it's all over but the shouting. But it's far from that. Although most of the Germans are suddenly getting sick of this mess, there are still a large number of SS troops that still believe in Adolf, and that will die rather than surrender.

However, I feel the help of your prayers but I would ask that you offer them also for all the members of my outfit. Pray for our success and safe return.

A few days ago we got the European Theatre of Operations ribbons. Nice looking. Maybe some day we'll get some gold stars for them.

Give my regards to Aunt Winnie.

All my love,
Morris

Somewhere in England
[V-mail, postmarked September 4, 1944]

Mr. William J. Hume
1321 Cambronne St.
New Orleans, Louisiana

Dear Uncle Billy,

Today, Sunday, offers the first opportunity that I have had since leaving the States of writing you. There isn't much one can write on one of these V-Mail forms, but then, there isn't much to write about.

It is now about a few minutes before ten and I am writing this on some slabs of concrete which will be used as stepping-stones to keep us from getting too muddy. The days are long here for I write this by daylight. The other fellows are still playing rugby out on the drill field. Others are letting down the sides of their tents and fixing their beds for the night.

Our trip over was very nice and we had the best accommodations that could be had. Far, however, from a first-class berth in peacetime. Our food over here is just about as good as it was in the States, and there is plenty of it. The English countryside presents a nice picture with its stone houses and fertile fields.

Well, I hope this finds you in the best of health, and I remain,

Sincerely,
Morris Jr.

* * * * *

Somewhere in England
[V-mail, postmarked September 4, 1944]

Dear Mom and Dad,

Today I received your letter of the thirteenth. It seems that it takes on an average of seven days for the mail to get through. Since today is Sunday I shall try to write to as many people as time and stationery will allow. Everything here is rationed. Soap, razor blades, and other necessities are strictly rationed even to GIs. Even we have ration cards. On this card items are divided into four categories: those that can be had over a week, once every two weeks, once every four weeks, and once every eight weeks.

I thank all of you for your Masses and prayers and I remember all of you in my prayers. Mass to-day was at four o'clock in the afternoon.

Last night I had a pass to Gloucester. Had a terrible time. Spent a lot of time getting there and then had only a couple of hours before starting back. There is nothing to do and no place to go. The restaurants can sell only fish and chips (fried potatoes). If you want wine, it is very expensive. The beer and cider run out too fast and the barkeepers hate to sell us a drop. So we came back to our tents rather disappointed. But the thought of the swell folks back home is always a lift.

Your loving son,
Morris

* * * * *

The following letter of September 11, 1944, is Morris's first since landing on Utah Beach, D-Day Plus 94, September 8, 1944.

Somewhere in France
September 11, 1944

Dear Mom and Dad,

This is just a letter to let you know that I am all right and in good health. Today I got your letters acknowledging that you had heard from me. I received six letters all together from Will, Richard, Kerry, you, Aunt Ogie, and Aunt Eleanor. I wish you would tell them all hello for me and give them all my love. If I ever get a chance to write them I will, but I doubt it.

To-day, Sunday, I went to a ten o'clock Mass held against the side of an old French house. When "les paysans" heard there was going to be a Mass, they changed from their everyday dirty rags into their walking-out clothes and attended. I received Communion.

This evening I went up and talked with some of the people in their big stone houses. When they speak slow, I can understand. I came back with some fresh milk and apple cider.

Enclosed is a hundred-franc note. It is Invasion money printed, I believe, in the United States, and backed, I presume, by the U.S. Treasury. It's pretty fancy, though it's worth only two dollars in American money. But the French have more faith in it than in their own fancy franc notes. Save it for me as a souvenir.

At present we're bivouacked in an apple orchard somewhere in France. We stew apples at every chance.

For Christmas I would appreciate a rosary along with some food. This is one year I won't be able to use toilet sets and bath slippers. Try to send a fruitcake if you think it will keep.

Love to all,
Morris

* * * * *

Somewhere in France
[Postmarked September 19, 1944]

Dear Mom and Dad,

Yesterday I received eleven letters dating as far back as the 19th of August. We're now in another apple orchard somewhere in France. I don't have the time to write much, nor the ink.

I had a lot of junk I had picked up, such as fuses, German ammunition, and one of their potato-masher grenades, but I got rid of them. After the war is over I'll probably be able to get anything I want for a souvenir.

For Christmas send me some candy—chocolate. The French children haven't seen candy in three years. Most of the towns are now in shambles. The French will need plenty of help after the war. When we pass through a town the people come out and stand and wave and yell like it was Mardi Gras back home. Sometimes they throw flowers and apples. We throw cigarettes and candy. I get along very well on my French, which is a good help in getting bread and butter, eggs, and sweet cider. The other night a Frenchman gave me and four of my buddies some of his best cognac. It's got a kick that would knock anybody's ears off.

I went to Mass and Communion twice last week. We were lucky to have had services.

Here's hoping this reaches you in a month.

All my love,
Morris

P.S. Heard from Aunt Hy and all the gang. Have Will tell Numa and all the boys hello. If you ever run into Monita Imbert, tell her hello for me.

Somewhere in France
September 26, 1944

Dear Mom and Dad,

I would like to ask you not to worry about not receiving more from me than you do. There will be times when you might not hear from me for weeks at a time. Please understand that circumstances do not permit any amount of continuity of mail. I don't think that again for the duration you will receive more than a few letters a month.

I am feeling fine and in the best of health. Yesterday the Chaplain said a special Mass and I attended and received Holy Communion. War has made prayer, with me, a serious habit.

I suppose that everyone is back in school getting used to the old grind. I sure would like to be back, and maybe someday when this is over I'll return, more serious, to the law books and instead of being a debit I'll become a sterling credit. So I pray and hope. I have on hand some 2,850 francs, which amounts to about $57. I shall never spend this. I would like to send it home. In which case I would like about $15 to go to Dr. Bonomo for a medal to be awarded to whom he deems the most deserving member of either of the Dramatic Societies. I shall continue this letter in another V-Mail.

September 26, continued...

I enjoy very much looking back on all the plays I was in. In my estimation I gained a lot from those plays. They offered good times and new friends. I never knew how good any of the productions were because friends never give adverse criticism in small matters such as those. But I enjoyed all the hullabaloo and congratulations that came after the final curtain fell. I appreciated very much winning the award for my portrayal of King Lear. I would now like to advance that amount of money for a medal to encourage the best of acting on the part of the players in the plays.

I hope that Will was able to start back to school in the best of health after his short rest period. Tell him to pay attention to his temper and his books and to drop any silly notions of joining up anything until he's called. Let him heed the voice of experience.

I can't answer all the letters I've received. But tell everybody hello for me—the Sellers, Stuarts, Kellys, Fonsecas, Joyces, and Redmanns. Tell them I appreciate hearing from them a lot. I don't want them to think that I am slighting them. I hope that all are well and I send all my love.

Morris

Somewhere in France
September 27, 1944

Dear Mom and Dad,

Today I got a wonderful boost in morale upon the receipt of twenty-one letters from all the folks. The one outstanding subject was the grand celebration of your twentieth wedding anniversary. Other subjects included everything from Kerry's letter telling of his trip to Abita Springs to your letter telling of your anniversary party. I really felt homesick after reading all the letters. The last was dated the twelfth.

I was glad to hear that David didn't mind starting school. I hope he gets along all right. I don't think William should interest himself in mechanics as a career. Perhaps it is a passing fancy which will vanish as he matures. I earnestly hope that he will settle down soon and go back to his laboratories. I am sure, if he persists on mechanics, that there are many courses in physics and chemistry concerning things which from a point of theory would be helpful in the practical work. The bulk of the letters were from the kids—most from Kerry—telling of their experiences, their acquisitions and accomplishments.

Tell Fr. Castel hello for me and all of the nuns who remember me. Give my regards to the Brunos and to any of the other people that you might run across from time to time. If you ever get a chance, read the GI Bill of Rights. If I ever get out of this, I'll let the government pay for my education for a while.

Regards to all the family. Thank them for their letters. I can't possibly answer them, but I appreciate them more than presents.

All my love,
Morris

* * * * *

Somewhere in France
September 30, 1944

Dear Mom and Dad,

At present the letters from you and the folks at home are fairly pouring in. Some days ago I got twenty-one letters at one mail call. Then the next day I got about eleven, and yesterday I got two. I don't know if you send the V-Mail by Air Mail. That is about the fastest way of all. Regular Air Mail is pretty fast, too.

Before I forget, the correct cable address is AMILEA as written on the typewritten letter sent out by the company. My letter had it wrong.

I have just received your letter of the 16th in which you speak of Ronnie's birthday and the advent of Uncle Paul's and Aunt Eleanor's silver wedding anniversary. To-day I will write them and extend congratulations. I doubt if the letter shall get there on time, but I will try.

Today, too, I also received a letter from Aunt Winnie. She asks what I should like for Christmas. There is no use to send V-Mail or any kind of stationery because the company supplies us with sufficient stationery. There is really nothing I need. In the last month I have spent only about three hundred francs. Some fancy food like you have sent before would be all right. Perhaps a sheet of six-cent Air-Mail stamps will help get my mail home faster.

Love,
Morris

* * * * *

Somewhere in France
September 30, 1944

Dear Aunt Eleanor & Uncle Paul,

Just a line to tell all of you at 1905 "Hello." There isn't much I can write about because almost everything I could say about me contains, perhaps, a little military information. Probably the only thing I can say is that I am somewhere in France and in the best of health. This may not sound like much, but over here it's a lot. Before coming into France I used to think of how much mud and rain and slop we'd have to live in. However, I was wrong. England may have been a rainy country, but France is mostly sunshine, apples, peaches, grapes, and wine. (It is right now at any rate.)

I know that I am a little early in regard to extending congratulations on your silver wedding anniversary, but I might not be writing again for some time. So I would like to wish both of you continued years of happiness and love. With lots of love and fondest regards, I remain,

Your loving nephew,
Morris

Somewhere in France
October 2, 1944

Dear Mom and Dad,

To-day I received your letter of Sept. 18. So you see, it takes some time for a letter to get home or, rather, to reach me. You ask if I know how much you miss me and how much you long for me to be with you again. Because of my own desires, the magnitude of which there is no comprehension, I can judge how much you miss me. There are no words that can describe the longing in my heart to see again the loved ones, the house, the walls, the lawns, the trees, wherein are wrapt the treasured memories of our normal time.

This war is far from over. Where once I read of victory by the first of October, I can now read of plans for a winter campaign. I guess we all thought too little of the quality of Nazi fanaticism. We should have known that a people that had made millions of personal sacrifices from 1933 on, and who had been so thoroughly educated with the criminal doctrines of a criminal leader, and whose every effort for the past ten years was toward World domination, that such a people would die rather than surrender. Their actions foretell their punishment. Germany must be destroyed.

Love to all,
Morris

* * * * *

Somewhere in France
October 5, 1944

Dear Mom and Dad,

I am using this kind of stationery instead of V-Mail because I am enclosing a money order for $60. I believe I told you about sending home some money before, about three or four letters back. I said I would send $57, but changed it to $60. If you want, you might get Aunt Eleanor and Uncle Paul a present for me for their silver wedding anniversary.

Since you will have probably been notified by now that I was wounded, I want to ask you not to worry. It was very slight and I didn't even know I was hit. The other day a few of us who had been injured or wounded were decorated by the Commanding General and given the Purple Heart. He asked me where I was wounded and how it happened. There was only a slight wound in the thigh, so there is nothing to worry about. I have been back with my outfit for a good while and was only absent from duty a few days. I am sending the medal in its box home for you folks to keep. I'll try to send it today if I can find suitable wrappings for it.

I get your letters in bunches. You all don't know how much I love you for them.

Well, here's hoping this thing will be over soon, at least by 1945.

All my love,
Your eldest son,
Morris

* * * * *

Somewhere in France
Saturday, October 14, 1944

Dear Mom and Dad,

Well, I'm back in a rest period again and glad to be here. While up on line it's impossible to write. There are so many interruptions, you know. If it isn't raining rain, it's raining something else. I'll take the rain. However, when it did rain, we had a chance of catching some of it in a tin can in order to shave. Some didn't shave for a long while and between the whiskers and the mud, 'twas enough to scare us.

I rode in a jeep one day back to the Battalion Aid Station to get the bandage on my leg changed. The mud and water were hub-deep, and we had a regular "hog wash." At least it sounded like the *Jennie Wilson* smashing through the groundswells of the Mississippi Sound. My leg is perfectly all right. I was only off my feet for about three days and that, because I didn't have any shoes. I couldn't afford to walk in my stocking feet for fear of catching cold.

Believe me, Mother, I have developed a fervent devotion to the Sacred Heart of Jesus. During an artillery barrage I was laying in my slit trench, which is a shallow trench just long enough and deep enough to allow you to get below ground level, and I was praying. I thought that I'd look through my pockets for a crucifix or a medal to hold in my hand during the fireworks. I came across the little leather case which Fr. O'Connor from up at the university had given me. I opened it and saw the three medals attached to the undercover. In the pocket of it was a badge of the Sacred Heart. It was the first time I had ever taken it out to look at it, and I read this sentence over the picture of the Sacred Heart: "Cease! The Sacred Heart is with me." Of that instant of which I read, the barrage ceased. I lay in my trench for a few minutes after it was over and I thanked God for the favor granted. You might give my regards to Fr. O'Connor and tell him this story and thank him again for the little leather case.

I have been getting your letters, all of which I save after I destroy my address on them. When getting ready for the night, I usually read through some of your old letters and then I read my prayers from one of the two prayer books that I got some time ago from the Chaplain. Then the long night begins, and I say Rosary after Rosary. The time passes fast this way. Over here there is about twelve hours of light and twelve hours of dark. Believe me, it really gets chilly.

Don't worry. Whatever happens can't be helped. These are unnatural times and the usual and natural course of things cannot be expected.

I got your letter telling me what you'd send for Christmas. Boy, it really sounds good. I was thinking this morning, when our Lieutenant passed out some cookies he'd gotten from home, what I could do to a box like you said you were sending. Send me about a box a week from now on. It'll take months to get here but I'll really appreciate it. Wrap it well and pack it so it won't get ruined.

I hear from every one in the family down to little Robert. I was glad to hear from Kerry and Richard that Jesuit started the season by defeating Peters. I hope that they cop the crown. I know that William is back from his trip by now. I hope he enjoyed himself as much as I used to with Roy and Numa and the Tri-Sig crowd. You remember how one of those trips ended? Daddy and I used to laugh when I told it. I can laugh right now when I think about it. I wonder if Sheriff Hebert got re-elected. That was some experience, but it'll never equal this for thrills and chills. "But I'm not looking for thrills and chills!" I keep telling them!

I get letters regularly from Esther telling me of her activities up at school and at the USO. I suppose I don't offer much encouragement to you to write letters, but I appreciate every one I get from you folks.

Give my love and best wishes to all the folks. I'll try to write everyone during this period. No telling where I'll be by the time you receive this. I'll write again this afternoon.

Your loving son,
Morris

P.S. Enclosed are some pictures taken a long time ago at camp at the old swimming hole. They finally arrived here in France. Love.

AMERICAN RED CROSS

Somewhere in France
October 15, 1944

Dear Mom and Dad,

Don't let the stationery scare you. It's all I can get my hands on. Can't even get V-Mail at present. Today I received your letter of the 26th. I know you worry a lot, but affairs to which Mr. Regan extended you an invitation are just the thing to lift your morale. Don't refrain from celebrating at any time on my account. You must know that when you are having a good time, I am happy. Go to those parties and then write me what a good time you had. We grow old too fast naturally without worrying ourselves into old age. I know that you think of me always. I spend every living moment thinking of you and remembering you in my prayers. I pray that you are well and that all are in God's graces.

Give my love and regard to the Kellys, the Stuarts, the Joyces, and Mrs. Murphy. Also to all my friends that you might run into from time to time.

Praying for the end of the war, I remain forever

Your loving son,
Morris

* * * * *

Somewhere in France
October 17, 1944

Mrs. Joseph Sellers
3020 Paris Ave.
New Orleans, Louisiana

Dear Aunt Hy,

Back in a rest period and having a pretty good time. Although after having been on line for a while they still give us a schedule back here, just like basic training. Today, for example, we had calisthenics, close-order drill, first aid, and other stuff. It isn't hard, just boring. Yesterday I had my first bath in a month, although I still haven't changed underwear—a bath isn't much good, is it? But it was good while it lasted. To show you how much it meant, I went thirty miles both ways to take it and I was allowed only three minutes under the water. So it goes.

Back here we are near a town and we can get passes to town. It's a pretty good-size town, and there is plenty of wine and food. The other night I went to a hotel for dinner. We had soup, then a very well-mixed meat salad of beef brisket, then the main course of potatoes brabant and beef steak. With this was served a salad of fresh lettuce. To drink we had some pretty good white wine. All of this cost forty francs per serving.

How are Uncle Joe and Margaret and Jodie Boy? When I get back, I'll probably recognize you and Joe, but Margaret and Joe Jr. I probably won't even know.

Hoping it ends soon, I remain,

Your loving nephew,
Morris

* * * * *

Somewhere in France
[V-mail, postmarked October 17, 1944]

Dear Aunt Winnie,

I would like to apologize for not answering your letters. I presume you understand that I couldn't because we've been on line. I am now back in a rest period which lasts for a few days, and which affords me the opportunity of catching up on some of my correspondence.

The war is far from over. The German people are now solidly behind the German Army. Our lightning-like drives have tended only to unite the civilian and military elements of the German nation. By the time you will get this, the German town of Aachen will probably have fallen, but it serves now as an example of the German desire for extermination rather than surrender.

However, the problem of winning the war is almost solved. But for the many years of Allied occupation there will continue fanatical underground resistance which shall cost us much. I said above that the problem is almost solved—but ahead there lies a rough and bloody road of many battles. There is so much talk about a quick end. Every doughboy's conversation deals with his hopes of returning home. But his dreams are only dreams. They keep us happy, though. During this period of rest we sit around the fire and recall the good times we've had back in civilian life and we talk of what we'll do when the Army sets us free. But each one wonders in his heart, "Will I ever see the day?"

I get plenty of mail from home. And like many other G.I. Joes, I live only for the letters and the PX rations. Darn, I read those letters from home and I change. If I'm in a bad mood I get melancholy and brood like an old dog. If I'm in a good mood I get even happier. A letter is so much like a visit home that I often sit and read and re-read the old mail to get a larger view of how the folks are living.

I hope that you and all the folks enjoy the best of health. Give my regards to Uncle Claude and to son and daughter.

Your loving nephew,
Morris

* * * * *

Somewhere in France
[V-mail, postmarked October 19, 1944]

Dear Mom and Dad,

To-day I had KP, or what might be called the equal of it. I and three others had the detail of cleaning the field ranges of the company kitchen. It was some job, this being the first time they were cleaned since we hit France. The dirt and hardened grease had to be scraped off with knives. Then the stoves were scrubbed with hot soapy water, then washed with gasoline, and finally brushed with a wire brush.

I received your letter of Oct. 3rd telling what and how you were sending my Christmas packages. It sounds very good. I am sure that I will enjoy it very much. In fact, your description of it made my mouth water. The whole trouble is that Christmas is two months away! I would like you to send me other packages from time to time with chocolate candy and cookies in them. They'd really come in handy. Some days when on line we had a hard time getting two meals. The food, when we got it, had to be carried up by a carrying party because of the German artillery and the condition of the roads, ruined by the rains. But whenever there was chow to be had, there were a bunch of hungry GIs willing to go back and get it.

Don't worry. This business is my duty, my present responsibility. It's a hard job. But God wills it.

Your loving son,
Morris

AMERICAN RED CROSS

Somewhere in France
October 19, 1944

Miss Ogie Joyce
1905 Calhoun St.
New Orleans, Louisiana

Dear Ogie,

Just a line to let you know I'm feeling fine and that I'm in the best of health. At present I'm back in a rest period, taking it easy for a few days. These rest periods are pretty good, but for obvious reasons they can't last too long. They usually last only a few days and then we go back on line.

I'm telling you a guy really gets to saying his prayers up there during the long, dark hours of the night and during the awful minutes of artillery barrages. It's a terrible life when compared to civilian life. Some of the fellows I used to buddy with are dead now. It's hard to conceive that they are gone. But in this game the players come and go. For us, it is our present job, there are no bonuses and no pink slips unless the Grim Sceptre hands them out. And there aren't any sit-down strikes and there are no forty-hour weeks with time and a half for overtime. And the better you do your job, the harder is the grind. But the harder you work, the sooner the job is done. But when it is finished, there is no product, no finished fabric. There is nothing but shattered dreams, ruined cities, broken houses, and bleeding hearts. But it's got to be, even though after the game is over, there is no winner.

How are the Stuarts, Aunt Eleanor and Uncle Paul, and Aunt Lala? How is Paul Jr.? I hope he hasn't run into any of this yet, and I hope he never shall. How is Miss Helen Clayton? I hear pretty much about her and Paul Jr.

Well, the most of luck and all my love to you. Give my regards to all, and give my love to Aunt Lala. Remember me to Paul.

Your loving nephew,
Morris

Somewhere in France
October 21, 1944

Dear Mom and Dad,

Today I received your cablegram of the twelfth. It took nine days. But it had me scared. I was afraid to open it even, fearing bad news from home.

Well, we're still resting, but I don't know for how long. I read in our Army newspaper that the Germans had formed a "pitchfork Army" which Herr Goering has ordered to defend "every house, every ditch, every bush." This shows you what the Allies are up against. This shows you how close to being finished the Germans think this war is. Germany is itself a fortress. Its people to a man guard its walls. Hitler in one of his latest speeches said that he would take peace now if we would guarantee the integrity of the German state. To quote Winston Churchill—"What kind of people does he think we are?"

Give my special regards to the Sellers. I don't think I have written them in a good while. Remember me to everyone.

Your loving son,
Morris

* * * * *

AMERICAN RED CROSS

Somewhere in France
Sunday, October 22, 1944

Dear Dad,

Today I received your letter of Oct. 5. It certainly was a pleasure to hear from you personally. Yes, Mother and the children write me all about the family, but I still appreciate getting a letter from you now and then.

During and after Mass this morning I kept thinking of home and all the folks. I guess the memory of home is a soldier's most precious possession, with one exception—his family. This is one of the reasons that I worry so much about your health and Mom's health and all the kids. You're all I've got. I have no worldly possession but you. I have no girlfriend to come home to, no wife and children, as have a good many of my friends. All I have and all I love are my parents, my brothers, and my sister. That's why you mean so much to me. I hoard every letter I get from home, and in my spare moments I re-read them. As I said before, they're like a touch of home.

Every GI dreams of getting home. And he knows that the sooner the war ends, the sooner he'll be able to go back home.

Lloyd's of London said the war would be over by Oct. 31. By the time this reaches you, we'll know if they were right. But if you ask any soldier when he thinks it'll be over, you're sure of a pessimistic reply. After all, can you blame us?

It would be a queer trick if you'd win the bank case in the Court of Appeals of the Supreme Court, wouldn't it?

Best of luck.

Son,
Morris

P.S. Have my allotments come through, and have you gotten my money order for $60 yet?

* * * * *

Somewhere in France
October 22, 1944

Dear Mom and Dad,

Today, Sunday, I attended Mass in town. It was a special Mass just for GIs. The sermon was preached in English by the French pastor. His accent was not pronounced as is the accent of most French who try to speak English. In his sermon he expressed thanks on behalf of himself and his country for the sacrifices the Americans have made in liberating France. This was perhaps the first time that any Frenchman has, to us, expressed his thanks in words. Many have thrown fruit and flowers to us as we passed through their towns; many have come to us in the field offering cider and wine; a little boy once screamed, "Vive les Americains!" as we neared the lines. But never had I heard a man's heartfelt thanks expressed so eloquently and so sincerely as they were in this priest's sermon. Tomorrow we are having a Mass offered for the repose of the souls of the dead in our company.

I hope all are well. I suppose you're going nuts with Christmas shopping coming up. I hope all are doing well at school. Tell Will I don't want to hear anything but good of him.

Love,
Morris

Somewhere in France
[V-mail, postmarked October 22, 1944]

Mrs. Claude J. Kelly
4139 Gen. Taylor St.
New Orleans, Louisiana

Dear Aunt Winnie,

I thought I'd drop you a few lines while hanging around the campfire waiting for mail call. I haven't received any mail in the last three days. I did, however, get a cablegram from Mom and Dad. It was sent out the twelfth of the month and I didn't receive it until the twenty-first. So cablegrams don't get here any faster than V-Mail. I believe regular Air Mail is the fastest of all. This letter will be sent Air Mail. Let me know how long it takes.

Well, I guess Winnie and Claude are getting ready for examinations now. Also at this time of year you're probably starting your Christmas shopping. Last year I was away for Christmas, and this year I'm even farther away. I hope that maybe by next Christmas I'll be at least back in the U.S. Of course, you never can tell. I haven't even seen this Noel yet.

I hope this letter finds you and Uncle Claude in the best of health, and Winnie and Claude in the firsts at school.

Your loving nephew,
Morris

* * * * *

Somewhere in France
Monday, October 23, 1944

Dear Mom and Dad,

Today the company attended a Requiem Mass for the deceased members of our company. For the first time in five years I served as an altar boy.

There isn't anything new to write because there isn't anything to write about. I am writing this letter by candlelight inside my pup tent. I say candlelight, but there are no candles over here. There is only waste fat with a piece of goods for a wick. It is held together by a pasteboard container.

In one of the cafés of a nearby town, which has not yet power enough for electric lights, they hollow out a big potato, pour the molten grease into it, stick a wick into it, and let the grease harden. This gives pretty good light, but the grease softens and the wick slips down into it. To remedy this the Frenchman usually sticks a needle through the potato and wick to hold the latter erect. "C'est la guerre." (Oh, well, Esther will tell you what the last word is.)

In your last letter of the 5th you said you wished that I was back sleeping in my "own nice bed." Well, if I ever get home I'm going to stay in bed for about a week. And if I still like the idea, I'll stay in it for a month!

At present we're getting plenty of very good food. There is so much food that I can eat only about two meals a day. No kidding, if I eat any more I get sick. They have bacon and eggs, fruit and cereal, bread, butter, and coffee in the morning. The next meals are, for example, pork chops and steaks with all the trimmings. Not that this is exceptional quality. But the quantity of the serving is tremendous.

Best regards to all.

Your loving son,
Morris

* * * * *

WESTERN UNION

A. N. WILLIAMS, PRESIDENT

CLASS OF SERVICE: This is a full-rate Telegram or Cablegram unless its deferred character is indicated by a suitable symbol above or preceding the address.

SYMBOLS: DL=Day Letter; NL=Night Letter; LC=Deferred Cable; NLT=Cable Night Letter; Ship Radiogram

(07)

The filing time shown in the date line on telegrams and day letters is STANDARD TIME at point of origin. Time of receipt is STANDARD TIME at point of destination

NSAH50 32 GOVT=VIA WUX WASHINGTON DC 11 220P

MRS ESTHER REDMANN=

7017 BROAD PLACE RTE MC NRLNS=

MC

October 11, 1944
2:08 PM

REGRET TO INFORM YOU YOUR SON PRIVATE FIRST CLASS MORRIS B REDMANN JR WAS SLIGHTLY WOUNDED IN ACTION EIGHTEEN SEPTEMBER IN FRANCE YOU WILL BE ADVISED AS REPORTS OF CONDITION ARE RECEIVED=

J A ULIO THE ADJUTANT GENERAL.

THE COMPANY WILL APPRECIATE SUGGESTIONS FROM ITS PATRONS CONCERNING ITS SERVICE

Somewhere in France
October 27, 1944

Dear Mom and Dad,

At present I am waiting for the mail clerk to send up to-day's mail. Yesterday I received your letters of the twelfth. Most of them deal with the War Department's telegram.

At present the sky's gray. The wind is blowing and there is the promise of rain. We have had a few days of sunshine, but even these were not enough to dry up the awful mud, and if the developing battle should see the complete defeat of the Jap Fleet, the war over there might be over in February. But this game over here will probably run into extra innings unless the Russians keep up their drive.

You asked me if I need any winter clothing. I could use a heavy turtleneck sweater, khaki in color. Get a large rather than a small one. If you can, send me chocolate candy every chance you get. Don't worry, it won't go to the French. I'm so disgusted with these people and their country that I don't do anything more for them than I have to. Some French are very pro-Nazi, many are collaborators, and many don't like Americans. Of course, the loyal French round them up and get rid of them as fast as they can. But France is still a mess, even though de Gaulle now rules it.

All my love to all.
Morris

Lloyd's of London had predicted the war would be over by the end of October 1944, creating uppermost in young soldiers' minds thoughts of peace, home, and loved ones. It was this frame of mind that prompted Morris to compose the following poem on October 30, 1944.

Peace

Ring out, ring out ye chapel bells
For peace is here once more.
Sing loud, sing loud ye birds of the sea,
Come rest upon the shore.

The trees shall blossom forth in green
The sun shall shine today
The people of the hamlet towns
Shall sing their grief away.

No more shall vultures rule the air
Nor seek a fallen prey
No more will men at other throats
For all is peace today.

Bring out the aged, crippled, maimed
For these will smile anew
On English boys from English towns
Passing in review.

They've just got back from over there,
From the trenches and the gore.
But some there are that march not here
They're gone forevermore.

The cathedral bells do peal the joy
Upon this happy day
As happy tears and joyous kisses
Chase the fears away.

But some there are that stand and wait
And clench their throats with fear
And choke themselves with muffled sobs—
They dare not shed a tear.

They are the mothers of the boys
Whose places go unfilled
Whose names appear on lengthy lists
Of the missing and the killed.

And as I stood there waving, waiting
Watching the troops go by,
I noticed a lady standing there
I heard her sniff and sigh.

"I guess wilna be home today,"
She said as she crossed the street
My heart beat hard in quickened time—
In time with the marching feet.

And a sadness crept into my soul
As the soldiers marched away
But the bells pealed forth their joyous songs
For all is peace today.

But many a wreck lies on the beach
And many a heart is torn,
And upon the breast of many a mother
The golden star is worn.

Oh, the crosses gleam white on Belgian fields
And they mark the shallow graves
Of those who fell on Belgian fields—
They will never be slaves.

The churches stand as hollow shells
Their bells shall ring no more.
And many a boy sleeps in the ground
At peace forevermore.

But from these battle graves
They all must rise some day
But, forget, forget them now
For all is peace today.

"Ah, peace, peace," the nation sighs
Forgets the things it said
Forgets the pledges made to God
Forgets, forgets—the dead.

—Morris B. Redmann Jr.
October 30, 1944

Somewhere in France
November 1, 1944

Dear Mom and Dad,

In the past few days I have received many letters from all in the family stating their concern over my being wounded. I think that is very nice of everyone. I have also gotten letters from all the children telling me of their schoolwork and of their participation in sports.

The thought of getting records from home for Christmas is a very pleasant one. I am sure I shall enjoy them very much. I shall thank you here and now for all the trouble you are taking to make my Christmas a happy one. It must have been some job getting everybody together to make the records.

I heard from Ogie, Aunt Eleanor, and Aunt Hy the other day. Hyie asked me to remember Jodie Boy in my prayers, which I do—day and night. I spend most of my time praying these days.

Today is gray with a little rain. It is also turning cold. The real winter is coming soon. I don't see how Germany can stand another winter of war. Of course, they are a very determined people. At any rate, pray God they get some sense.

Love,
Morris

The following poem written for his parents is somewhat melancholy, but reflects his deep love for them and his thoughts and longing for home.

To Mom and Dad

I feel your love shine down on me
In everything I strive to do.
It warms this heart across the sea
Much as the sun that sips the dew.

It reaches as your hand to mine
It helps me through the weary days
And makes the darkened skies near shine
And takes me where the music plays.

In all your letters that I read
The tales are of another year.
They are the tonic that I need—
The drink that brings to life good cheer.

Your words are like the rays of sun
That cast no shadows in their way
But leave the darkness all undone
And give my world eternal day.

Much as the flame set by the spark
Is this heart when yours is near.
Sweet as the song of the meadowlark
Is your love—so rich, so clear.

Perhaps there comes another day
When all the earth is warm and fair,
And children once again shall play
Without a thought, without a care.

But though that be far or near
Your love and words must be my light
My warmth and my companion dear
Through this journey, through this fight.

—Your devoted son, Morris
Somewhere in France, November 1, 1944

* * * * *

Somewhere in France
November 1, 1944

Mrs. Joseph R. Sellers
3020 Paris Ave.
New Orleans, Louisiana

Dear Aunt Hy,

I received your most welcome letter of the fourteenth just a couple of days ago. Today things seem to be quiet, so I am taking the time to write a few lines.

I hope you and Uncle Joe enjoyed yourselves on your ninth wedding anniversary and birthday celebration. I guess Margaret enjoyed the circus. Ogie, in a letter of the same day, asked me if I remembered the time she took Paul and me to the circus. I most certainly do. I seem to remember even more clearly now all the nice things that you and the whole family have done for me and my family. Such as the weeks we used to spend together, and those family gatherings on Sunday at your home in the country. Those days are among some of the most pleasant memories I have.

I hope Jodie Boy is getting along OK. I remember him in my prayers day and night as you requested. Thank you for your prayers and novenas. Give my best regards to Uncle Joe. Love to Ogie—I'll write her next chance I get.

Loving nephew,
Morris

* * * * *

WAR DEPARTMENT
THE ADJUTANT GENERAL'S OFFICE
WASHINGTON 25, D.C.

In reply refer to:
AG 201 Redmann, Morris B., Jr., 38 499 577
PC-N ETO 213
5 November 1944

Mrs. Esther Redmann
7017 Broad Place
New Orleans, Louisiana

Dear Mrs. Redmann:

I am pleased to inform you that a report has been received from the theater of operations stating that on 28 September your son, Private First Class Morris B. Redmann Jr., was returned to duty.

In view of this report, it is not expected that additional informationwill be received regarding his condition.

Sincerely yours,
J. A. Ulio
Major General
The Adjutant General

Somewhere in France
[V-Mail postmarked November 6, 1944]

Miss Ogie Joyce
1905 Calhoun
New Orleans, Louisiana

Dear Ogie,

I have before me two of your letters dated the 19th and 20th. I received them some days ago. In re your letter of the 19th: I was wounded very slightly, so slight that I didn't think anything would be done about it. I was hit by shrapnel in the leg in two places—in the knee and in the thigh. I never felt any pain, and within two minutes I had medical aid and morphine. Within an hour and a half I was on an operating table where the piece from my knee was removed. The next day they probed the wound in my thigh but could not extract the piece in it. At no time did I suffer the loss of the use of the leg, and today I am perfectly all right. The piece in the thigh does not bother me at all. In fact, I don't know it's there. My wounds have been completely healed for the past three or four weeks. But it was a miracle it wasn't worse. One large piece ripped through the shoulder and sleeve of my jacket, and only scratched me; another large piece tore the wrist of my sleeve without even touching me. My helmet was blown off but my head was untouched. Don't worry. Use discretion in repeating this.

Love to all,
Morris

P.S. Don't know the major.

* * * * *

Somewhere in France
[V-Mail postmarked November 6, 1944]

Mrs. Claude J. Kelly
4139 Gen'l Taylor
New Orleans, Louisiana

Dear Aunt Winnie,

I have before me your letter of the 19th which I received some days ago. At that time I could not answer; today, however, I have a chance of catching up on my mail. On Sunday we came back off line for a few days' rest. I went to eleven o'clock Mass and Communion, and in the afternoon to a picture show some miles back. I felt pretty good then by that night. I had a choice of taking a bath or going to the show. Well, I hadn't washed, even, in some nine days. But the show held more appeal than even the nice warm bath, so I went to it. It was very good. There were also selected "short subjects."

I know how much a stir I cause because I know how much you people worry about me. I have asked you time and time again not to worry. What's done 'tis done.

> *"The moving finger writes and having writ moves on*
> *And all our piety nor wit can lure it back to cancel half a line.*
> *Nor all our tears wash out a word of it."*

Those Christmas packages really sound good. I'll thank you now for all the trouble you have taken to make my Christmas a happy one.

Glad to hear that Claude is doing grand in his Greek; also, that he has had some affiliation with Dr. Bonomo on the radio. For myself, those radio programs meant a lot, and I enjoyed being on the air very much. In that business one meets many very nice people. I think that during my college career I participated in about 100 radio plays either as a sound technician or as "dramatic personae."

With best regards to Uncle Claude, Claude, and Winnie, I remain

Your loving nephew,
Morris

* * * * *

Somewhere in France
November 7, 1944

Dear Mom and Dad,

Today is Tuesday. I have just finished pulling twenty-four hours of guard back in our reserve area. We were relieved Sunday morning early, and I had the opportunity of attending Mass and receiving Holy Communion. The Mass was said inside a private chapel which constitutes part of an old château. Right after Mass I ate dinner and then got ready to go to the picture show. I had a choice of going to the show or taking a bath. I took the show, because I hadn't seen one in months, whereas I had had a bath only three weeks ago! But the show was very good and I enjoyed it very much. It was called *Take It or Leave It.* (after the radio program of the same name). The leading role was, of course, played by Phil Baker.

Besides the "feature presentation," there were several "short subjects." That Sunday was much like the ones I used to spend back home. By the time I got back to the bivouac area it was suppertime. So I ate supper and then afterwards, since it was dark and I couldn't write, I stood around and talked until I got sleepy.

Yesterday, Monday, I went on guard at eleven in the morning and I only managed to write two letters all day—one to Aunt Winnie and one to Aunt Ogie. I did not write you because I had only V-Mail and I wanted to write a long letter and send it by Air Mail. Sometimes I think V-Mail is good, and other times I think that regular Air Mail is the quickest. I can't say which is the faster from the States because lately, the weather in the Channel has been very bad and no mail could get here at all.

The rain had held up for a few days but at present, the wind is blowing a heavy mist through the fields and woods, and the roads are becoming seas of mud and floating islands. But we have big rubber overshoes which keep our feet both warm and dry, so the mud isn't too much of a problem.

I want to ask you again not to worry. Almost everybody in their letters tells me how much you worry. And now I'm beginning to worry about your health and welfare. I know that you are not well and that you have an extremely nervous condition. And I know that because you love me so much you worry too much. Now I don't go for this worrying business at all. I used to worry about what to do if this should happen or if that should happen. And I soon found that I was imagining all sorts of things. So I decided that I wouldn't worry about anything and that I would worry about something when it happened, and only then. I know there wasn't any detail to the W.D.'s telegram. But you should not start imagining things. To tell the truth, I thought the wound was so slight that nothing would be said about it. The reason I did not write anything about it in my letters was because I didn't think you would ever find out. Then I learned that the record had been sent to Washington and that a telegram would be sent home. Then I wrote and told you what had happened, which letter you have probably received by now. I did not want to cause undue alarm. I think the telegram was rather silly anyway. Most of us don't like to have them sent home. I believe it should be our judgment as to whether we want our folks notified or not. But very few ever have anything their way in the Army.

I have before me your letters of the eighteenth and twentieth and one of Dad's of the thirteenth. I am glad to hear that everything at the firm is working to Dad's advantage and that the law business is good. One thing I would like to ask: Does the Supreme Court of the U.S. have jurisdiction over such a case, or does its jurisdiction not extend over the law and material involved?

With regard to the chocolate—I think you can forget about it. We get a chocolate ration over here along with our cigarettes. I don't smoke, so I trade off with the other fellows who don't care for the chocolate. In this manner I get pretty much of the candy.

Today is Election Day, but there isn't too much talk over here as to who will win or lose. Of more interest is the result of the Notre Dame–Navy game and other results of similar great games. In this season as in every previous season there have been startling upsets that make men's pocketbooks fluctuate. (Not mine, however; I'm very unlucky—I don't play at all.) Many attach much to the outcome of the election—even the end of the war. However, I am not of that opinion. But whoever is the next president I pray that God will guide him in the right direction so that he might contribute his share to a lasting peace. Making peace will not be an easy job, and I am sure that France will spoil the broth. For my money the present government of France isn't worth a continental. The Communists are very strong and well armed, as many are members of the FFI [French Forces of the Interior], which was ordered disbanded and disarmed by General de Gaulle but which defied the latter's order. I hate to think that our beloved democracy is fighting to make France safe for a good Communist government. But what beats me is the passive attitude that the French Catholics take to the rising red tide. I think they are only lukewarm. Politically France is divided into many different groups, and de Gaulle does not have as much backing as his committee would have us believe. If he were to enforce his order that the FFI disband, he would bring France into a state of near civil war. From the few French I have spoken with, I would say that the de Gaulle government—unless it can acquire the cooperation of all political elements—could not carry a general election.

Well, Christmas is coming, and while I have the time and while the stores still have some things that would make nice presents, I am going to ask that you would take twenty dollars out of my account and get a nice present for each of the nine children. I would like that they be left around the fireplace at the foot of the mantelpiece in the music room, so that they would find them there on Xmas morn.

I hope that Abry Bros. do a good job on the house. As you say, it's got be done. I hope for your convenience they make a fast job of it.

I'm glad to hear that David likes school. Aunt Winnie was telling me of your propaganda methods used in making him think it wasn't too bad.

If you still have the paper in which is contained the new president's statements, send me a clipping; also, the figures on the actual votes and then the electoral votes.

That's all for now. I remember everybody in my prayers and am thinking of you always.

Your loving son,
Morris

P.S. Request some stationery. This is borrowed.

* * * * *

Somewhere in France
November 7, 1944

Dear Will,

I suppose it's about time I answered some of your letters. I would like to be able to write you as often as you write me, but alas, I cannot. I'm glad to hear from you and learn of what you are doing. I am sorry you declined nomination to office in your fraternity, but perhaps it is just as well and will allow you to devote more time to your studies. By the way, how is school? How are all the girl friends? Marie Frey and Elaine Mouledoux?

Most of the time over here I'm thinking of the times I used to have back home with all the gang. I think a lot of Monita Imbert, Arthur Appfel, Numa, Parker, Raymond, Marie Louise, and the others I used to run around with. And when I'm not thinking of them I'm wishing I were home. During the long hours of the night I pray and plan for the things I'd like to do after the war. There are hundreds of them. But one that seems pretty good is, if I have the money, going up to Detroit and buying a brand-new car and driving it home. That is, if Mom and Dad wouldn't object. And if I did do this I'd take you along in case anything should go wrong. You might know how to fix it. Then I'd go back to school looking for another degree, or perhaps I'll have some other vocation. It's hard during these times to make up one's mind as to what one really wants to be. But I'll be seeing you, not soon, but someday. After this is over I'll probably have to pull Army of Occupation. Study hard.

Your brother,
Morris

Somewhere in France
Sunday, November 12, 1944

Dear Mom and Dad,

Today is Sunday and we're up on line. The weather and days now are quite different from the weather and days we first knew when we first landed in France. Instead of beautiful, warm, sunshiny days, when the birds sang and the bees buzzed all around, we now have cold, gray, rainy days. The birds still sing but not in their big green houses. Their houses remain, but the color, like the season, has changed because of the fast-approaching winter. During those first days on the continent we usually had from fourteen to sixteen hours of daylight. But now we have a time eking out eleven.

This morning I couldn't attend Mass, but while sitting in our straw-insulated dug-out I read the Mass from the little prayer book that I always carry with me. I picked up a French prayer book (minus a cover) which has the Latin of the Mass in it. However, I seldom use it. I stick to the little "Military Missal" which I got from the chaplain back in England. I almost forgot, but I also have a little prayer book called *Shield of Faith*, written by Msgr. Fulton J. Sheen. It contains reflections on prayer and other meditations. I often read through it. It helps me a lot.

Today is Aunt Eleanor's and Uncle Paul's twenty-fifth wedding anniversary. Again, I extend to them my congratulations and best wishes for continued happiness. I will not say that I thought more of them today, or prayed more for them today than usual, because as you know I am always thinking of all the folks back home and long for the day when I shall return home. And yet home seems a long ways off. I guess it's because the end here isn't yet in sight. I don't believe that Gen. Marshall knew how true he spoke when he said, "Victory of the democracies can only be complete upon the successful and complete destruction of the war machines of Germany and Japan." He might have been more correct if he had added also, the people of these two nations.

I hope that all are well. I seem to be doing all right. I think I've been gaining weight again, or else my pants have shrunk.

How is Will getting along in school? I hope you don't have any more monkey business with him. He's really a smart fellow and could really become something if he'd only settle down to some serious hard work. I guess the same might be said of Kerry—but as you said, he shouldn't expect to pray his way through school. I guess the rest of the children are all studying hard. Give my love to all of them.

Had some fruitcake the other day. One of my friends got it. It was very good. I await anxiously my packages! I have some stuff coming from Aunt Winnie, too.

Well, I think I'll close. In a week or two you might mail me another fruitcake. I would certainly appreciate it. I'll start requesting those about once every two weeks now.

Love to all the folks.

Your loving son,
Morris

* * * * *

Somewhere in France
November 15, 1944

William J. Hume
1321 Cambronne St.
New Orleans, Louisiana

Dear Uncle Billy,

Yesterday I received your most welcome letter of October 31. We are "on line" somewhere in France. Today has been pretty quiet so far, and the sun has been shining bright since it first came up at about eight o'clock. Today is the first in many that we have seen where the sun was shining, not obscured by heavy black clouds. There was, however, a heavy frost on the ground. But this was all melted away by ten in the morning.

Over here, while on line, we live mostly in holes. We have dug-in positions in which we sleep and stand guard during the night. These positions are pretty close to blockhouses. We build them of logs, corrugated iron (from garages or barns), and sandbags. This should survive almost anything but a direct hit of artillery. Then, if they ever have a direct hit, we won't ever know it. They say you never hear the shell that gets you. That's probably true, but I don't believe there are any witnesses.

It was almost two months ago that I was wounded, and I have been back on line twice since. The first time was right after I left the hospital where they kept me for about ten days. Believe that telegram when it said I was only slightly wounded. That's the truth. When I come home I'll tell how it happened and then I'll forget everything I ever knew about war or Europe. Maybe someday I'll come back to Europe, but by that time it'll be changed from the Europe I knew. It'll probably be a more beautiful, modern continent, but I suppose some of its battle scars shall still remain.

I believe that I'll probably be part of the Army of Occupation, although I wish I could come home as soon as it's over. There's no place like home.

Glad to hear you are enjoying good health. Sorry about your lack of appetite, though. I hope you enjoy a happy holiday season and I extend my best wishes now, should I be unable to write again.

With kindest regards,
Morris Jr.

* * * * *

Somewhere in France
November 15, 1944

Dear Mom and Dad,

As I write this our artillery is pounding away out to our front. A loudspeaker is set up on the right and is broadcasting to the Germans, asking them to surrender. (I don't know if this will be cut out.) I have heard of such methods, but this is the first time I have seen or heard them employed. I am sitting at the entrance to our dug-out enjoying a little of the rare sunshine that we hardly ever have these days. Today has been exceptional in that it was warm and bright. (The Germans just threw some artillery at the loudspeaker. They're doing it again.) The loudspeaker is off now and I guess our artillery will put in some punctuation. Our artillery always gets the last word. If the Germans throw one shell our way, they get about twenty-five back. So it goes.

Yesterday, I got two nice letters from old friends: Uncle Billy and Roy Guste. He's (Roy) written quite a bit lately and I've only answered once. I just finished a letter to Uncle Billy, and I shall try to borrow some more stationery and write him (Roy).

So David has started to learn how to write, eh? Well, he don't do too bad. Of course, I can see Mother's hand in Robert's. Their notes were in your letter of the 28th. On the same day that I received your letter, I received Uncle Billy's of Nov. 3, which came Air Mail. So I think Air Mail is faster.

I am expecting some of the first packages you mailed any day now. The boxes are beginning to roll in at every mail call. But so far I haven't received one.

What is the name of the play Will is in? And when will it be produced? I hope he studies his lines and acts serious during rehearsals. Doc gets awfully irritated when a cast starts cutting up. I know; Bertel, Guste, and I were about the worst.

That's all for now. Give my regards to Fr. Castel and to my old professors out at school. Hope all are well. All my love.

Morris

P.S.The crows are flying South. Sure sign of winter.

* * * * *

Holiday Greeting Card

Don't Tread on Me
Joyeux Noël

Meilleurs Souhaits du Continent

From Your Loving Son,
Morris
376th Infantry U.S.A.

[On reverse side]

Dear Folks,

Here it is Christmas again. Though I am far away, I extend to Mom and Dad, Esther, William, Kerry, Richard, Ralph, Ronald, Jerome, David, and Robert, my

Kindest Regards and Best Wishes for
A Happy Holiday Season

Morris

Somewhere in France
Sunday, November 26, 1944

Dear Mom and Dad,

I am trying to write this in a crowded, makeshift day room. It's pretty noisy in here. The fellows are discussing the week-end's football results and the radio-phonograph is flaring forth with Sinatra and "I'll Get By." Some are trying to sing along with him. The boy next to me, from Georgia, has just remarked that this time about four months ago, he and I were eating Sunday dinner at our homes. I agree with him. It's now about 7:30 European Time, which is about two o'clock your time. As I write you're probably finishing up a wonderful Sunday dinner.

We're back in reserve for a few days. Joe Heinkels got kinda mad the last night we were on line and threw a little artillery at us. He came close but nobody got hurt. Our guns silenced them after a two-hour duel.

Yesterday the rain and wind let up, and after a clear, cold night we got up at dawn (which is at eight o'clock) to frozen mud, frost-covered fields, and hot pancakes and coffee. While on line we never have pancakes because they're too much trouble. But when we come off line we have them almost every morning.

Tonight at the picture show is *Dragon Seed* with Katie Hepburn. The shows in the rest period here change every three days. Everybody gets to go at least once. We get a chance to take showers too. So many men from each platoon are allowed to go each day.

A day or so ago I had a pass to a big French city. I had a wonderful time. Many of the city's buildings lie in ruins, but the French carry on as usual. The stores are full. There are more toys in the windows than back home, and the people are well dressed. I had everything I wanted to eat and also to drink. I am broke now but I had a swell time. I even rode all over town on the tramways. I saw many beautiful buildings and centuries-old castles with deer running around inside the walls.

My three buddies and I drank champagne—1934—at 160 francs a bottle, and had beef steaks at 25 francs the serving. On that day the four of us were far from the war. Then we found a restaurant that had ice cream at six francs the serving. The manager got mad when we got three rounds apiece before he knew it. But I explained that it was the first time in four months that we had even seen ice cream.

But a sour note was to see the pitifully small number of men digging in the ruins, trying to clean up the ruins, and once in a while finding in the broken stone and twisted steel another body of some innocent. And on some walls to see painted the words DÉTRUIT PAR LES LIBERATEURS and in another place THE LIBERATORS HAVE KILLED AS MANY AS THE BOCHE. But as one of the workers explained to me, "C'est la guerre." This with a shrug and a smile from a man who had seen his two small children killed during the air bombardment. It will be a long time until the buildings will be rebuilt. It will take generations to restore France to a real world power.

This morning I went to Mass and received Communion. We have a dispensation from fasting and can receive at any time without fasting.

Give my regards to all the folks. I'll write more tomorrow.

Love,
Morris

* * * * *

Somewhere in France
Monday, November 27, 1944

Dear Mom and Dad,

Probably you have already received my Christmas card. While in Nantes I bought several other Christmas cards to send to the people back home. I wrote up a list of people to whom I would like to send cards, and there were twenty names on it. Well, I had bought more than enough cards so I gave some to the other boys who had not been as fortunate as I in getting a pass.

When I wrote yesterday I didn't think I could mention the name of the town to which I had gone on account of censorship. But today Lt. Goldenzweig said it was all right. I don't know if you and Dad were there when you visited Europe.

Nantes is a pretty big city. Although it has been bombed heavily by the Allied Air Force, it is still a beautiful city. Some of its more famous buildings and some of its more beautiful buildings were destroyed or severely damaged, but it was necessary to run the Heinkels out. While there I visited the Château des Ducs de Bretagne. It's about 700 years old and is very beautiful. Its walls are very thick, and it is a perfect example of the medieval castle. The moat still surrounds it, and deer roam its grounds. One of these is pure white—the first white deer I had ever seen, and a very beautiful animal at that.

In the city's biggest cathedral there is not one pane of glass left. All had been blown out by the bombardment. The most modern building of all, "Le Magasin Decré" which was a huge department store, is just so much twisted steel.

As I said in yesterday's letter, I had a swell time. The people are still gay. The markets are full. There seems to be no food shortage. Perhaps they'll spend a cold winter but they have lights, and I suppose everybody can dress warm. They dress just like N.O. people, and a Nantes crowd looks like a home crowd in the French Quarter.

Well, lots of love to all. Tell those boys and that girl to study hard. I'm well and want to stay in the Infantry. So, don't worry.

Your loving son,
Morris

* * * * *

Somewhere in France
Monday, November 27, 1944

Dear Aunt Winnie,

I received several of your letters during our last tour on line. I also got letters from all the rest of the family, from Hyie, Ogie, and Aunt Eleanor. Really, you people flatter me with your letters. They're really nice and they sound just like you. But understand me, I won't be home before it's over and then I might walk through parts of China on my way back home. It's true my eyes aren't good. But with glasses they're perfect. Glasses are no handicap. There are millions of GIs that wear glasses, and they're in the Infantry. I'll take the Infantry and I intend to stay in it.

Today is a beautiful, sunshiny day and I feel fine. It's even money, so it seems, that war will be over by Christmas. However, I have bet 100 francs that it won't. It's true that I am pessimistic. But I can't help it. A peaceful world seems a long way off, and being a civilian is just a dream.

When we first came off line this time, I got a pass to a big French city. I really had a good time—even better than when I was in New York. I had fine meals, which included everything from soup to ice cream. This is no lie either. Of the latter I had three servings, which made the manager glower at us. Then in the evening before we started back we drank champagne from Bordeaux 1934 at only 160 francs a quart. It was really good.

During the day, three of my buddies and I walked through the department stores and visited the old famous buildings. But a little girl who spoke perfect English informed me that the museum pieces had been stolen by the Germans, and that the main salon was occupied by corpses brought in for identification from the ruined sections of the city. That was a day in the once beautiful city of Nantes. I have several sets of photographs of the city and its port, but I'll send them home later.

Glad to hear Claude Jr. is doing well in school.

Best regards to all.

Morris

* * * * *

Somewhere in France
Monday, November 27, 1944

Mr. & Mrs. Paul S. Stuart
1905 Calhoun St.
New Orleans, Louisiana

Dear Aunt Eleanor,

Today I received your letter and others giving the details of your silver wedding celebration. I hope you and Uncle Paul enjoyed yourselves as much as everybody else seems to have. Of course, and this is an old complaint, I wish I could have been there to either add or detract to the gaiety of the occasion.

You know it's funny the way things go. The Army is always trying to boost your morale. They come out with statements like "ETO Vets to fight in China." Of course, this makes us happy to know that after this Cook's tour of France, the Army will open up its offices and send a select group of vets to China. I think as soon as this gets over I'll go crazy and get a discharge. I don't want to continue this GI World Tour in China. Let some other stay-at-home get out and see the world. But all kidding aside, I'm a pessimist. I even bet 100 francs the war wouldn't be over by Christmas. Then if the war gets over I'll either go to the Pacific or go play hide-and-seek with the German underground as a soldier in the A.O.

So-o-o-o, as Ed Wynn the old fire chief says, this means I won't be home soon. But that won't affect the price of eggs in Alaska.

Well, I have just changed pens so I'll change subjects. I got a letter from Paul Jr. a few days ago, and I shall answer tonight if time will allow.

The other day I had a pass to the big French city of Nantes in the province of Brittany. This city had been given an awful pasting by us and the English in the drive to push the Germans out. Here, I and three buddies had a swell time. Drank the first champagne since I left for the Army. It was Bordeaux 1934 and had as much fizz as a hot Coca-Cola. I even found ice cream, the first since New York, in one of their big restaurants. The people are well dressed and aren't by any means starving. There are a good number of autos running around the streets also. And of course I got back into the habit of dodging streetcars again. Oh well, lots of love to all,

Morris

* * * * *

Somewhere in France
Monday, November 27, 1944

Dear Aunt Hy,

Got your letter of some weeks ago, some days ago. Ah, after looking through my pile of letters I have found it. It was written November 2. I have just re-read it to see if you had asked me anything that I might be able to answer. Nope, you're not as inquisitive as most people. It's just as well. I can't ever answer the questions asked anyway.

Little Jodie certainly seems to get around from all accounts. I guess all children his age begin to feel their strength by pulling tablecloths off the table, et cetera. I can remember times when my younger brothers pulled stunts like that. Only I think most of those boys favored rolling down steps in kiddie-cars or "taylor-tots," or cutting their own hair Indian style. Then as they grew older they drove Mother almost crazy with such cute tricks as getting locked in the bathroom, tracking mud over the seats of the car, or walking through fresh-laid cement. But these experiences and the stern corrections all go toward forming strong character. Yeah, but what characters? Ah me, such is life.

The weather has been not too bad in the last few days. It's growing cold over here. But when we get back on line again we'll have a full moon to light up the fields if the clouds stay away.

We've got to wade through mud back here in the rest area to get to and from chow. Then we have to take hikes almost every day back here. But I don't mind the hikes. It's almost a pleasure to march along again with all your buddies, yelling at each other and coming out with cracks like "You look like the south end of a horse going north." It's really good to see all the guys in the company again, and shoot the bull with them and get the dope on all the latest rumors.

A few days ago I got a pass to visit the big seaport city of Nantes on the Loire River. I had a good time eating strawberry ice cream and drinking champagne. Spent my whole month's pay almost, but it was worth it. Acted like a big-time operator in the cafés and restaurants. Different from living in a wet hole and eating cold meals sometimes, and sweating out the cold rainy nights.

Best wishes to all,

Love,
Morris

* * * * *

Somewhere in France
December 10, 1944

Dear Mom and Dad,

I am writing this with hopes that it will reach you by Christmas. I am writing it in an old French château a few hundred yards behind the lines. Our squad of twelve men were brought back for two days of rest. In these two days I hope to do a number of things. One is to dry out; the other is to unearth myself. As soon as we got in this morning we got fresh clothes and clean pairs of sox. I then cleaned and oiled my rifle and then had chow.

We have a nice room in the place here. There is a radio in here and a good fire in the fireplace. Our executive officer passed out some good cough medicine to us. I think Dad might appreciate a drink of it. It was White Horse Scotch—which reminds me to express the hope that you have plenty of Christmas spirits in the house for the holidays. I won't be there to fill the ice bucket or pass the hors d'oeuvres, but don't think I won't be thinking of you and all the family and such great friends as the Hoggs, the Cokers, and Uncle Billy Hume. Give them all my regards when they invade on Xmas Day.

Tho' I may be far away on that day, I'll attend Mass and be joined with you when I receive Holy Communion. We'll be in divisional reserve for Christmas, which is a swell break for the whole battalion. I hope I'll get some of those Christmas boxes while back in reserve. I'll really go for them. I have received all the Christmas letters, but was previously seven days without a letter. Mail is awful over here. Got letters from everybody. Rec'd two from Roy Guste. He's really on the ball. Got several cards from Gissie Burton and Kent Zimmermann. The latter was mailed the 3rd of December; took only seven days. That was out of Chicago. Wish you'd call his mother and tell her hello for me and give the family my regards.

As soon as I get the Combat Infantry decorations I'll be eligible for a pass to Paris. Perhaps I'll get some souvenirs if I get there. You probably have read of the Paris Pass Plan that is in effect in the ETO. The lights have gone out, but we have a bunch of kerosene lamps going which give light to write by.

The weather is cold and wet. Too wet to snow. But after it stops raining the pools of water and the incessant mud freeze. We put straw around the holes to keep from being muddy, and the straw freezes. Our outer clothes are usually wet, but we have so many layers of clothes on that we don't mind. Shucks, I'm used to the worst conditions there are now.

By the way, two of my buddies are getting the Silver Star for Action Above and Beyond the Call to Duty during a shelling of some nights ago.

Well, Merry Xmas.

Your loving son,
Morris

* * * * *

Somewhere in France
December 10, 1944

Dear Aunt Hyie,

The other day I received a very nice letter from you telling about the Thanksgiving celebration. Sounded like old times. House must have been crowded as a dug-out during an artillery barrage with the eleven Redmanns, the Kellys, Stuarts, and Joyces there.

You said that you had heard that I forsook a bath for a show. Well, Aunt Hy, I would have been better off if I had taken the bath. The other day a GI from the company our platoon was attached to comes over to my hole and says: "Hey, I hear "I" Company is lousy!" This with an air of shock. Well, I just kept on scratching and said sarcastically, "You don't say."

It took me about three days to get rid of my little friends. They have some good insect powder that can rid you of all in forty minutes. Amazing, isn't it?

This last time on line was a little rough because our platoon stayed up when the company went back into reserve. The dug-out leaked, and then the next night caved in. It rained every night and the water froze in the morning. And every morning we wrung out the bedrolls and the blankets and prayed for sun to dry them. Oh boy! Rough! To top it off we were in a hot spot. Artillery, rifle grenades, mortars, every night. But most of the time I can sleep right through it. Winter is here. But I don't think any G.I. Joe will go cold unless it's his own carelessness. There's plenty of food and clothing. There is a shortage of ammunition for the big guns. But I guess the people back home have heard of it by now.

Glad to hear Jodie is getting along OK. Best wishes to all for the holidays.

Love,
Morris

* * * * *

Somewhere in France
[V-Mail postmarked December 10, 1944]

Mrs. Claude J. Kelly
4139 Gen'l Taylor
New Orleans, Louisiana

Dear Aunt Winnie,

Would you please get Mom and Dad a Christmas present for me. I realize that this comes as a late request, but couldn't help it.

I shall forward a money order of ten dollars as soon as possible to cover.

Love and best wishes for a happy holiday season.

Morris Jr.

* * * * *

Somewhere in France
December 10, 1944

Dear Dad,

This is just a letter to shoot the breeze. I haven't written in twelve days because it's been pretty rough. Not the Jerries but the weather. There was an article in *Stars and Stripes* calling us the "Muddy Bloody Men of the Line." Well, I've been "bloody"; now I'm "muddy." Such weather! Cold, rainy, windy—awful! We live in holes, and when the line moves we've got to make new holes. This last time our platoon didn't go back into reserve when the company did, but remained on line to strengthen another company. We just shifted over to their sector of the front, which was somewhat of a hot spot. We had a hole dug into a hedgerow into which the rain swept for the first three nights straight. You can't see a thing. This gives one an excellent opportunity to develop one's sense of hearing. It causes one to throw a lot of grenades at sounds that his imagination leads him to believe that even a bn. [battalion] of Heinkels are just in front of him. I've got an automatic rifle with me that sprays at a rate of five hundred and fifty a minute. It's a pretty good gun, altho' Jerry has an MG43 or 42 which has a cyclic rate of fire of between 1,100 and 1,500 rounds per minute (woo-woo!). But it ain't accurate, it sez here. Jerry also has some other good weapons of high velocity (2,700 ft. per sec.) and fast cyclic rates of fire. But whenever he uses them, he learns what an American artillery battery can do to him.

I'm getting to be the real old soldier type. Go for weeks without shaving, eating two meals a day, swapping cigarette rations for cigars or candy.

But besides the inconvenience of the weather and Herman the German, I have other troubles too. A fellow from "K" Co. comes over to the hole the other day and says with a look of surprise, "Hey, I hear "I" Company is lousy!"

"You don't say so!" I answer, scratching my back furiously.

We've been up on line for twelve days already and face about six or eight more. The Colonel told me, when he visited us on line for a heart-to-heart talk a few days ago, that we'd be in divisional reserve for Christmas. Our division has been in action now for three months. I think we have two battle-stars for our ETO ribbon. Probably get more before it's over.

Being on divisional reserve for Christmas is about the best news I have heard since on the line. Perhaps I'll get some of the those boxes by that time.

I don't know anything about the Democratic senator from Louisiana named Overton Brooks. But if he can do what he says, or, rather, get Congress to do what he wants, I would remember him for the rest of my natural life as a good Joe. He says that Congress should pass a bill permitting soldiers who have been in combat, or those who have been in the ETO for two years or more, to return home immediately after the end of the war. In other words, we shouldn't have to pull Army of Occupation. I believe A.O. would be rougher than combat. Imagine trying to police a nation of diabolical criminals. I'd rather fight in China or in the Islands of the Pacific than live amongst a nation of such horrible, inhuman, monstrous creatures as are these degenerate generations of Nazi Germany. If this war were to continue for ten years, it wouldn't matter to me, as long as this despicable breed of men is crushed in the end. How the world can forgive Germany is beyond me. People back home can preach an easy peace because they don't know all that the Germans have done. When I was in Nantes I passed a plot of ground in the middle of a street. And on this plot was a sign: HERE ARE THE BODIES OF 40 HOSTAGES SHOT BY THE GERMANS, SEPT. 23, 1943. I asked questions and found out that these forty French lives were taken for four Germans killed by the Underground. That's a ratio of ten to one. If we could kill 10 Germans for every Pole, Russian, Jew, etc., that the Nazis have murdered in the past four years, I think the Germans would have plenty of "lebensraum." Any American soldier that even speaks to a German faces a fine of $65. Strictly, no fraternization.

To the Germans, Gen. Ike has said, "We come as conquerors. . . ." And if we, the Americans, British, and French—and Russians, too—don't crush Germany and blot out the last vestige of National Socialism and its methods, then the sacrifices of Dunkirk, Coventry, Arnheim, Dieppe, St. Lô, and all others are in vain.

I hope and pray that someday peace will come again to the world. But it must be a lasting peace, or I and millions of others will feel that the greatest effort of our lives is for naught.

Love,
Morris

* * * * *

Somewhere in France
December 13, 1944

Dear Mom and Dad,

Let this penciled epistle serve as a request for a fountain pen. Nothing too good, you understand, because I'll lose it in a few days after receipt. That's the way it goes. I've had about five different ones over here, but somehow I always manage to get rid of them.

Well, we're back in reserve but not the reserve I thought I would be in. And we're back early too, so that means I'll be sweating Christmas and New Year's out on line. I mean sweating too. Though the mercury is sub-freezing during those midnight hours, there isn't one guy who isn't sweating the minutes of his guard out. Listening for every sound, watching the eerie silhouettes of hedgerows and trees. Just waiting, watching, and praying. Maybe if I were younger I'd go for this Boy Scout–cowboy and Indian stuff.

But now we're back in reserve, I don't know for how long. But our platoon had just completed thirteen days' continuous action on line. We missed going into battalion reserve when the rest of the company went in for a few days.

Had a wonderful shower the other day (courtesy of Division Quartermaster—Showers Division). It was really nice. A shower can mean all the difference in the world. It gives you such a refreshed feeling. Sometimes I have gone without shaving or washing for quite some time. Really, after coming back and cleaning and shaving, I hardly recognize myself.

The other day I received two packages dated Oct. 14. They were from aunts Winnie and Eleanor. In the latter's I found the record. Don't have any means of playing it, but I'll get to it sometime, someplace. I'll write them and thank them. I enjoyed them very much. But I'm beginning to believe that the ship yours were on was sunk. No kidding. They were mailed in September, weren't they? The postal system—it's *wonderful.*

I'm in good health. A slim, tall, 160 pounds of soldier (it sez here). Heh-Heh. When I come marching home again (hurrah, boys, hurrah) the children will be "verboten" to play soldier. And if there's any Fourth of July celebration going on, I'll go visit the Sharps. (Don't take me serious; I'm trying in a dull way to be humorous.)

I've got about twenty-eight ounces of concentrate chocolate. I traded cigarettes for it. What I don't eat I'll give to some French kids that look like they could stand some.

Got an excellent letter for Fr. Emmett Bienvenue, S.J. from St. Mary's College the other day. It gives a very simple explanation of the Mass. I shall try to send it home. He was my professor of Greek some years ago—one of the best profs that have undertaken the task of teaching me.

You should read some of Kerry's letters to me before he mails them. They're gems! You'd think he was my elder brother. I think he is a very talented letter-writer. If he were, around home, of the caliber he portrays himself by his letters to me, he would be your pride and joy. Maybe he isn't as self-centered as in his younger days. (I write like an old fogie.)

Glad to hear that Uncle Billy has spent some of the holidays with you. Maybe he can take my place at the Sunday dinner table.

Got a nice letter from Peggy Mc the other day, which I have yet to answer. She told me of the Song of Bernadette play and of her activities. Closed by giving me her family's "special" regards.

Got Christmas cards from old friend Bernie Ward, from Kent Zimmermann, from both of you and all the kids.

To-day medical officer came and checked on my eyes. Asked a lot of questions—if I had two pr. of glasses and all that. I told him my eyes with glasses were as correct as could be, which they are. They don't bother me. I know you worry. But I'm in the Infantry and I like it, and I'm here to stay. It's my job and I'll see it through. I've criticized many for being in the rear echelon because they give orders without fully appreciating the G.I. Joe's conditions while on line. I could never do any other job because I'd want to go back. Back to the friends, the holes, the guns, the grenades, back to the Muddy, Bloody Men of the Line. I've gone this far in the game and it's the last inning. There's two out, nobody on base, a weak hitter up, and our team is way up in the lead.

But the people who must keep us in the lead are people back home. We depend on them for the guns and shells and tires to move the trucks and supplies. I don't know just how critical the ammo supply is. But we can only fire our artillery as counter-battery fire. In other words, if we see some Jerries out front, we can't call artillery. We can use it only when Jerry starts shelling us, in order to make him stop.

Lots of love to all and best wishes.

Your loving son,
Morris

* * * * *

Somewhere in France
December 14, 1944

Dear Mom and Dad,

Just a few lines to let you know that "everything is still all right," as the song says. It's half-past eleven at night. There's just four of us sitting around in the "day room." Two of us writing, one fixing the fire, and the other listening to the radio. This place was once a German barracks. It's got a good stove in it, and I'm sitting here in my shirtsleeves. Outside it's sub-freezing. I hate to think of going out to the tents. Once we get in our sleeping bags, tho', we warm up pretty fast.

I don't smoke cigarettes—but I have a little taste for cigars. If you must send smoking material, I'll take the latter. Still haven't got a package from you.

Answered a letter from Norris Mary Murphy tonight. Thank her mother, please, for the Christmas present you wrote about.

Lots of love,
Morris

Somewhere in France
December 14, 1944

Mrs. Paul S. Stuart
1905 Calhoun St.
New Orleans, Louisiana

Dear Aunt Eleanor,

A few days ago I received your package of the fourteenth of October, and I would like to thank you very much for your kind consideration.

I am in the best of health but am not enjoying my sojourn in France. Of course, if this were a self-appointed exile, I'd come home right now. But alas, there are certain little forces and obligations that keep me here, don'tcha know.

We're back in reserve now for a few days, but we won't be here for Christmas. Of course, that's our luck. First, they definitely say you will be off line for Xmas, and in their next action they do just the opposite. So it goes.

"Tis a nipping and an eager air" outside. It can't rain because it's too cold. I'm beginning to wonder just how cold it gets here. Regards to all. Please send Paul's address; I lost his letter.

Your loving nephew,
Morris

* * * * *

Somewhere in France
[V-Mail postmarked December 14, 1944]

Miss Ogie Joyce
1905 Calhoun St.
New Orleans, Louisiana

Dear Ogie,

Just a few lines to say hello and let you folks at 1905 know I'm thinking of you. I haven't had much chance to write—but then there isn't much to write about. Same old stuff. Winter's here. It's cold and gray. But I like those days. It makes me remember and appreciate the good warm homes we had back home. You know those days—too cold to go out, so you listen to the radio close to a nice fire—all peace and contentment.

I hope to see those days again—but—I've got to sweat it out with every other GI. Please thank aunts Eleanor and Winnie for their packages. I'll write them tomorrow. It's midnight now.

Love,
Morris

* * * * *

Somewhere in France
December 15, 1944

Dear Mom and Dad,

Last night I wrote you before I went to the picture show and saw *Saratoga Trunk* with Gary Cooper and Ingrid Bergman. Much of the action took place in New Orleans; I liked it, but I would have liked to have seen it end another way.

Tonight I am sitting in a French café, writing and eating sandwiches and drinking non-alcoholic beer. The sandwiches are of chopped pork seasoned with garlic and chopped onions. (Pardon me while I order another sandwich.) I have just about caught up on my back mail. I have written almost everybody except my good friends Roy and Shelby Trice. I received one regular letter from Roy and a newsletter telling of the activity of the whole Tri-Sig Fraternity members. He plays me up big—heh, heh.

Comes the New Year I'll probably be in Germany or some other place if rumors run true. Well, that's all for now. Love to all the children.

Your loving son,
Morris

* * * * *

Somewhere in France
[V-Mail postmarked December 15, 1944]

Mrs. Claude J. Kelly
4139 General Taylor
New Orleans, Louisiana

Dear Aunt Winnie,

Some days I receive two boxes—one from you and one from Aunt Eleanor. I enjoyed the fruitcake and cookies very much, and I want to tell you that they were delicious. Those were the first boxes I have received, although Mother said in her letter of the 26th that she had sent nineteen so far. I guess they'll catch up with me some months from now. If you like, I'd like another box of cookies.

I'm writing this while waiting for a haircut. A couple of fellows from our company are cutting hair here in what looks like it was once a German barracks. It's a long, low building made of corrugated sheet metal. We have a few tables in here, a couple of stoves, and an electric system which dimly lights the place. We sleep in tents over which there is a thin coat of white ice when we get up in the morning. Happy New Year to all the Kellys.

Your loving nephew,
Morris

* * * * *

Somewhere in France
Sunday, December 17, 1944

Dear Mom and Dad,

Yesterday afternoon on a rain-soaked field we had a parade at which were awarded the Silver and Bronze Star medals to the members of our battalion who had showed gallantry and intrepidity in action. Our company took all the Silver Stars and a few Bronze Stars. We are, I think, the most decorated battalion in action in the division. The band led the parade after playing the National Anthem and the Missouri Waltz.

Two of the Silver Stars went to two buddies of mine who had taken telephones up into trees with them one night during an enemy artillery barrage, and directed counter-battery fire on the German guns, silencing them.

I would have written last night but I went to the show to see Ronald Coleman and Marlene Dietrich in *Kismet.* The technicolor was magnificent, but the actors were wasted.

What a country—what a country? Why the Germans ever wanted it, I'll never know. Our bivouac area is dramatically under water and mud. All of France is soaked and drenched with rain. To keep dry is impossible. But it could be worse, yes, it could be worse. It could be cold. But then if it would turn cold, the rain would stop. And that can't happen!

I still haven't gotten a package from home and this irritates me no end. But I've seen the mail screwed up too long to worry too much. Some letters take as much as forty days, and others as little as eight days. And the peculiar thing is, you'll get one of each at the same mail call.

It is now three o'clock in the afternoon. I am waiting to go to Mass at four o'clock in the big church in this little town. I shall pray for peace in the early New Year.

However, I think that peace is impossible without total occupation of Germany. The German radio broadcast the other night was an appeal for peace—but on their terms, which, to one who wishes only for unconditional surrender, must be rejected as unsuited to the end for which we strive.

I am an idealist in that I would love to see a war-free world and happy people. I would love to see a World Federation as advocated by Eli Culbertson and others. But at the same time I am realist enough to know that the different natures and dispositions of nations would never permit it.

I still have to write Marie Louise, Roy, and Shelby Trice. Also Fr. Bienvenue, S.J. I don't feel like writing—things are miserable. But perhaps I'll get some letters at mail call. They'll help a lot.

Your loving son,
Morris

* * * * *

Somewhere in France
December 23, 1944

Dear Mom and Dad,

All news is bad. The Germans have smashed the front and have penetrated at least thirty-five miles. The Germans have promised Hitler Aachen for a Christmas present, and the commanders have promised their troops to be in Paris for New Year's. The headlines of *Stars and Stripes* are BIGGEST BATTLE SINCE D-DAY and REICH HURLS ITS BEST MENCHUTO ATTACK. The plans for the present counteroffensive are thorough, as were those that humbled France in a matter of days back in 1940. Perhaps this is the final roar of the dying lion. Perhaps the effort is backed by everything the Germans can muster. If this can be smashed, the war will probably be over by the time this reaches you. If the war isn't over when you get this, please make a novena to our Lady of Prompt Succor, the patron saint and savior of New Orleans.

Also from the *S&S,* I find this bit of advice to parents of fond children. "A pat on the back develops character—if administered often enough, young enough, and low enough."

I will have remembered you all at Mass and Communion on Christmas Day.

Love,
Morris

Somewhere in France
Wednesday, December 27, 1944

Dear Mom and Dad,

Christmas has come and gone, almost unnoticed. I didn't even have the opportunity to attend Mass and Communion. But I guess the war must go on. Xmas morning, long before dawn, we were eating good hot chow. Still before dawn we moved out through our own lines and into enemy territory, with rifles loaded for bear. This was Christmas and we were going out on combat patrol to smash Jerry behind his own lines. We were looking for trouble because we had to get prisoners and they just don't come in with hands up to accommodate us. Cautiously we moved ahead, up into the shelled villages, through the pockmarked apple orchards, past the German positions, until at last we reached the highest ground where we could see the whole countryside. But all was quiet. Nothing stirred in the broken houses or in the roofless barns. In the hazy distance could be seen a church tower. But there were no beings around. No animals, save for a dead rabbit, which lay in a road, no birds, and mysteriously enough, no Germans. And we were deep into their lines. We waited and watched and listened. In the distance, very, very faint, a church bell rang. Off to the left some dogs were barking. Otherwise, all was quiet. We turned and came back. At two-thirty in the afternoon we had our Christmas dinner of turkey and all the trimmings, just like in the States. So, though we might have had it otherwise, peace was with us on Christmas Day.

I know I haven't written in quite some time, but first, it's almost too cold to write (the temperature is in the low twenties—altho' one of the fellows said that it was five below), and second, there are too many distractions.

I have received a few boxes which I enjoyed very much. I use the rosary over and over during the night, praying to our Lady of Prompt Succor. I gave some of the Sacred Hearts to the other fellows in the squad. I carry one in my wallet.

I never have written to Marie Louise. I am really ashamed. She sent Christmas cards, get well cards, and a box of delicious Heavenly Hash. Oh well, maybe I'll get off a letter to her to-day. Besides the aforementioned, I have never written to answer her last letter. Hm-m-m, I won't have any girlfriends, will I?

Things are getting to be pretty rough. The weather is bitter cold. The ditches and paths which were covered with water a few days ago are now covered with a white sheet of ice. The trees have taken on a winter coat of white along with the whole countryside. Really beautiful, if it weren't that there's a war going on.

There is nothing that I want or need. The mail situation is still one grand mess. I have received only about six letters in the last two weeks or more. They were from Dad written on Will's birthday, one from Mama, Esther, Jerome, and Claude Jr. I am still waiting for the other packages and the back mail.

I am in good health and spirits. Wish I could write more but I just "ain't up to it." Watch the newspapers for news from this outfit. Many articles appear in the papers over here, so I guess they show up back home. I have seen some clippings sent from home, of the stories of this division.

Give my regards to all. And I mean *all,* because I haven't dropped a line to anybody in over three weeks or a month. Have Will give my regards to all my old friends. Will Dad please tell Mr. Guste I have heard from Roy, but that I have not written because of the various reasons that one might surmise? Roy is a very regular correspondent.

I hope everyone is doing well at school. All my love to all,

Your loving son,
Morris Jr.

* * * * *

Somewhere in France
December 28, 1944

Dear Mom and Dad,

Yesterday I received a bunch of Christmas cards and a few letters from both of you, Ogie, and Richard. I received a Mass card from Mrs. Mary Cologne, and also a Christmas card. I received a card from the Stuarts and also from someone else whom I do not remember at present—oh yes, Peggy McGinity. Please ring Mrs. Cologne and thank her for me. You might also call Mrs. Murphy and thank her for the box of Creole pralines. I thought the handwriting was yours. Tell her I also heard from Norris. I'd write her (the mama), but I don't remember the address.

Before me I have your letters of the 10th of the current. Glad you liked my Christmas cards. I sent Fr. Crandall and Uncle Billy ones like yours. The others I managed to pick up in tobacco stores in Nantes while on pass there some time ago. Those stores sell everything but tobacco.

There isn't much to write about. I was glad to hear that Will did well on Talent Night. Maybe next year he should go on by himself. Speaking of piano players, Dad closed by saying that you were playing "I'll See You Again," as he wrote. I never got a chance to play your records, and yesterday I packed them away in my duffel bag and probably won't see them until after the war.

Glad to hear that the law business was good this year. Hope it's still good ten years from now when I'll be starting out as a "barrister at law."

Well, I'm always thinking of you, although I'm not always writing to you.

Give my regards to the Kellys, Stuarts, Joyces, and Sellers.

Your loving son,
Morris

* * * * *

Somewhere in France
December 31, 1944

Dear Mom and Dad,

This is the last breath from a dying year. A memorable chapter in the life of every living being. In the latter half it much affected the emotions and feelings of the people of the United Nations, and in particular, those of our own. From the sixth of June when the liberation of Europe began, the emotions of many became fluid and inconsistent, changing from fear to joy, from joy perhaps to sadness, from the watchful silence of those first D-Plus days, to jubilant optimism, and from optimism to realism, as the official communiqués announced the winnings and the losings.

But perhaps one of the most notable notes of the year of 1944 was that it was a year of sacrifice never before witnessed by anyone. For one who lived through this potent year, and saw the effort put forth by ourselves and our Allies, that one, could say he knew us "in our finest hour."

I doubt, if ever before, in all history, has there been such grand cooperation and friendship between the nations of such an alliance as that to which we belong. Perhaps this spirit is owed in part to the great threat posed by the aggressive spirit and military might of mankind's common enemy. And thus, there is a somewhat saddening and sober note that now appears upon the global field. I believe that in the defeat of Germany, there shall end the cooperative spirit of the greater nations. Already the signs can be seen. As victory comes nearer, the obligations of mutual aid and security seem to dissolve in the grand confusion of statements already spoken and those expected to be spoken. The integrity of decimated Poland is no more sacred today than it was Sept. 1, 1939, when the panzers roared into its towns and villages. Because as the two signing parties agree, "The Atlantic Charter exists only in notes." Nations have turned against nations. In Greece the dog has bit the hand that fed it.

However, as far as the war goes, one could say the general situation was good and victory seems sure by the spring or early summer of 1945. The greatest battles have yet to be fought. These will be battles for the Rhine, for there lies the last natural barrier to Greater Germany. There lies the last grand line of defense. Perhaps by the beginning of March, our armies shall have removed the Rhine Valley from German hands. Someday in May a German Plenipotentiary Commission shall once again seat themselves and sign the line—in a railroad car in a famous forest. But the road is long and peace is still a dream.

We can say with certainty that the war will be over by Christmas.

This morning I went back and heard Mass and received Communion. I hope to get the chance to attend and receive tomorrow. To-day is exceptional—warm sunshine and cool breezes. The ground is thawing out and things are getting muddy again.

Yesterday I got a very rich and delicious fruitcake from Mr. and Mrs. Kahrs. I presume that's "Doc" Kahrs of Cloverland Dairy, and Daddy's friend. They live at thirty-four something St. Charles. I wish Dad would express my thanks, for I do not believe I shall really have the opportunity of writing them for some time.

I suppose you follow the war news closely and have probably heard of us from commentators or the like. However, as a New Year's resolution, pray more for me, and worry less about me, and both better off shall be.

Love to all,

Your loving son,
Morris

P.S. Shall send another money order home soon. The bonds should come every month. Send further info. Shall inquire to-day.

* * * * *

In the following letter to his parents, dated January 11, 1945—the last letter of his life—Morris writes of a wonderful afternoon and evening spent the previous week with a buddy from Tennessee. He doesn't mention this buddy's name, but if this person is still alive and recognizes this episode, I ask him to please contact me: Kerry Redmann, 68243 Taulla Drive, Covington, LA 70433, telephone number (985) 875–9899.

Morris's ability to speak the language made the visit with this French family enjoyable, and a welcomed interlude to the harshness of war. It is my belief that Morris fully intended to see them again after the war, should the opportunity have presented itself. He was not one to forget acts of kindness, especially in the situation they were in.

It is my hope that members of this family recognize this account of Morris and his buddy's visit as recalled in his letter, and understand how grateful he was. I would be pleased to hear from them at the above listed address.

Festung Europa
January 11, 1945

Dear Mom and Dad,

I realize I probably have caused you a lot of unnecessary worry by not writing, but for some time I haven't had much chance. For some days we've had much snow that piles up in drifts and blankets the villages and mountains of the countryside. It's really beautiful, and for me—a new experience. There isn't much wind so it's not too bad. The days are short and gray with never a sign of the sun. The days seem to fade in and out. The nights are never too dark, and days are never too bright. One has one heck of a time digging a hole in the snow. It's usually an all-day job.

Haven't had any mail in over a week, but shall try to write a letter on some of the subjects you wrote in your V-Mail of the 14th. It speaks of your Christmas shopping tour in the Vieux Carré. Exorbitant prices? Whew! You should try to buy stuff over here. In theory the rate of exchange here is 50 francs to the dollar. In reality, it's 300 francs to the dollar. Silver articles and other souvenirs which would sell for two dollars in the best clip joints in Royal Street run as high as six hundred francs. That's far beyond my means, since I only draw 788 francs a month. Although in American dollars that's the equivalent of $15.90, the purchasing value of 788 francs is just about $2.62 American. But I shouldn't worry. I never get a chance to spend the works. "What, never?" "Well, hardly ever." About a week ago or so, through a French butcher with whom I had become good friends, I got eight bottles of champagne for an exceptionally reasonable price. I also had three beautiful beef steaks from him (about six pounds) for the equivalent of $1.20.

I and a buddy from Tennessee took these to a café to have them fixed, but the proprietors were unwilling. A few minutes later while walking down a street I asked a little boy where I could get them cooked; he asked me to wait a minute. I waited, while he obligingly ran inside and asked his mother if she could cook for two American soldiers. Well, the little boy beckoned and we hurried in out of the snow to a nice warm house. It was a rather large affair of many rooms. We went and seated ourselves in the kitchen. The kitchen was very modernly equipped with an electric stove and a beautiful radio. This was a surprise, since most kitchens I had seen in the abandoned houses near the line were just open, smoked-black fireplaces.

The family was large also. Something like ours—seven children. They ranged from thirteen months to fifteen years. The eldest was studying English in high school. He could read a little, but couldn't speak it.

Well, for dinner we had soup with croutons, plenty of french fries with the beef steak, bread and butter, cider to drink with the meal, and stewed apples. All during the meal, I'm batting the breeze with the "père de famille," so I'm in pretty good with him. So after dinner he goes upstairs and brings down a bottle of very fine cognac. He then tried to get an English broadcast for us. We got some war news. Yes, I thought the broadcast was English—all English. That's all you hear from BBC. "The English did this . . . the English did that. . . ." And whenever the Americans do anything, the English pull that Lindbergh stuff and say "We."

So, we quit listening to the radio and began talking about South America, where the best coffee comes from, the Germans, the weather, and politics. Had a couple of cognacs, and after an invitation to visit them again the next time I was in their city, I left. If, after the war, I am again in that town I shall visit them, for I am sure that I spent a very enjoyable evening.

Then my buddy and I walked out of the city back to a snow-covered field, to snow-covered tents, pitched on frozen ground. At present we're in reserve and have a pretty good deal. We're billeted in houses—the few left in this little town that are still habitable. We're back on three meals a day. To-day I had the first fresh beef since England. It was really good. In the mornings we have hotcakes, syrup, bacon, and cereal, coffee to drink. However, I prefer only two meals a day. I always feel overstuffed when I eat three.

The other day a buddy and I made some very good ice cream in a bucket, and we made it in about three minutes. We took two cans of milk, about six or eight ounces of sugar (in 2-oz. boxes), and about ten ounces of Nestle's cocoa mix, which is also in 2-oz. pkgs. (C-ration stuff). You mix the above together and then add plenty of snow, and stir as you add. It makes excellent ice cream. All the comforts of home! (Some bull.)

Hope all are well at home and in school.

Give my love to all.

Your loving son,
Morris

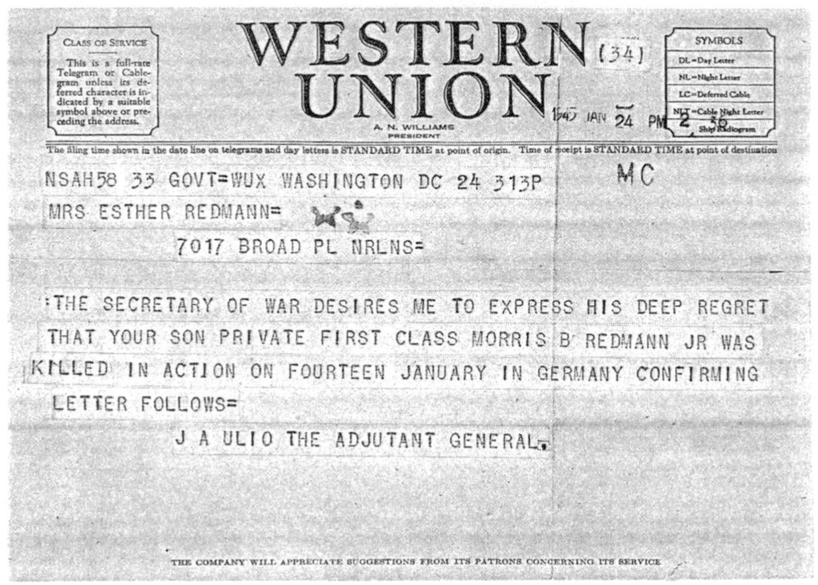
WESTERN UNION

CLASS OF SERVICE: This is a full-rate Telegram or Cablegram unless its deferred character is indicated by a suitable symbol above or preceding the address.

A. N. WILLIAMS, PRESIDENT

SYMBOLS: DL=Day Letter; NL=Night Letter; LC=Deferred Cable; NLT=Cable Night Letter; Ship Radiogram

1945 JAN 24 PM 2 35

The filing time shown in the date line on telegrams and day letters is STANDARD TIME at point of origin. Time of receipt is STANDARD TIME at point of destination

NSAH58 33 GOVT=WUX WASHINGTON DC 24 313P MC

MRS ESTHER REDMANN=

7017 BROAD PL NRLNS=

:THE SECRETARY OF WAR DESIRES ME TO EXPRESS HIS DEEP REGRET THAT YOUR SON PRIVATE FIRST CLASS MORRIS B REDMANN JR WAS KILLED IN ACTION ON FOURTEEN JANUARY IN GERMANY CONFIRMING LETTER FOLLOWS=

J A ULIO THE ADJUTANT GENERAL.

THE COMPANY WILL APPRECIATE SUGGESTIONS FROM ITS PATRONS CONCERNING ITS SERVICE

HEADQUARTERS 376TH INFANTRY
APO 94 c/o PM New York, NY
Office of the Commanding Officer

18 January 1945

Mrs. Esther Redmann
7017 Broad Plac
New Orleans, Louisiana

Dear Mrs. Redmann:

It is with deep sympathy that I write to you of the death of your son, Private First Class Morris B. Redmann Jr., 38499577. Morris was killed 14 January 1945 in Germany while engaged in action against the enemy. He was buried with fitting burial rites read by a Catholic chaplain in an Army Cemetery in Luxembourg.

Morris joined this regiment 10 months ago and had served his country well as a good soldier until the day of his death. By his excellent conduct in action against the enemy, he had been awarded the right to wear the Combat Infantryman Badge.

The company and the regiment feel his loss keenly. His comrades join with me in extending our heartfelt sympathy. We shall do our part to bring the war to an early and successful conclusion so that his sacrifice will not have been in vain.

Very sincerely,
H. H. McClune
Colonel, Infantry Commanding

A Combat Infantryman's Burial

Not midst tolling dirge of church bells,
Nor with solemn prayers and Requiem mass,
'Neath misty shadows emerging through stained-glass windows,
And air so filled with scent of incense was he interred;

But in the subtle stillness of after battle,
In dawn's first light that quietly ushers in the day,
We carried his body all caked with mud,
And placed it, gently bagged, into the clay.

Yet who shall say that he was not content,
Or missed the incessant prayers and chanting choir,
He who had heard all day the battle anthems,
Echoed a thousand times by the 88's screeching fire.

What oriel glass can lovelier images cast,
Than those the evening skies majestically unfold,
Their mingling light creating magic colors o'er the dead,
Softly illuminating the spangled banner for which he died.

—*Kerry P. Redmann*

PART FIVE

LUXEMBOURG AMERICAN MILITARY CEMETERY

Morris B. Redmann Jr. remains buried in the Luxembourg American Military Cemetery, which comprises over fifty acres and is situated in a glade enframed by spruce, beech, oak, and other trees of the forest in a hilly wooded area called Hamm. The entrance is through tall, wrought-iron gates—each section weighing more than one ton—and bears gilded laurel wreaths, the ancient award for valor. The massive stone pillars supporting the gates are surmounted by gilded bronze eagles.

The memorial itself consists of a tall, columnar, square chapel of stone, set upon a podium, reached by two flights of steps, and a terrace overlooking the burial areas. The chapel rises fifty feet above its podium, and is made of white valore stone from the Jura Mountain region of central France. The interior walls are of Hauteville Perle stone, also from France.

Above the altar is a tall, narrow window of stained glass portraying the insignia of the five major U.S. commands that operated in the region—the Twelfth Army Group, the First Army, the Third Army, the Eighth Air Force, and the Ninth Air Force.

The floor of the chapel is made of four different marbles from Italy, and inset into the floor is a bronze circular plaque containing the thirteen stars of the Seal of the United States of America, wreathed in oak, pine, and laurel.

The burial plots are broken by two radial malls, each containing two fountains with pylons of valore stone. The fountains flow into three small terraced pools embellished by bronze dolphins and turtles—the dolphins symbolizing the resurrection, and the turtles symbolizing eternal life. Carved on the reverse side of the pylons is a symbol of the four

Evangelists—an angel for St. Matthew, a lion for St. Mark, a horse for St. Luke, and an eagle for St. John. Interspaced between the fountains are long planters of different species of American roses.

Originally, there were 13,016 American military buried in this cemetery—all of whom gave their lives in the Battle of the Bulge and the Advance to the Rhine. Of this number, 7,940 were returned to the United States as requested by their next of kin, leaving 5,076 permanently buried at Luxembourg. Included in this permanent number is General George S. Patton Jr., Commanding General of the United States Third Army.

Visit to Morris's Grave: Final Closure

After fifty-five years, one of my younger brothers, Ralph, joined me with our wives in visiting Morris's grave at the Luxembourg American Military Cemetery in Hamm. We had signed up for a tour called "D-Day to the Rhine," which was specially designed by renowned author and historian, Stephen E. Ambrose. At the cemetery, with the sensitive and kind assistance of retired Marine Captain Ron Drez and his wife Judy, we paid our respects to Morris's memory, encircled his marble headstone with the 94th Infantry Division flag, and placed a bouquet of flowers and a small American flag upon his grave. Carol Harangody and Gayle Ray of Littleton, Colorado, assisted Captain Drez by filling the lettering on the marble cross with river sand, furnished by the cemetery administrator's office, so the name and other information would stand out for picture taking. I was truly grateful for their help. Captain Drez concluded our ceremony at the gravesite with a toast: "To Morris Redmann—soldier—warrior—American."

At the end of the grave ceremony at the Luxembourg American Military Ceremony, I offered a prayer which I had composed upon arriving in Luxembourg, not only for our brother, Morris, but for all those interred:

> *Almighty Father, we come here today—to this hallowed ground—to this place of honored glory—to pay our respects to the memory of Morris B. Redmann Jr., and his comrades-in-arms, who made the supreme sacrifice during the Battle of the Bulge.*
>
> *Though we are still burdened by our loss, even after all these years, we are strengthened with the knowledge that sadness gives way to the bright promise of immortality—and if we truly believe, we must accept that death was their portal to eternal happiness.*

Father, we are reminded of the words of St. John, the Evangelist, chapter 10, verse 28, wherein he affirms the promise of Your Son: "I give unto them eternal life and they shall never perish." What comforting and befitting words in a place like this.

Father, we thank You for including those interred here among the flock of Your elect—and we ask that You sustain and bless their surviving families.

Finally, Father, we implore Your help in making certain that what was endured here and what was sacrificed here will never be obscured by the passage of time nor the dimming of memory—so that we here remaining and generations yet unborn will inherit and preserve our distinctive way of life—our purple mountain's majesty—our fruited plain—our fortress built by nature—our bastion of freedom—our blessed plot of land—our United States of America.

Amen. Amen. Amen.

Upon leaving the cemetery, I thought of a saying attributed to the Emperor Napoleon: "The boundaries of a nation's greatness are marked by the graves of her soldiers."

PART SIX

LETTERS FROM FRIENDS AND FAMILY

The following are a few letters from Morris's close army buddies, written to his parents after his death.

Loyola University
School of Law, Dean's Office
New Orleans, Louisiana

January 25, 1945

Mr. Morris B. Redmann
7017 Broad Place
New Orleans, Louisiana

Dear Mr. Redmann:

Morris was a student in the law school just a few months. He knew many of the boys in law school before he entered as a student, so I learned to know him when he was in the Arts College. Those of us who knew Morris will not forget him.

Whatever I write now is inadequate. Please tell his mother how sorry we are.

Very truly yours,
Vernon X. Miller, Dean

My dear Mr. and Mrs Redmann and the dear Little Ones,

I am sorry, so very sorry.

I am remembering your dear boy in Holy Communion these mornings and shall attend Holy Mass in requiem on Monday.

May God bless you and comfort you.

Sincerely,
Lil Garvey

* * * * *

Saturday, January 28, 1945

Mr. & Mrs. Redmann

Dear Friends:

I want to express to you my sincerest sympathy in the loss of your dear son. "No greater love is there than to lay down one's life for another," and surely this dear boy has given his all for us.

Nothing that I can say will compensate for the loss, but there is this satisfaction that he died as he had lived, a noble boy with a Christian life behind him.

May God give you the strength to submit to His will and find comfort in your sweet family.

With kindest regards.
Sincerely,
Adelaide C. Henican

* * * * *

DOMINICAN SISTERS MOTHERHOUSE
CONGREGATION OF ST. MARY
7214 St. Charles Avenue
New Orleans 18, Louisiana

January 28, 1945

My dear Mr. and Mrs. Redmann:

Our hearts are torn with tender sympathy for you, your daughter and young sons, sister and brothers to a gallant young hero who courageously battled against the enemy of his country and the enemies of his faith.

We cannot comfort you; in Morris, your firstborn, was centered your dreams of future achievements and happiness—then, our country called him. No words of ours can assuage your grief—yet, we do beg you *not* to think of your darling boy as resting beneath German soil, but to *know* that his is the shining splendor of glory encompassing God's heroes for all eternity.

That Morris was a staunch, true soldier of Christ and an undefeated soldier of America, constant in endurance and noble in sacrifice, is owing to the strong faith and beautiful love in his love, and the noble example of virtue surrounding him from infancy. He is now with God, obtaining grace and strength for you.

Our prayers have been for him—and we are asking Jesus and Mary to console you.

Sincerely yours in St. Dominic,
Sister Mary Dominica, O.P.
Mother General

* * * * *

Long Beach, Calif.
January 29, 1945

My dear Mrs. Redmann,

While in Los Angeles to-day, we bought a N.O. *Times-Picayune* and read where a requiem mass was being said for Morris Jr. Please accept our heartfelt sympathy on your great loss. Needless to say, it upset us terribly and we want you to know that we join you in prayers for him.

Sincerely,
Hazel Bruno

* * * * *

ARMY AIR FORCES
B-29 SUPERFORTRESS

January 29, 1945

Dear Mr. and Mrs. Redmann,

Letters today from both Numa and my mother brought me first news of Morris's death. The loss of one of my dearest friends and beloved schoolmates was a crushing blow.

I think perhaps you knew how close Morris and Numa and I were during our school days, so you can understand how we felt about him.

May I add my condolences and prayers to those of Tri-Sigs and Morris's friends all over the world in your hour of sorrow.

Sincerely,
Charlie Brennan

* * * * *

1925 Biltmore St., NW,
Washington 9, D.C.
January 30, 1945

Dear Mr. Redmann;

I learned of your son's death this evening and wish to express my deepest sympathy to you and your family.

I feel sure that you do not remember me, because you met me only once at a Pegasus gathering in your home. Morris was an acquaintance of mine at Loyola, even though we pursued widely different degrees. It was a pleasure to have been associated with him, and this tragic news shocks me deeply.

It has been more than a year since I last saw him as I left for Midshipmens school in September of 1943. Since then I have been able to spend but a brief twelve-day period in New Orleans. After being commissioned at Notre Dame University, I was sent to the Navy Department for a short while. I was then detached and reported to the Naval Research Laboratory, where I have been engaged in research work ever since.

In closing I wish to again extend my sympathies. I will remember Morris in my prayers.

Sincerely,
Charles P. Smith Jr.

5727 Cabanne Avenue
Saint Louis, Missouri
February 3, 1945

Mr. and Mrs. Morris B. Redmann

Dear friends:

Today's post has brought the tidings of your bereavement, and our hearts, believe me, are heavy with the grief that has pierced your own. Your chief solace in these days of poignant sorrow must be the Faith in which you have been reared and the love that indissolutely binds you and your dear children to one another—whether in this life or in that beyond. If reason, religion, and the universe itself mean anything at all, that shining young soul who so recently gave up his life did not lose it; he but exchanged it for a wider, brighter fuller one with Him who also laid down His young earthly life for our salvation.

Though grief-torn, your own lives are exalted and enriched through your priceless sacrificial gift. Whatever your beloved boy might have achieved had he been longer spared to you and to his country, his name is now written with fadeless honor on the page of history, as it is also in God's own Book of Life.

These considerations have of course occurred to you, and perhaps with but little softening of your present hearts' distress; but we trust that with the passing of time they may become a source of genuine comfort.

Words cannot convey the measure of our sympathy; but, dear Esther and Morris, we do share in your sorrow, deeply and keenly. You and yours have and will long have an intimate place in our thoughts and prayers. Our love to you all.

Samuel and Grace Stewart

REVEREND CHARLES MCCONVILLE
OUR LADY OF MOUNT CARMEL CHURCH
St. Francisville, Louisiana

February 3, 1945

Mr. Morris Redmann
Canal Buildings
New Orleans, Louisiana

Dear Morris:

I am deeply grieved to hear that your dear son Morris B. has been killed in action somewhere on the Western Front. I feel almost as if he belonged to my own family. I know what a terrible blow it must be to you and his good mother. May your splendid family be a comfort to you both in this hour of sorrow.

I suppose he must have belonged to the First or Third Armies opposing the attempted breakthrough in December and January. It was one of the most glorious victories in American history. The brave boys who died there will be ever remembered by their countrymen.

Dear Morris, you and Mrs. Redmann are in my thoughts and prayers. I shall say a special Mass tomorrow for Morris B., and all the family. May God comfort you. Our prayer must be the prayer of the holy patriarch: "Though the Lord shall slay me, yet will I keep my trust in Him."

With deep sympathy,
Sincerely yours in Christ,
Charles McConville

4601 South Galvez Place
New Orleans, Louisiana
February 4, 1945

Dear Mr. & Mrs. Redmann,

Please permit me, on behalf of the friends and companions of Morris Jr., in Sigma, Sigma, Sigma, Fraternity, and particularly myself, to inform you that I have asked Father Soniat at Loyola to say ten Masses for Morris, beginning this week.

All of us wish to be remembered to your family.

Sincerely yours,
Numa V. Bertel Jr.

* * * * *

NAVY SUPPLY CORPS SCHOOL

February 4, 1945

Dear Mr. & Mrs. Redmann:

The news about Morris reached me this past week, and its tragic contents have struck me very deeply. Needless to say, all the Tri-Sig fellows have the same feeling as I do at this time. To lose one so very close to us is very hard to take.

However, our feelings must certainly be at a minimum when the thought of how you must feel at the loss of Morris comes to mind. My deepest and most heartfelt sympathies are with you in this hour of your great sorrow.

I pray to God that Morris and others like him have not given their lives in vain, but that a new world of peace and friendship will result from their glorious sacrifice.

May your loss be replaced by all the good graces that God may bring to you and your family.

Sincerely yours,
Parker Schneidau

HOLY GHOST RECTORY
117 Hooper Street
North Tiverton, Rhode Island

February 9, 1945

Mr. & Mrs. Morris Redmann

My Dear Mr. & Mrs. Redmann,

I cannot tell you how shocked I was when I received the sad news that Morris had died. His death was a glorious one; nevertheless, a cloud of sorrow has appeared over your home and lovely family. I have said Mass for him & for you all. I had no idea that he was in the battleline, as I thought he was attending a military college somewhere. I know he is all right. He was a splendid boy. Praying that the Blessed Mother shall comfort you. She knew what it was, to lose her "boy" also. We are snowbound here for weeks, and so I miss Louisiana in many ways. Kind regards to the children, especially Kerry, and again my sincere condolences on your sorrow.

Sincerely,
Kerry O'Connor Keane

* * * * *

February 13, 1945

Mr. Morris Redmann
Canal Bank Building
New Orleans, Louisiana

Dear Mr. Redmann,

News has reached me here, where I am taking a good rest, that your eldest son has been killed in action. My heartfelt sympathy goes out to you in this hour of great trial. I have included your martyred son in one of my Masses, and I will include him in several others I shall take soon for my own intentions. I am also including him in the daily Memento at Mass.

Here's hoping and praying that this terrible war will soon be over. I have given up trying to fathom it, and I have resigned myself to a blind faith in Providence.

As to myself, I am happy to report that the rest is proving a great help. With sincerest personal regards and again with my sincerest condolence.

Yours in Christ,
Columban Thuis, O.S.B.
Abbott

* * * * *

Wednesday, February 14, 1945

Dear Aunt Esther and Uncle Morris,

Mother's letter telling me about my cousin arrived on 2 February when I was at a distant port. We had never received mail there before this time, and when I heard "Mail call," a very strange feeling came over me and I sensed bad news. I almost knew before I opened her letter, what she would say. This lessened the shock, but I have been terribly grieved ever since. Lately, however, I have come to realize that all trouble is over for our Morris, and I firmly believe that he is, at this moment, sharing in a rich reward, happy with our dear Lord in Heaven, for he was a wonderful person. You have my deepest sympathy and are remembered every night in my prayers. Very often, my ship is at sea on Sunday, but as soon as I have the opportunity I shall offer a Communion for him.

How are the other children getting along? Tell Kerry that I have just one picture left and he shall have it very soon, as I'm sending it today.

Still the same routine with me down here. I have a very slight chance of getting home perhaps in July. I will have a year at sea then.

I want to thank all of you for your prayers and for remembering me in your letters. Drop me a line again when you have time.

My love to all,
Paul

1345 Logan St.
Denver, Colorado
March 4, 1945

Dear Esther and Mr. Redmann:

We have received the very sad account of your beloved son's death, and, again, we try to extend to you our sincere and deepest sympathy. We know, indeed, the tragic meaning of having to give up one's beloved children, for, as we believe we told you, some years ago, we have had to give up all three of our loved ones. However, we realize, too,—though, that your sorrow is very hard to bear, inasmuch as you could not be with your darling son, at the time of his death.

We know, from his picture, that he was a happy, fine young man, who enjoyed life and loved his parents, his brothers, and sister, as well as his Aunt Lala, and other relatives. His letter to his Aunt Lala proves the nobility of his character, his very kind thoughtfulness of others, and gratitude for everything that had been done for him from his childhood, up to young manhood. We can imagine how tenderly you will always cherish his dear letters. Then, too, we have noticed that he was a brilliant student, and a leader in college activities. There will always be a great consolation in the fact that you gave him such a fine Catholic education. No doubt you will hear later on from the chaplain of his division. This will also be a great comfort to you all.

We are so very sorry, also, to learn from Mr. Redmann's letter, of the illness of your young son, David, but we do hope he has improved, although we fully realize that his injury was most painful, and unfortunate.

We will try to remember your dear son, Morris, in our poor prayers, as well as all the members of your family. Please give our love also to Aunt Lala, who was so kind to all the children, including Morris.

We are about as usual and trying to attend some of the Lenten services. Again, with our deepest sympathy and prayers.

Lovingly,
Ralph and Elizabeth Kelly

U.I.O.G.D.
St. Joseph's Abbey
Benedictine Fathers
St. Benedict, Louisiana

March 5, 1945

Morris Redmann
New Orleans, Louisiana

Dear Mr. Redmann:

Your request for twelve Gregorian masses every day for three hundred and sixty days was referred to me a few days ago. Fortunately I found someone that was willing to take this extra burden. As to the stipend, there should also be an extra offering. The Rev. Father is ready to start the Gregorian masses this week. So please let me know immediately. The enclosed literature is to enlighten you on the subject.

Yours truly,
Rev. Clement Steinacker,
O.S.B

* * * * *

March 7, 1945

Reverend Clement Steinacker, O.S.B.
St. Joseph's Abbey
St. Benedict, Louisiana

Reverend and Dear Father:

Reference is made to your letter of March 5, 1945, and to our telephone conversation of today regarding the twelve Gregorian Masses to be said every day for 360 days for the repose of the soul of my son, Morris B. Redmann Jr.

In accordance with our understanding reached on the telephone, I enclose herewith my check to the order of St. Joseph's Abbey for $420.00.

With kindest regards to you and all the Community, I remain

Sincerely,
Morris B. Redmann

The Gregorian Mass takes its name from the originator, Pope St. Gregory the Great, who governed the Church from the year 590 to 605. This pious practice is an ancient teaching of the Church, confirmed by the Council of Lyons, Florence, and Trent. This early form of devotion consisted of the offering of 30 Masses for 30 consecutive days, without interruption. Its intention is for a particular soul, recently departed, whose release from Purgatory is thereby implored of the Divine Mercy of God. The initial offering was by Pope St. Gregory the Great while he ruled as Abbott of the Monastery of St. Andreas, on the Coelian Hill in Rome. When Abbott Gregory was elevated to the Papal Throne, his influence caused this practice to be known throughout Christendom and is still offered even to this day.

* * * * *

March 7, 1945

Dear Esther & Morris:

Words are so futile in times of trouble like yours, but I must tell you that my heart goes out to you in sympathy so deep that I cannot express what I feel.

Your boy was so fine in every way that you have the consolation of knowing that he met his Maker with a clear conscience, having done everything that was asked of him. Ogie has told me so much about his sweet and wonderful character. I prayed for him while he was in this world, and he still has my prayers. May God comfort you and give you strength to bear this sorrow. I am so glad I sent Morris a Christmas card to let him know that I was thinking of him.

Sincerely,
Gissie

CONGRESS OF THE UNITED STATES
HOUSE OF REPRESENTATIVES
WASHINGTON, D.C.

March 10, 1945

Mrs. Esther Redmann
7017 Broad Place,
New Orleans, Louisiana

Dear Friend:

I am deeply grieved to learn that your son has been killed in action in the service of his country. While I am anxious to do something to soften the distressing information you have received, I realize that no words or action on my part can restore to you the son that you have given to help win the struggle for the preservation of humanity and the principles of liberty and justice on which this country was founded. Any words or message are, of course, totally inadequate; however, I do want you to know that you have my sincere sympathy in your bereavement.

Sincerely yours,
James H. Morrison, M.C.

* * * * *

CITY OF NEW ORLEANS
OFFICE OF THE MAYOR

March 20, 1945

Mr. and Mrs. Redmann
7017 Broad Place
New Orleans, Louisiana

Dear Mr. and Mrs. Redmann:

I have just learned of the death of your son, Morris B. Redmann Jr., Private First Class of the United States Army, who has been reported killed in action. I wish to extend my deepest sympathy.

I trust that you may find comfort in the memory that your son has made the supreme sacrifice in upholding the tradition of the United States in defense of his country.

It is my sincere hope that time will temper your grief, and that you will gain comfort in the realization that to men, like your son, who have died that the American Way of Life can continue, the nation owes an everlasting debt of gratitude.

Again, my deepest sympathy to you and the other members of your family.

Faithfully yours,
Robt. S. Maestri

* * * * *

94th Signal Co. APO 94
March 23, 1945

Dear Mr. and Mrs. Redmann,

I realize that this letter will not lessen your sorrow but I want you to know that I, too, am deeply grieved by the death of Morris Jr.

As you know, we were inducted together, we went to Camp Beauregard together, and during basic training at Fort Benning, we were in the same platoon and the same barracks. He was a likeable person and I can think of no one, outside of my family, whom I liked as well as him.

I last saw him on the *Queen Elizabeth* when we came across. In Brittany I wrote to him, but I was never close enough to see him. In Germany I wrote to him but received no reply, so I tried to find him. When I went to his company I was told that he had been killed. I was too shocked then to ask any questions, so I only knew what they told me.

Later, Georgine wrote that she had called and was told that he had been killed.

There is nothing I can say to tell you how sorry I am. I will come to see you when I return to New Orleans.

Sincerely,
Shelby C. Trice

Germany
May 22, 1945

Mrs. Morris B. Redmann
7017 Broad Place
New Orleans, Louisiana

Dear Mrs. Redmann:

In reply to your letter of February 17 addressed to Lt. Foster of this organization, and held pending his return from the hospital, I shall be most happy to answer and give you the information desired by you, even tho' there is little that I can say. You see, I always find this sort of a hard task and not entirely to my liking, since but for the grace of God and a lot of luck the same letter might be as well going to my mother.

Your son Morris joined us, as I recall, in Camp McCain, Mississippi, just a few months before we came overseas and became a member of the first platoon. He served with the company while we had the mission of containing the Germans in the St. Nazaire, Lorient pocket, which was left behind in the push thru France last year. We remained there until around the first of the year, and at that time moved up to the big front.

We were at first in reserve in a little village near the town of Perl in Germany, and the day Morris was killed was the first action we participated in on the big front. At that time the first battalion of our regiment was attacking from the town of Wochern to take the towns of Tettingen and Butzdorf, and we were held in reserve of them to be used only if there was any danger of the attack being held up, or in case of counterattack. We dug in just behind the town in a woods, and no sooner had we started digging in than the Heinkels started shelling the woods.

We had some casualties from the first barrage, and Morris at that time helped take these casualties from the woods to the road for evacuation. After helping the wounded out, he returned and again they started shelling, and it was this time that he was killed and as fate would have it, in the same hole that he had just helped one of his wounded buddies out of. The night before we pushed off on this operation he had told some of his buddies that he was sure he would never come back, as has been the case with many of the men, and even then he didn't hesitate but went anyway.

There are no words of praise that I might use that I should consider praiseworthy of his act, so I shall not try. The names you mentioned as friends of Morris's are no longer with us, so I'm afraid you'll have to be content with this, and if I can be of any further help just let me know.

Sincerely yours,
Charles P. Macke, 1st. Lt.

Monday, August 13, 1945

Dear Mrs. Redmann,

I have thought of you quite often since January. I haven't written because I honestly didn't know what to say. I still don't, but I should think you'd like for me to tell you about my friendship with Morris.

I met him at Fort Benning; we were in the same company. However, it was at McCain that I really got to know him. We were in the same platoon through it all. Things weren't too bad while we were in France. We occasionally had time off, and it was almost like living. Morris and I spent all of our off time together. I'm sure he wrote you of our trip to Nantes, France, last Thanksgiving. It was one of the most enjoyable trips I have ever taken.

After we left France, everything changed. We didn't go into action when we first got there, and Morris and I had a room together in a German home. Incidentally, Morris received a check from his father (or some money) on or about the 10th of Jan. I know he never spent it; have you gotten it? I think it was on the 14th that we left to go into action. L Company was not to fight; we were going to wait in some woods until another element took a small town. We got safely in the woods just before daylight. We were told it wouldn't be necessary to dig in, so we didn't, except for a few boys. We sat there for about an hour, listening to the battle on the next hill. Morris and I ate C rations together. All of a sudden the Germans dropped six shells in the woods. It was like murder; the shells exploded in the trees and covered us with shrapnel. Just as suddenly they stopped. Morris and I were lucky enough to be unharmed. Dreading more shells, Morris and I dug slit trenches. I was standing, talking to him, when they came again. They dropped five more and then stopped. I called to Morris and he didn't answer; I ran to his hole and raised him up. He was already dead; a piece of shrapnel had gone through his back. Mrs. Redmann, he died instantly. He was hit by the last shell in the second group. I was to him in less than a minute, and he was already gone. I hope this is some consolation, if there is any such thing. I have seen so many die in pain and agony, that I can understand; but I know that can't be the case with you. We called a medic, but I knew it was useless. Smith, Gallagher, Hambly, DeMase, and I were like lost babies after that. These boys were other friends of Morris's.

Things got continually worse after that; I sometimes almost lost faith in the intelligence of the whole awful thing. I lasted until the 26th and then I stepped on a *schü* mine. I'm sure that my sister told you about that, however.

I am doing fine now. Of course I have lost lots of weight, but that'll come back in time. I am supposed to be fitted with a prosthesis this week, so things are finally "looking up"; it's a good feeling to be able to look ahead again.

I hope this letter will be a little help for you. I just thought you might feel better if you knew. If it's otherwise, just mark it up to my stupidity. I do want to tell you that Morris was one of the nicest, cleanest boys I ever knew. He was popular in the company; he was unusually bright, and lots of the boys looked to him for leadership. I'll never forget one night in La Gacilly, France. We held Mass for a boy who had been killed. Morris assisted the French father. It was beautiful. That's just the way he was; he could handle almost any situation. I know your family must be awfully nice, because for him to be as he was, it just couldn't be otherwise. He certainly was a credit to you.

Well, I guess I had better close. Maybe I'll get to see you someday; I'd certainly like to. I hope you are all fine and well, and please give my regards to Mr. Redmann.

Respectfully,
Tom Moore

P.S. How is Morris's brother (the one in college now—or just out)? Morris was awfully proud of him.

* * * * *

469 Clinton Avenue
Albany 5, N.Y.
September 12, 1945

Dear Mr. Redmann:

I'm not much of a letter writer, and I'm not quite sure as to just where to begin. Hence, if this letter seems disjointed, or incorrect in any way, I do hope you'll overlook it.

In the year of 1944, your son joined my old outfit—Company L, 94th Division. We, having mutual interests, soon became fast friends. He was a swell guy and I grew quite fond of him.

In August of the same year we went overseas. First—to England—where we trained a lil. Then in September we boarded the LCIs for the trip across the Channel. We were soon to see action.

Because of our position in the squad, Morris & I were due to sweat it out together. I was the automatic rifleman & he was my assistant. This setup suited us fine.

Well, poor Morris wasn't long in action before he was wounded. If memory serves me well—it was on September 18th. I sure felt sorry for him—but he did get a lil rest, & for that I was glad.

After he returned there were many more days that we sweated out 88's and 155's shelling us. Going on patrols, etc., etc.

Then in January, the 14th day of the year 1945—Morris passed on. It was easy for him—no pain. Knowing him, I know that he died with a prayer on his lips.

As I looked at him, I made a silent promise to tell you & his mother all the details leading up to his death. I'm sure he'd have done that for me.

If there is any details you'd like to know—please advise. I regret that it's impossible to write further now. My most heartfelt sympathy to you & Mrs. Redmann.

Sincerely,
Vincent A. DeMase

* * * * *

Mr. Vincent A. DeMase
469 Clinton Avenue
Albany 5, New York

September 26, 1945

Dear Mr. DeMase:

I was indeed very glad to receive your letter of September 12, 1945, and regret that I did not sooner find opportunity to write you.

I shall be glad to hear from you as often as you have the time and the inclination to write, and any details that you can give about Morris's activities as a G.I. Joe will be most welcome.

We have had the pleasure of having Tom Moore of Columbus, Georgia, visit with us between trains on his way from Atlanta to California. He told us what great friends you and Morris were.

If you have the addresses of any of Morris's other friends, including any people in France who may have been nice to him, we would appreciate your letting us have them.

If you are ever coming this way, please be sure to let us know, as we would be happy to see you.

With the hope that you will write me again, and with kindest regards and best wishes, I remain

Sincerely,
M. B. Redmann

* * * * *

469 Clinton Avenue
Albany 5, N.Y.
4th June, 1946

Dear Mr. & Mrs. Redmann:

I've been meaning to write to you ever since the turn of the year—but—it just couldn't be done. I won't try to explain or make excuses. There is no possible explanation.

I'd be glad to answer any questions relative to Morris if you'd let me know what you'd like to know. I'll be a bit more prompt in reply, too.

We—Morris & I—became good friends in Camp McCain prior to going overseas. Our friendship grew with the months that followed due to close contact we had during our march thru France.

Morris's passing was a great blow to me—a shock from which I don't think I'll ever recover. I've tried to forget it, but never knew that forgetting could be so difficult—but—that's my problem. Anyway, it'll take time.

Morris often talked of you folks—so much so I almost felt that I knew you personally. His most cherished memory was his last visit home. He told of spending the evening at home with you folks and another fellow and his wife. I believe the fellow was in "H" Company of our regiment. I don't recall his name. I believe you had a nice fish dinner—if I remember correctly. Anyway, he certainly enjoyed that evening, and his description of it was that it was just perfect.

He often spoke of his younger brothers and of the pranks that they pulled—such as how they pulled the chair out when their father went to sit down, etc., etc.

He always spoke very affectionately of both you folks. One day he received a letter from his mother wherein she mentioned missing him so. This letter touched him deeply and inspired him to put his feelings into words—verse, to be exact. He permitted me to copy his poem and send it to my mother, too. This I copied from his original copy, which he scribbled off on the back of an envelope which contained a letter from his dad. Funny about this—there were about one or two stanzas of another poem that he'd started there, too.

I can't remember exactly how it went, or just what had inspired it. I can't seem to remember whether he'd mentioned having visualized it in a dream. Anyway, the theme of it was his own death. It's so long ago that I just can't remember how it went, but it seems as though he imagined seeing the Lord. He explained it to me and told me he wanted to send it to his mother, but was afraid she'd be frightened. I agreed with him on this, and told him he shouldn't be thinking such things.

It seems that Morris had one wish—one dream—to return home. At the same time he was possessed with the terrible thought that *he knew* he never would.

The day of his passing he mentioned having had a bad dream the nite before. I don't recall the contents of the dream—but I believe in it, he'd foreseen his own death. He mentioned his pride in his outfit—in his lack of fear in following them anywhere. Yet he said he wished himself away from the field of battle on that particular day.

I don't know what else to say, so I believe I'd better close now. I enclose a few snapshots I found—these were all taken in the States. I have no pictures taken overseas. I don't recall Morris ever having had a picture taken overseas—yet he may have. I also enclose the V-Mail of the poem I'd sent my mother as copied from Morris's original. I'd appreciate the return of the poem—unless you'd rather keep it. The pictures you may have. If I find any others, I'll forward them.

If there are any questions you'd like to ask, I'll do my best to answer them. Good-bye for now.

Sincerely yours,
Vincent A. DeMase

PART SEVEN

LETTERS FROM THE WAR DEPARTMENT

THE SECRETARY OF WAR
WASHINGTON
Official Business

February 12, 1945

Mr. Morris B. Redmann
7017 Broad Place
New Orleans, Louisiana

My dear Mr. Redmann:

You will shortly receive the Purple Heart medal, which has been posthumously awarded by direction of the President to your son, Private First Class Morris B. Redmann Jr., Infantry. It is sent as a tangible expression of the country's gratitude for his gallantry and devotion.

It is sent to you, as well, with my deepest personal sympathy for your bereavement. The loss of a loved one is beyond man's repairing, and the medal is of slight value; not so, however, the message it carries. We are all comrades-in-arms in this battle for our country, and those who have gone are not, and never will be, forgotten by those of us who remain. I hope you will accept the medal in evidence of such remembrance.

Sincerely yours,
Henry L. Stimson

War Department
The Adjutant General's Office
Demobilized Personnel Records Branch
High Point, N.C.

In reply Refer to
AGRD-C 201 Redmann, Morris B.
(26 Feb 45)

29 March 1945

Mr. Morris B. Redmann
Canal Building
New Orleans, Louisiana

Dear Mr. Redmann:

Reference is again made to your letter requesting a record of service in the case of your late son.

Additional records now available show that your son, Morris B. Redmann, Army serial number 38 499 577, who gave his address as 7017 Broad Place, New Orleans, Louisiana, was inducted into the military service on 27 September 1943 at New Orleans, Louisiana. He left the United States for the European Theater of Operations on 6 August 1944, and served in Scotland, England, France, and Germany. He was killed in action in Germany on 14 January 1945, while serving as a private first class in the Infantry. His Army specialty was rifleman. He was authorized to wear the Expert Infantryman Badge, European-African-Middle Eastern Ribbon, Purple Heart, and Combat Infantryman Badge. His character and efficiency rating as a soldier were recorded as excellent.

Permit me again to extend my sympathy to you and Mrs. Redmann.

Sincerely yours,
E. C. Gault
Colonel, AGD
Chief of Branch

WAR DEPARTMENT
OFFICE OF THE QUARTERMASTER GENERAL
WASHINGTON 25, D.C.

25 September 1946

Mr. Morris B. Redmann
7017 Broad Place
New Orleans, Louisiana

Dear Mr. Redmann:

The War Department is most desirous that you be furnished information regarding the burial location of your son, the late Private First Class Morris B. Redmann Jr., ASN 38 499 577.

The records of this office disclose that his remains are interred in the U.S. Military Cemetery Hamm, plot L, row 1, grave 1. You may be assured that the identification and interment have been accomplished with fitting dignity and solemnity.

This cemetery is located two and one half miles east of the city of Luxembourg, and is under the constant care and supervision of United States military personnel.

The War Department has now been authorized to comply, at Government expense, with the feasible wishes of the next of kin regarding final interment, here or abroad, of the remains of your loved one. At a later date, this office will, without any action on your part, provide the next of kin with full information and solicit his detailed desires.

Please accept my sincere sympathy in your great loss.

Sincerely yours,
T. B. Larkin
Major General
The Quartermaster General

WAR DEPARTMENT
OFFICE OF THE QUARTERMASTER GENERAL
WASHINGTON 25, D.C.

8 February 1949

Pfc. Morris B. Redmann Jr.,
ASN 38 499 577
Plot H, Row 1, Grave 20
Headstone: Cross
Hamm U. S. Military Cemetery

Mr. Morris B. Redmann
7017 Broad Place
New Orleans, Louisiana

Dear Mr. Redmann:

This is to inform you that the remains of your loved one have been permanently interred, as recorded above, side by side with comrades who also gave their lives for their country. Customary military funeral services were conducted over their graves at the time of burial.

After the Department of the Army has completed all final interments, the cemetery will be transferred, as authorized by the Congress, to the care and supervision of the American Battle Monuments Commission. The Commission will also have the responsibility for permanent construction and beautification of the cemetery, including erection of the permanent headstone. The headstone will be inscribed with the name exactly as recorded above, the rank or rating where appropriate, organization, state, and date of death. Any inquiries related to the type of headstone or the spelling of the name to be inscribed thereon, should be addressed to the American Battle Monuments Commission, Washington 25, D.C. Your letter should include the full name, rank, serial number, grave location, and name of the cemetery.

While interments are in progress, the cemetery will not be open to visitors. You may rest assured that this final interment was conducted with fitting dignity and solemnity, and that the gravesite will be carefully and conscientiously maintained by the United States Government.

Sincerely yours,
Thomas B. Larkin
Major General
The Quartermaster General

LIST OF MORRIS'S BADGES, MEDALS, AND CITATIONS

Expert Rifleman
Expert in Browning Automatic Rifle (BAR)
Expert in 30-Caliber Machine Gun
Purple Heart—St. Nazaire, France
Expert Infantryman Badge
Combat Infantryman Badge
Presidential Unit Emblem
Army Good Conduct Medal
European-African-Middle Eastern Campaign Medal
Purple Heart with Oak Leaf Cluster—Germany (posthumously)
Bronze Star Medal with Oak Leaf Cluster—Germany (posthumously)
Victory World War II Medal (posthumously)
Army of Occupation, World War II Medal (posthumously)

GLOSSARY

A.O.	Army of Occupation
ASTP	Army Specialized Training Program
Aux Petits	To the little ones
BAR	Browning Automatic Rifle
CBI Theater	China-Burma-India Theater
ETOUSA	European Theater of Operations, U.S. Army
EWT	European War Theater
Festung Europa	Fortress Europe
F.F.I.	*Forces Française de l'Intérieur* (French Forces of the Interior)
Jennie Wilson	One of the "pilot boats" of the "Associated Branch Pilots" Organization that operated in the Gulf of Mexico from South Pass at the mouth of the Mississippi River, during World War II
lebensraum	Space required for life, growth, or activity
ODs	Army olive drab uniform
OPA	Office of Price Administration
P.O.E.	Port of Embarkation
PX	Post Exchange
Schü mine	*Schützen* mine—Anti-personnel Mine
SS	*Schutzstaffel* (German elite guard)
Widerstandsnests	German six-foot-thick pillboxes

NAMES OF FAMILY AND FRIENDS

Morris's Family:

Mother and Father (Mama and Daddy); Folks
Esther, Morris's only sister

Morris's eight younger brothers (oldest to youngest):

Will
Kerry
Richard
Ralph
Ronald
Jerome
David
Robert

Bertha	Morris's mother's cook
Lizzie	Morris's mother's maid

Aunts:

Eleanor	Morris's mother's sister; Mrs. Paul S. Stuart
Hy/Hyie	Morris's mother's sister Hyacinth; Mrs. Joseph R. Sellers
Jeanne	Jeanne Girot Redmann; wife of Dad's brother, Stephen
Lala	Lala Joyce, Morris's great-aunt

Ogie Joyce	One of Morris's mother's sisters, unmarried
Winnie	Morris's godmother and sister of his mother; Mrs. Claude J. Kelly

Uncles:

Claude	(Kelly) Morris's mother's sister Winifred's husband, Claude J. Kelly
Paul	Morris's mother's sister Eleanor's husband; Paul S. Stuart
Stephen	Stephen M. Redmann; Dad's brother
Sharps family	Mr. and Mrs. Thomas V. Sharp; Dad's sister and husband

Cousins:

Claude Jr.	Claude J. Kelly Jr.
Gregory	Gregory Redmann (Marine, killed at Battle of Tarawa)
Jodie Boy	Aunt Hy's son
Little Winnie	Winifred Kelly, daughter of Mrs. Claude J. Kelly
Margaret	Aunt Hy's daughter
Paul Jr.	Morris's first cousin Paul S. Stuart Jr.

Morris's Friends:

Billy (Uncle)	William J. Hume; good friend of Morris's dad; former amateur tennis and golf champion in New Orleans
Cologne, Mary	"Mamie" Cologne; organist and choir director, St. Mathias Church
Cokers	Mr. and Mrs. William Coker, good friends of Morris's parents
Father Bienvenue, S.J.	Jesuit priest who taught Morris Greek at Jesuit High School; they later became good friends
Father Castel	Pastor of St. Rita's Catholic Church, New Orleans

Fonseca family	Next-door neighbors at 7011 Broad Place, New Orleans
Gissie	Gissie Burton; friend of Aunt Ogie's and Morris's family
Hoggs	Mr. and Mrs. Edwin T. Hogg, good friends of Morris's parents
Murphy family	Mrs. James C. Murphy and family; Norris Mary, classmate
Randall, John	Friend at Camp McCain, Mississippi
Mrs. Schreder	Head nurse in nursery at Mercy Hospital
Trice, Shelby	Inducted in Army with Morris, close friend

Good Friends and Classmates at Loyola University:

Bernie	Bernie Ward
Charlie	Charlie Brennan
Frank	Frank Schneider
George	George Reinecke
Howard	Howard Taylor
Kent	Kent Zimmermann
Lolita	Lolita Martinez
Luke (Bruno)	Lucas F. Bruno; also known as Pvt. L-F-B
Marie Louise	Marie Louise Salatich
Monita	Monita Imbert
Norris Mary	Norris Mary Murphy
Numa	Numa Bertel Jr
Peggy Mc	Peggy McGinity
Roy	Roy Guste
Warren	Warren Mouledoux